BRITISH ELECTIONS: MYTH AND REALITY

FOR MARION JOAN

Geoffrey Alderman

BRITISH ELECTIONS:
Myth and Reality

B. T. BATSFORD
London

First published 1978

© Geoffrey Alderman 1978

ISBN 0 7134 0195 8 (cased)
      0 7134 0196 6 (limp)

Phototypeset by Granada Graphics Ltd.

Printed and bound in Great Britain
by Billing & Sons Ltd., London, Guildford and Worcester.

for the Publishers
B. T. Batsford Ltd.,
4 Fitzhardinge Street,
London W1H 0AH

CONTENTS

List of Tables
Preface

Chapter One:	**The Framework**	9
	The historical legacy	9
	Dissolutions, manifestos and mandates	22
	Some votes are more equal than others	29
Chapter Two:	**Legal Constraints**	42
	Universal suffrage?	42
	Free elections?	48
	The distribution of seats	58
Chapter Three:	**Politics**	69
	The Parties	69
	Choosing candidates	73
	Election by the few	87
	Campaigning	93
Chapter Four:	**Ritual**	104
	The legitimation of government	106
	The myth of the media	114
	The Press	115
	Radio and Television	122
	The Impact of the Media	133
	Opinion polls	138
Chapter Five:	**Results**	147
	Politics and class	148
	The decline of class-based partisanship	159
	New voting alignments	167
	Sex, Age, Religion, Region	168
	Third Parties, Local Parties, No Parties	177
Chapter Six:	**Conclusion**	192
	Unrepresentative democracy	192
	Referendums	196
	Do elections matter?	202
	Notes	208
	Appendix: General Election Results, 1945-1974	229
	Guide to Further Reading	230
	Index	232

LIST OF TABLES

1:1	Ebbw Vale & Ilford North, October 1974	29
1:2	Votes and seats for the governing party, 1945–74	31
1:3	The relationship between votes and seats, October 1974	32
2:1	Examples of disparities in constituency size, 1955–70	62
2:2	Unequal parliamentary representation in the United Kingdom	66
2:3	Party strengths, had there been equal constituencies, October 1974	67
2:4	Gerrymandering in Londonderry, 1967	68
3:1	Women candidates & MPs, 1964–October 1974	84
3:2	Women candidates in the Conservative and Labour parties, 1964–October 1974	84
3:3	Conservative and Labour candidates, 1966–74: socio-economic background	87
3:4	Variations in swing, February & October 1974	91
3:5	Swing and turnover of seats, 1950–74	92
4:1	Circulation of national daily newspapers 1951–74	116
4:2	Opinion poll forecasts, 1945–74	141
5:1	Conservative and Labour party preferences by class, 1964–74	155
5:2	Electoral support for the Conservative and Labour parties, 1945–74	160
5:3	Performance of the government at by-elections, 1950-77	162
5:4	Fluctuations in the Gallup Poll, 1947–74	162
5:5	The performance of Plaid Cymru, 1959–74	180
5:6	The performance of the Scottish National Party, 1959–74	180
5:7	The Liberal vote, 1945–74	182
5:8	Liberal party preference by class, 1964–74	183
5:9	Average Communist vote per candidate, 1945–74	184
6:1	The Common Market Referendum	198
6:2	Occupations of MPs, 1951, 1964 & October 1974	204
6:3	Educational background of MPs, 1951, 1964 & October 1974	205

PREFACE

I have written this volume as a text rather than as a textbook. Accordingly it does not aim at exhaustive or comprehensive coverage of its subject. It is conceived as an extended essay, a commentary on British elections, and it concentrates on the often sharp differences between what is commonly supposed to take place at and as a result of the electoral process, and what actually does take place. It is designed to provoke; and if my readers are moved only to disagree profoundly with me (and I hope in that case they will write and tell me so), I shall count this book a success.

Strictly speaking, a study of British elections ought to confine itself to Great Britain. In fact, though I have included material on Northern Ireland wherever this has seemed appropriate from the point of view of the overall picture, I have not ventured into the intricacies of Northern Irish domestic politics.

Except where otherwise stated, all election statistics are based on my own computations.

The author of a book such as this is bound to rely heavily on the writings of others. The references in the notes will, I trust, serve as an acknowledgment of my own debt in this respect. I should, however, like to thank here Messrs Ladbrokes and William Hill for supplying me with information concerning betting at elections. I am also indebted to the British Election Study at the University of Essex for permission to cite unpublished survey data.

My friend Dr Rodney Barker cast his critical eye over the entire draft of this work, and has saved me from many errors of fact and interpretation. For those which remain I alone am responsible.

I have derived much inspiration from conversations with a number of politicians, journalists, teachers of politics, and students. Each encounter has helped me to define and re-define my own position, and to ask new questions. Fortunately, the woman to whom I am married is neither an academic nor a political animal. She has been a wonderful refining influence on me.

GEOFFREY ALDERMAN

London, 12 January 1978

Chapter One

THE FRAMEWORK

The historical legacy

The modern British electoral system, though it has evolved from eighteenth- and nineteenth-century notions of representation long discarded, is often portrayed as a direct lineal descendant of the system familiar to Peel and Palmerston, Gladstone and Disraeli. It is commonplace to read that the Reform Act of 1832 marked the beginning of the movement towards what is termed 'parliamentary democracy'. As one standard textbook puts it, 'in 1832 British parlimentary representation . . . took an irreversible, but incomplete, step towards democracy'.[1] The standard view would then go on to argue that the franchise, the right to vote, modestly extended in 1832, was further enlarged by the reforms of 1867, 1884 and 1918, after which it was simply a matter of dotting the 'i's' and crossing the 't's': that is, of ironing out anomalies and removing minor irregularities. Meanwhile, steps had been taken, notably by the Ballot Act of 1872 and the Corrupt Practices Act of 1883, to remove bribery and intimidation of electors. By the end of the Great War, therefore, universal adult male suffrage, involving also limited female suffrage, the elimination of illegitimate pressure on electors, and the construction of reasonably equal electoral districts, had been achieved. If the electoral system of the 1930s was not entirely democratic, it was as near democratic as made no difference, and the remaining blemishes were removed by the Attlee government in 1948.

The above account is, of course, grossly oversimplified;

nonetheless, it does mirror a widespread view of the march of British parliamentary democracy, as taught to thousands of schoolchildren and undergraduates. It stresses evolution not revolution. It places much emphasis upon the legalistic mechanics of electoral reform, and has little to say about the climate of politics at any given time in the story; changing views of politics, political culture and rhetoric are seldom mentioned. For instance, so-called 'corruption' of electors in the mid-Victorian period, through the distribution of guineas and pints of beer, is regarded as inherently evil, though the equally reprehensible corruption of electors in the 1960s, by means of promises made at elections and then forgotten, is ignored.[2] The Whig historians may be almost extinct, but their *modus operandi* is very much alive. It will be a recurrent theme of this book that politics is about the acquisition and retention of power in society. Ambition is its driving force, and it can be safely asserted that no British politician has ever pronounced upon the electoral system, or made an appeal to his voters, without these factors weighing heavily in his mind. This is as true of theories of representation as of arguments about electoral reform.

The growth of the House of Commons as an important adjunct of government dates from the matrimonial difficulties of Henry VIII. That monarch used the Commons as a counterweight to the influence of Rome, and he knew that the confiscation of church lands, and the sale of them to the *nouveaux riches* of Tudor England, would provide much popular backing for his break with the Papacy. In so doing, however, he sowed the seeds of future bloody conflict. The peers, in the House of Lords, had always had an important part in royal government. The 296 members of the Commons, elected for 37 counties and 110 boroughs, but representing new wealthy interests in the community, became increasingly restive. Determined to put an end to the absolute prerogative of the monarch, they eventually took up arms against Charles I, allowed his son, Charles II, to return on their terms, ousted *his* Catholic brother, James II, and installed in his stead a Dutch Calvinist, William III. The Glorious Revolution of 1688, and the constitutional and religious settlement which followed it, marked the beginning of 'limited monarchy' but, more importantly, marked the triumph of property in the political system.

Wealth thus formed the basis of power in eighteenth-century Britain. The events of 1688, Christopher Hill writes, 'demonstrated the ultimate solidarity of the propertied class'.[3] The wealth of the country was founded upon agriculture; those who owned the land arrogated to themselves the right to decide the affairs of the realm; those who did not own land aspired to acquire some. The right to vote was restricted to freeholders whose tenements were worth at least forty shillings per annum. It was taken for granted that the interests of these people were synonymous with the national interest, and that they would always act in conformity with it. 'Universal manhood suffrage' was, by this argument, unnecessary, a waste of time, an irrelevance. Those who did not have the vote were represented 'through the land on which they lived'.[4] It was, moreover, open to them to bring influence to bear on those who did have the vote. Finally, members of Parliament did not regard themselves as specially beholden to those who had voted for them, or supported them; to have declared themselves, in any way, prisoners of their electorates would have been playing with fire. Burke's speech of 1774 to the Bristol electors is often quoted in this context:

> Parliament is not a *congress* of ambassadors from different and hostile interests . . . but . . . a deliberative assembly of *one* nation. . . . You choose a member indeed; but when you have chosen him, he is not member of Bristol, but he is a member of *parliament*. If the local constituent should have an interest . . . evidently opposite to the real good of the rest of the community, the member for that place ought to be as far, as any other, from any endeavour to give it effect.[5]

Perhaps more revealing, and a good deal blunter, was the view of Charles James Fox:

> I pay no regard whatever to the voice of the people; it is our duty to do what is proper without considering what may be agreeable; their business is tho chuse us; it is ours to act constitutionally and to maintain the independence of Parliament.[6]

The contrast between this philosophy and late twentieth-century attitudes could not be starker. In 1976 the prospective Labour parliamentary candidate in Kensington gave an undertaking to her local party general management committee that, in respect of certain subjects, she would, if elected, vote in Parliament in accordance with decisions reached at management committee meetings; she also agreed to retire at a general election if the committee so requested, subject to her constitutional rights of appeal. 'What the undertaking *mandates* me to', she declared, 'are the election *pledges* on which the electorate vote.'[7]

Such deference to the views of electors was entirely foreign to eighteenth-century politicians. In its place was the representation of interests, or more specifically the legitimate interests – the social and economic groups – of which the nation was composed. Thus, while extra-parliamentary organisations, such as the Yorkshire Association of 1779–80, formed with the avowed aim of putting pressure upon MPs, were regarded with suspicion, the political power exercised by such groups as the East India Company, the Bank of England, the West India Interest and the Canal Interest, power based partly upon a bloc of MPs and partly upon financial potency, was taken for granted.[8]

By the end of the Napoleonic wars, this concept of political representation was under strain. The industrial revolution had brought into existence a manufacturing class whose wealth was not based upon land, and never would be. Hard-headed businessmen in Manchester, Birmingham or Sheffield resented the fact that they helped create the wealth of the country but were not able to elect MPs because none of these towns was represented in Parliament. New interests had arisen and were demanding entry into some at least of the corridors of power. At the same time there were renewed demands for a purification of the electoral system, and especially for the rationalization of the voting qualification and a curb on the 'nomination' or 'rotten' boroughs in which election was, in practice, in the hands of one landed magnate or a small group.

The eighteenth-century had been littered with attempts

to reform Parliament and root out corruption. A series of Place Acts had attempted to diminish the influence of the Crown by preventing certain categories of government servants from sitting in the House of Commons, or influencing elections. Acts of 1729 and 1770 had attempted to take disputes over the franchise and election returns out of party politics. In May 1783 William Pitt had introduced resolutions in the Commons in favour of parliamentary reform. And Curwen's Act, passed in 1809, had, in the words of Lord Liverpool, 'put an end to all money transactions between Government and the supposed proprietors of boroughs'.[9] Twelve years later the notorious nomination borough of Grampound had been disfranchised, and its two seats given to Yorkshire.

All these measures had, as their rationale, the purification and refinement of the system, not its replacement by any other. The Reform Act of 1832 was very much in this mould. Lord John Russell, introducing the bill in March 1831, stressed that the effect of the proposed £10 householder vote would be the extension of the franchise to 'about half a million of persons, and these all connected with the property of the country, having a valuable stake amongst us, and deeply interested in our institutions'.[10] Frome was enfranchised because it had a woollen industry and would 'represent' the south-west of England. Whitby and Sunderland would 'represent' shipbuilding. Totnes, with 179 voters, returned two MPs, but so did Liverpool, whose electors numbered over 8,000.[11] County MPs now totalled 253 as against 188 in the unreformed House of Commons; borough representation dropped from 465 to 399. There was certainly no statistical consistency about the 1832 Act; its guiding principle was rather the preservation of the eighteenth-century constitution. Although it increased the British electorate by about 38 per cent, less than three-quarters of a million persons were entitled to vote as a result of it, or about 1 in 5 of the adult male population in England and Wales, and about 1 in 8 in Scotland.[12] It was not, and was not meant to be, even remotely democratic.

It is clear, however, that the terms of the Act were less

important, in the long run, than the fact of its passage. The election of 1831 was dominated by the proposed reform and many candidates pledged themselves to support the bill. Those who were successful could indeed claim that they had been 'mandated' by their electors; the Burkean concept of parliamentary representation had thus been struck a blow from which it was never to recover.[13] The electorate may have been very small, but it existed nonetheless, and had to be deferred to.[14]

After 1832 franchise reform ceased to be an issue of immediate importance. The country was as apathetic about manhood suffrage as it was about the secret ballot. Chartism, which espoused these causes among others, was a damp squib. But the mandate, or rather the nature of the relationship between an MP and his constituents, became a topic of intense interest. Peel's 1834 address to his Tamworth constituents raised many eyebrows, for it was nothing less than an appeal for election to Parliament on the basis of a programme of measures. The voter registration provisions of the 1832 Act fostered the growth of Whig and Tory registration societies in each constituency. The development of a national press, the growth of the railway system and the spread of the electric telegraph all tended to erode the local nature of electioneering which had prevailed hitherto. People looked to Parliament to legislate on important domestic matters, many of them the consequences of the rapid industrialization which had itself brought about parliamentary reform. MPs found, whether they liked it or not, that their constituents held them accountable for their parliamentary activities. Party feeling intensified as a result. New, more professionally organized political clubs came into existence – the Tory Carlton (1832) and the Whig Reform (1836) – and came to have some say in the choice of candidates and the disbursement of election expenses.[15] Henceforth, electors were at least as interested in what a parliamentary candidate stood for, as in who and what manner of person he was.

It was the realization of the influence which electorates might assert over MPs which stamped out wild, speculative theories concerning the wisdom of universal suffrage. More important than the Hyde Park fiasco which put an end to Chartism, in 1848, was the rejection, by John Stuart Mill, of his father's plea that all men over 40 years of age be given the vote. In 1820, in his *Essay on Government*, James Mill had succinctly, but cautiously, stated the considered Benthamite view of the desirability of a system of universal manhood suffrage in which, however, the older men in the community would represent the views of the younger and of the women. By rebelling against his father's views, John Stuart Mill demonstrated admirably the shortcomings of this utilitarian paternalism. For him, the danger was not in rule by the minority, but in rule by the majority. He was adamant that men and women should be treated equally in the matter of the franchise.[16] He was equally adamant that the right to vote be withheld from those not proficient in reading, writing and simple arithmetic, while extra votes should be given to those with superior intelligence.[17] Voting would become an intellectual exercise. Geographical constituencies would disappear, to be replaced by a system of proportional representation in which the entire country would become one constituency, allowing for the representation in Parliament of any opinion gaining a minimum quota of votes.[18] Education was thus to replace property as the basis of the franchise, and of its future extension.

In their details, the observations of the younger Mill had no popular support. But for the politicians of the mid-Victorian period they contained valuable lessons. If electoral reform was to come, it had better come slowly and cautiously. The fact that reform was a subject of little popular interest was beside the point. The newly-enfranchised would, it was hoped, reward with their allegiance those who conferred the benefit upon them. Reform became a political football. It was the Liberal Russell who first took up the cause, in 1851. It was the Conservative Disraeli who eventually carried a bill, in 1867. Determined to pass a bill at almost any cost, Disraeli was content to see a very modest measure turn into an Act of radical proportions. All borough householders in England, Wales and Scotland were enfranchised, adding nearly a million mostly urban voters to the electorate.[19]

In the long run, it was the Conservatives who reaped the reward. Though they lost the ensuing general election, their victories in Middlesex, Westminister and south Lancashire foretold the arrival of suburban Toryism which, in part at least, made possible their victory in 1874, when a Conservative majority was returned for the first time in over thirty years. But it was Gladstone who won the short-term tactical victory. He was able to cement the alliance between Liberalism and Nonconformity, and to attract Irish support by favouring the disestablishment of the Irish church. When he became Prime Minister in 1868, with a majority of over a hundred seats, he headed a party committed to a full programme of legislative reforms. The election had, in fact, decided not merely who should sit at Westminster, but what measures should be passed there.

It was not, therefore, the inconsistencies of the 1832 reform which somehow made inevitable the passage of the 1867 Act. But the inconsistencies of the 1867 Act were glaring enough for their eradication to become a matter of political concern. The Reform Act of 1884 put the county franchise on the same basis as that for boroughs, and applied to Ireland the voting qualifications in force in the rest of the United Kingdom. The net result was an increase in the electorate from three to five millions, so that about 60 per cent of adult males had the vote.[20] The Redistribution Act of 1885 rationalized the arrangement of constituencies: Wales, Scotland and the north of England gained at the expense of the south of England. Rural and urban areas were equally treated. Single-member constituencies became the order of the day, and only 24 two-member boroughs survived.

The reforms of 1884-5 are often taken as a watershed in British electoral history. It is true that, after 1885, it was individuals who were represented in Parliament, not communities. It is also true that the Ballot Act of 1872, and the Corrupt Practices Act of 1883, had done much to reduce bribery, intimidation, and election expenditure. But old habits died hard. There was much about politics which remained essentially local; the personal vote which an MP could attract mattered a great deal. Renegade Liberals, such as Sir Edward Watkin at Hythe and Joseph Chamberlain at Birmingham, were able to desert their party but retain their constituency support. Local newspapers still carried verbatim reports of parliamentary proceedings. Gladstone's Midlothian campaigns of 1879–80 were, to be sure, a new departure, an attempt to turn elections into national rather than local contests; they were, however, undertaken in that constituency – Midlothian – for which Gladstone had already agreed to stand at the next general election.

Nor was the secret vote an infallible guarantee against intimidation. Coercion of tenants by landlords in rural areas persisted long after 1872.[21] As late as 1911 it was possible for an election result (that of Exeter, December 1910) to be reversed on the grounds that certain votes had been improperly cast.[22] The Municipal Franchise Act of 1868 had given women who were ratepayers the right to vote in local borough elections; at parliamentary elections there was no female suffrage. Above all, property remained the basis of the franchise. The property qualification had been lowered, not abolished. Only householders and lodgers paying more than £10 a year in rent were allowed to vote. Those who owned land or business premises in a constituency other than that in which they resided, were allowed two votes; so too were those who held a university degree, for the principle of the representation of the seats of learning in Parliament had been extended during the course of the century. The Third Reform Act resulted, in short, in the extension of the franchise to a mere 29 per cent of all adults. In 1910, only 58 per cent of the adult male population had the vote.[23]

Put another way, a man in his late sixties on the eve of the Great War, who had been born in, say, the year of Peel's repeal of the Corn Laws (1846), and who had first voted in 1868, would have had little difficulty in adapting himself to the various electoral changes in the late nineteenth century. What he may have found novel, even uncongenial, was the way in which his vote was solicited by the politicians. The two great parties had thrown up extra-parliamentary organisations to mobilize support among the newly-enfranchised. The National Union of Conservative & Constitutional Associations, founded in 1867, was the brainchild of Disraeli, who hoped it would bring the working classes to his side. It held an annual conference with no powers, neither did it determine policy nor did it choose candidates. In the early 1880s, after Disraeli's death, Lord Randolph Churchill attempted to use it to strengthen his own position vis-à-vis Lord Salisbury. In 1884 the two came to an agreement and the National Union, having served Churchill's purpose, was allowed to languish.

The National Liberal Federation was a much more serious affair. It orginated in the Birmingham Liberal Association, which had worked hard in the election of 1868 to defeat the 'minority' clause of the Second Reform Act, under which, in the twelve three-member constituencies, a voter could have only two votes, and in the City of London (four MPs) only three. The purpose of this clause, which was Conservative-inspired, was to allow for minority representation in the big cities. Birmingham Liberals hoped that by the minute organisation of Liberal voters they could sweep the board; and they did. Moreover, it was possible for all members of the association, through a complicated system of committees, to take some part in the choice of candidates. The National Liberal Federation was organised by Chamberlain and other Birmingham Liberals in 1877, to bring together all local Liberal associations under one umbrella. There were sporadic attempts to make election candidates conform to its policies. The 'caucus' had arrived.

The growth of these extra-parliamentary bodies profoundly worried contemporary observers. Few politicians wished to see a situation develop in which MPs were formally accountable to their constituency supporters, whose bidding they would have to do at Westminster. In 1885 the 'minority' clause therefore disappeared. The National Liberal Federation lived on as Chamberlain's tool in his campaign for the leadership of the Liberal party. In the event, he was unable to carry the federation with him in his opposition to Gladstone's Irish policy. Partly as a result, he left the party. Gladstone, moving the federation's headquarters from Birmingham to London, brought it firmly under his aegis; it never gained the formal right to make policy.

But if the caucus had been 'tamed', it nonetheless lived on. Surveying the situation in 1902, the Russian liberal Ostrogorski argued that the caucus was essentially undemocratic, attracting 'only the enthusiasts, the bigots of the party, and the busybodies. The great mass remained outside, sunk in its apathy and indifference'.[24] 'Every attempt at asserting the freedom and independence of political thought' was repressed;[25] political agitation was erected 'into the system'.[26] Machine politics had crossed the Atlantic and was sucking the life-blood of British liberal political traditions. Superficially, the object was to hasten the onset of democracy; actually, to stifle dissent and entrench oligarchy.

Ostrogorski undoubtedly overstated his case. But it was a case for all that, and the formation of the Labour Representation Committee in 1900 seemed to confirm his pessimistic outlook. Here was an organisation, aspiring to political power, which was, *ab origine*, extra-parliamentary. It sought to sponsor parliamentary candidates who, if successful, would be pledged to carry out *its* policies. The tail at last seemed to be wagging the dog. Could a Labour MP ever call his soul his own? This question has never been resolved. Some Labour MPs have had rough rides from their constituency parties, and some have been disowned by them. In 1909 Lord Justice Farewell quoted Burke with approval when he dismissed, in the famous Osborne judgment, the claim of the Amalgamated Society of Railway Servants that it had the right to collect 1s 1d annually from each of its members to provide for the representation of railwaymen in the House of Commons, on condition that MPs so sponsored accepted the Labour whip. An MP, he held, 'cannot be deprived of his independence, nor can he free himself from the great duty to the country that he undertakes by becoming a member'.[27]

As a matter of fact, Ramsay MacDonald, as leader of the infant Labour party in the Commons, acted without continually referring himself to the dictates of the caucus. Yet – and here was the novelty – the party claimed the right, through its conference, to instruct MPs. The Parliamentary Labour Party, to a very great extent, 'acted in response to the initiative of extra-parliamentary sources'.[28] The 1907 conference resolution of the party made it clear:

> That resolutions instructing the Parliamentary Party as to their action in the House of Commons be taken as the opinions of the Conference, on the understanding that the time and method of giving effect to these instructions be left to the Party in the House, in conjuction with the National Executive.[29]

The implication was evident: an elector who voted for a Labour party candidate was voting primarily for a set of policies, not for an individual.

Was this really as new a departure as it seemed at the time? The formal embodiment of the new philosophy in the constitutional framework of the party certainly was. But the tendency for elections to centre on measures, not men, had been manifest for some time. The election of 1886 had been largely about Irish Home Rule. That of 1906 had centred on Tariff Reform. The elections of January and December 1910 and been exclusively concerned with, respectively, the Lloyd George budget and the reform of the House of Lords.

It is clear that by 1914 the nature of the electoral contest had outstripped the limits of electoral law. When elections were concerned with choosing the best men, a franchise restricted to those men best fitted to do the choosing could perhaps be justified. But if elections were about policy and, moreover, policy which increasingly affected the entire population, ought not the individual citizen, irrespective of sex or wealth, to have some say in the composition of the legislature? After 1906, and not merely because of the colourful and often violent campaigns for women's suffrage, electoral reform became, for the first time since 1831, a subject of popular concern. In 1906, 1912 and 1913 bills abolishing plural voting were passed by the Commons but defeated in the Lords. In 1909 a Royal Commission on Electoral Systems was set up, and reported the following year unanimously in favour of the 'alternative vote' proposal (explained on p.33 below).[30] In 1911 the maximum period between general elections was reduced from seven years to five. The payment of MPs was begun as an attempt to free aspiring politicians from the obligation to be wealthy. In 1913 the Osborne judgment was reversed; it was henceforth possible for a working man to help sponsor an MP through his union, even though he himself was denied the vote.

The national sacrifice involved in the Great War dealt a mortal blow to the old system. After the passage of the Representation of the People Act in 1918, the British electoral system was unrecognisable. Hitherto, the suffrage had been linked to the payment of rates; henceforth, universal manhood suffrage was bestowed on the basis of six months' residence. The university franchise was preserved, but extended to graduates of provincial universities. Occupancy of business premises worth £10 per annum bestowed an additional vote. Women over 30 were enfranchised if they themselves were local government electors or the wives of such electors; the local franchise was, at the same time, extended to all owners or tenants of property. The principle of approximately equal electoral districts was, in general, accepted, and the ratio between the largest and smallest constituency was reduced from 8 to 1 (in 1885) to a maximum of 5 to 1.[31]

The extension of the franchise was alone enough to make the 1918 act revolutionary in its implications. The total electorate jumped from about 7.5 millions, in 1910, to nearly 20 millions, or approximately three-quarters of the adult population. When the voting age for women was lowered to 21, in 1928, the electorate embraced over 90 per cent of all adults. Without this massive increase in the enfranchised population, it is difficult to see how the growth of the Labour party in the 1920s could have taken place. The principle of the representation of individual citizens, regardless of their wealth, was thus largely accepted; representation was no longer based on taxation. It is noteworthy that, as a result of the 1918 act, the receipt of poor relief ceased to be a voting disqualification.

Vestiges of the old system did however remain. Only in 1948 were the university seats and all forms of plural voting abolished, as also was the residence qualification. Strictly speaking, therefore, the principle of 'one man, one vote' did not arrive until 30 years after the passage of the 1918 act. The net effect of the 1948 act was, indeed, to bring about a slight decrease in the percentage of adults enfranchised. Even the lowering of the voting age to 18, in 1969, only added about 800,000 to an electorate of 39 millions, or about two per cent.[32] The reform of 1918 was indeed the beginning of a new era. The enormous increase in the size of the electorate called for new methods and styles of political communication. The idea of a mandate took on greater potency. The measurement of public opinion had political relevance. The systematic organisation of parties at constituency level became a necessity. The number of uncontested seats, which had been as high as 114 in 1906 and 163 in December 1910, fell to 7 in 1929 and to 3 in 1945.[33] Turnout, which had stood at 57.2 per cent in 1918, reached 73 per cent in 1922 and has never, since then, dropped below 70 per cent. It is true that turnout figures just as high, or higher, had been recorded earlier. In 1906 the figure was over 83 per cent. But there is a world of difference between a turnout of 83 per cent in an electorate of 7,264,608, and, say, in October 1974, a turnout of just under 73 per cent in an electorate of 40,072,971. The possession of the right to vote has now become the rule rather than the exception. The turning-point came in 1918.

Dissolutions, manifestos and mandates
The process by which the franchise has been widened in the United Kingdom has been a typically pragmatic one. There has been nothing 'merely logical' about it.[34] In 1832

the principle aim was to preserve the eighteenth-century system of representation; in 1918 to give the vote to all men and some women; in 1969 to bring the voting age into line with changing views of adult maturity. At every stage the hope of political profit has, in part at least, motivated the reformers. But it would be a grave mistake to suppose that the franchise has been democratized, that all adults have the vote, that all votes are equally valuable, or that the possession of the vote ensures to the elector a continuing say in how the United Kingdom should be governed.

To begin with, the dissolution of Parliament and the calling of a general election are acts of the royal prerogative, exercised by the monarch on the advice of the Prime Minister. There is thus no need for an Act of Parliament authorizing an appeal to the people; neither the electorate nor their parliamentary representatives are consulted. Elections are foisted on the people whether they like them or not. And the timing of a general election places enormous power in the hands of the Prime Minister. In 1951 Clement Attlee, the Labour premier, dissatisfied with a majority of only five, forced the electors to go to the polls again, after an interval of only twenty months, in the hope of increasing Labour party support; the result was a Conservative government. In October 1974 Harold Wilson called an election after less than eight months in office, hoping to turn a minority Labour government into a majority one; he obtained an overall majority of three seats. In May 1955 Sir Anthony Eden called a general election (though one was not due till February 1956) in the hope of capitalizing on a reduction in the standard rate of income tax the previous month. The next election need not have taken place till 1960, but Harold Macmillan called one in 1959, when the damage done to the reputation of the Conservative party by the Suez affair and economic recession had been forgotten, and the opinion polls were giving the Conservatives a convincing lead.[35]

The timing of a general election is obviously crucial. In theory the monarch has the right to refuse a dissolution. In May 1950, in a pseudonymous letter to *The Times*, Sir Alan

Lascelles, George VI's private secretary, argued that the monarch could refuse a dissolution if he were satisfied that the existing Parliament 'was still vital, viable, and capable of doing its job', that an election would be detrimental to the national economy, and that another Prime Minister could be found to carry on government business, with a working majority in the Commons, for a limited period.[36] In practice, the refusal of a dissolution has not occurred in modern British history. A Prime Minister, on the other hand, can use the threat of a dissolution to quell internal criticism in his party, or bring rebels to heel, as Harold Wilson did shortly before his resignation in the spring of 1976. When a dissolution is called, the timing of it will generally be of the Prime Minister's own choosing, and it will serve purposes which are peculiarly his own.

Nor do the general public have much say in the issues upon which an election is fought. More will be said on this subject, in so far as the election campaign is concerned, in a later chapter. Here it will suffice to concentrate on the election manifestos, which few people buy and even fewer read. The manifesto is part of the elaborate ritual by which party stalwarts are able to reassure themselves of their political identity. It is both the war-cry and the war-paint of the warrior braves; the mixture of sound and fury, the patches of light and darkness, all must be just right. Since victorious parties seldom stick to their manifestos, the whole exercise might seem academic. But victorious governments also have a habit of claiming a mandate for whatever their manifesto happened to contain.

For these reasons, the compilation of the manifesto is accorded a great deal of time and energy, even though the conditions under which it is compiled are of necessity very different from those under which the policies it enumerates may have to be implemented. The incongruity of making pledges and promises under these conditions is further enhanced when one remembers that no opposition party has the research facilities and technical data available to the government, and without which prognostications of future action can only be very imperfectly rehearsed. A really honest opposition manifesto would declare: 'We don't know what problems we shall have to face if returned to power, we haven't the expertise at our command to make reliable predictions. These are our policies, but we warn you that we cannot guarantee that any of them will ever see the light of day.' But it would be foolish to deny that no opposition in its right mind would dream of couching an appeal to the electors in those terms. Hence sweeping, incomplete or vaguely defined policy statements are made, only to be abandoned in whole or in part later on. The 1970 Conservative manifesto, *A Better Tomorrow*, stated: 'We will stop further nationalisation'; in fact, Rolls-Royce was nationalized by Edward Heath's government after only eight months in office. The manifesto also stated: 'We utterly reject the philosophy of compulsory wage control'; in November 1972 such a philosophy was implemented.[37] The entire February 1974 Labour manifesto, *Let Us Work Together*, assumed that Labour, if returned to office, would have a parliamentary majority to carry out its pledges. The fact that no such majority was forthcoming did not deter Harold Wilson from taking office.

Nor is there any evidence that manifestos sway votes. During the three weeks between the dissolution of Parliament and polling day, issues may arise spontaneously. From the point of view of the electors, there is a world of difference between support for a party and support for its policies. A survey of the 1950 general election campaign in Greenwich showed that support among Labour supporters for Labour policies averaged only 61 per cent; but 41 per cent of Labour supporters said they approved of Conservative policies, and, on average, 31 per cent of Conservative supporters approved of Labour policies.[38] Professor J. Blondel has analysed opinions on 22 questions asked by the British Institute of Public Opinion in the period 1959-61. He found a large measure of agreement between Conservative and Labour supporters on 'humanitarian' issues, such as capital punishment, and on questions of foreign policy. There was more partisanship on economic and social questions, but even here it was not extreme.[39] David Butler and Donald Stokes, the authors of *Political Change in Britain: The Evolution of Electoral Choice*, do not even bother to include 'manifesto' in their index.[40] This is not to deny that *issues* play an important part in the determination of party preference;economic issues, in particular, can be crucial.[41] The attraction of *policies*, especially policies put forward at the time of a general election, must however be open to doubt. Voting is a complex matter, but the manifesto is irrelevant to it.[42]

Why, then, do manifestos continue to appear? The answer seems to be that they are 'house' publications of the political parties, designed mainly for internal consumption. Party research workers expend considerable energy in devising new policies; they want to see them in print. Party candidates want a compact statement of policy for reference purposes, and as a shield when facing awkward questions at press conferences; here the manifesto serves its turn.[43] Most important of all, party activists want some assurance that the party 'image' has not changed in theory, especially where it has changed in practice. They want to be sure that the tablets of stone still exist, however battered and broken they may be.

This function of the manifesto is most clearly seen in the case of the Labour party. As befits the offspring of extra-parliamentary forces, the constitution of the Labour party deliberately gives its party conference a major say in policy decisions. Proposals which receive a two-thirds majority on a card vote are included in the party programme; the National Executive Committee and the Parliamentary Committee of the party decide which items from the party programme shall be included in the manifesto. The drafting of a Labour manifesto can thus become a tug-of-war between a cautious leadership and the appointed guardians of the socialist conscience. The references, in the October 1974 manifesto, to the party's as yet incomplete plans to nationalize banking and insurance, and to the February pledge to cut 'several hundred million pounds' of defence expenditure, are cases in point.[44]

In the Conservative and Liberal parties, the drafting of

the manifesto rests, ultimately, with the parliamentary leaders, though due deference is expected to be paid to extra-parliamentary opinion. The Conservative Research Department has an Advisory Committee on Policy, composed of MPs, peers, members of the National Union and Central Office, as well as co-opted members, to comment on manifesto proposals. In February 1974 the manifesto was prudently silent on the nationalisation of Rolls-Royce, but pledged the party to oppose Labour's policy of 'massive nationalisation on an unprecedented scale'; the October manifesto promised the electorate that the party would remove threats of further nationalisation. Again, the February manifesto referred to the party's continued opposition to the imposition of 'a universal system of comprehensive education', without explaining how it was that comprehensive education had actually spread (for instance in the Inner London Education Authority) under Conservative rule. The descriptive label on the package is, apparently, more important than the ingredients. So long as the policy remains unchanged, party adherents are expected to forgive deviations in practice; and the vast majority of them undoubtedly do so.

For the 90 per cent of the electorate who do not even subscribe to a local political party[45] these ideological nuances would be irrelevant were it not for the fact that a party winning office (if not power or a majority of popular support) invariably claims a 'mandate' for those parts of its policy which were included in its manifesto. At this stage, two points need to be made. The first, and fairly obvious, is that the reverse is not true – i.e. governments are not particularly reluctant to pursue policies which were not in their manifestos. Stanley Baldwin passed the Trade Disputes Act (1927); Clement Attlee curbed the power of the House of Lords (1949); Harold Wilson passed the Commonwealth Immigration Act (1968); Edward Heath took the United Kingdom into the European Economic Community (1973). None of these acts, each of which vitally affected the interests of British citizens, had previously been submitted to the electorate or included in a manifesto.[46]

The second point is that manifestos, running into several thousand words, say many things, often in a very woolly fashion. It can hardly be supposed that every voter agrees with every item of policy of the party for which he votes. On the strength of the evidence already cited, it seems highly probable that many do not. If every general election were fought on a single issue, as in December 1910 (reform of the Lords) or 1923 (tariff reform), voters would have a clear policy choice. No election since the Second World War has been fought on a single issue; only the EEC referendum of 5 June 1975 was a true plebiscite of the people. In this respect, the fact that many election promises *are* carried out is beside the point. Nor does it matter what proportion of the electorate vote for a victorious party. The notion of the mandate, not merely as a mandate to govern, but as a mandate to pass more or less controversial measures which happen to have been included in the manifesto, implies a degree of popular support which rarely exists. Against this background, the power of those who draft the manifestos is great indeed.

The promulgation of the manifesto is closely bound up with the doctrine of the mandate. The mandate is a twentieth-century device. A hundred years ago most politicians did not recognise it. 'I am perfectly aware', Lord Hartington instructed the House of Commons in 1886, 'that there exists in our Constitution no principle of the mandate. I know that the mandate of the constituencies is . . . unknown to our Constitution.'[47] With the constitutional crisis of 1909, when the House of Lords refused to pass a Liberal, budget of avowedly radical proportions, which had not been submitted to the people,[48] and the election of January 1910, which confirmed the Liberals in office if not in power, the doctrine of the mandate came into its own.

It is a doctrine with peculiar appeal to the Labour party, whose roots are embedded firmly in the practice of the trade union movement mandating delegates to support certain policies and oppose others. It has taken firm hold on the Conservative party, on whose behalf the peers were acting in 1909. Thus in 1923 Baldwin felt he had to have a mandate from the people for protective tariffs. In 1973 many Conservatives claimed it was wrong for trade unions to flout or ignore the Industrial Relations Act, for had not the government obtained a mandate for it in 1970? Minor parties, too, are fond of exploiting the doctrine. The Scottish National Party (SNP) proclaims: 'if the SNP gets a majority of the [Scottish] seats at a General Election, this will produce an unquestionable mandate for self-government. The Westminster government will then have to comply with the wishes of the Scottish people.'[49] In other words, if the party won 36 of the 71 Scottish seats, it would claim to speak for an electorate of over three million and a population even larger. When one realizes that such a majority of seats could be obtained with a mere minority of the votes cast, the enormity of the SNP claim to a mandate becomes apparent.

If the electoral system ensured that an MP could only be elected, and a party installed in office, by obtaining a majority of the votes cast, such a claim would be extravagant but not absurd. As it happens, the electoral system of the United Kingdom provides no such guarantee.

Some votes are more equal than others

No voter may exercise more than one vote. But votes are not of equal potency. A comparison of two results in October 1974 will illustrate this point:

1.1 Ebbw Vale and Ilford North, October 1974

	Ebbw Vale (electorate 37,640)	Ilford North (electorate 65,195)
Labour	12,226 (74.1 per cent)	20,621 (42.5 per cent)
Liberal	3,167 (11.0 per cent)	8.080 (16.6 per cent)
Conservative	2,153 (7.5 per cent)	19,843 (40.9 per cent)
Plaid Cymru	2,101 (7.3 per cent)	—
Labour majority:	18,059 (63.1 per cent)	778 (1.6 per cent)

A voter in Ebbw Vale is clearly not in the same position to influence the result of a general election as a voter in Ilford North. At Ebbw Vale it would need 9,030 Labour voters to vote Liberal for the seat to change hands. Since electorates change in size, as does turnout, this is most unlikely to happen, except perhaps over a period of time. At Ilford North, a switch to Conservative by only 390 disgruntled Labour supporters would produce a different result next time. This margin is small enough to remain unaffected by, say, a surge in Liberal support or the entry of a fourth party. Ilford North was, in fact, the only London constituency to change hands in the October 1974 election. In February the Conservatives had had a majority of 285; the total Conservative vote remained exactly the same in October. It is probable, therefore, that a switch to Labour by a few hundred Liberal voters gave Labour the seat and, unintentionally perhaps, helped Labour nationally to its narrow 3-seat majority over all other parties. Put another way, Michael Foot, the Labour MP for Ebbw Vale, can afford to support policies which are unpopular with his constituents. At Ilford North, the late Millie Miller might have jeopardized her security as an MP if she had done so. The voters of both constituencies exercise political choice; those at Ilford North also exercise political power.

The above examples illustrate two further inequities of the present electoral system. One is that electorates of different sizes have the same representation. If one MP represents over 65,000 electors at Ilford North, the 37,000 electors at Ebbw Vale ought not to have an MP all to themselves. The other is that it is possible for an MP to be elected – as Millie Miller was – with only a minority of the votes cast. Fifty-seven per cent of the electors in Ilford North expressed a preference not to be represented by Labour in Parliament. The system brushed aside their views. In fact, 60 per cent of the seats in the October 1974 election were won by a minority vote; in February the proportion had been 64 per cent, the highest in modern British electoral history. 'Plurality voting' – or the-first-past-the-post system – ensures that the candidate who obtains the most votes is elected, no matter how many votes are obtained by other candidates. A small turnover in votes from one party to another in individual constituencies can, when translated into seats at Westminster, lead to disproportionately large majorities.[50] No government since 1945 has polled more than 50 per cent of the votes cast, but all but one have obtained more than 50 per cent of the seats (see table 1:2).

1.2 Votes and Seats for the governing party, 1945–74

Election	Government	Votes cast (percentage)	Seats obtained (percentage)
1945	Labour	47.8	61.4
1950	Labour	46.1	50.4
1951	Conservative	48.0	51.4
1955	Conservative	49.7	54.6
1959	Conservative	49.4	58.0
1964	Labour	44.1	50.3
1966	Labour	47.9	57.6
1970	Conservative	46.4	52.4
1974 (February)	Labour	37.1	47.4
1974 (October)	Labour	39.2	50.2

The nearest correlation between seats and votes for the government was in 1951, when the difference was still over 3 per cent. In fact, in 1951 Labour actually obtained a larger share of the votes cast (48.8 per cent) than did the Conservative party; but the Conservatives obtained more seats (321 out of a total of 625) and so formed the government. In February 1974 the system favoured Labour. The Conservative share of the vote was higher (37.9 per cent), but the number of seats was lower (297 against Labour's 301). The distorting effects of the system have, however, hit the minor parties hardest.

Table 1:3 shows the results of the October 1974 election. The final column tells its own story. The Liberals polled over half the Conservative vote, but obtained less than five per cent of the Conservative representation in terms of seats. Plaid Cymru obtained 0.6 per cent of the votes cast, giving it three seats; other minor parties in Great Britain obtained a slightly higher proportion of votes, but no seats at all. The National Front, for instance, obtained 0.4 per cent of the votes, which ought to have entitled it to at least

1.3 **The Relationship between votes and seats, October 1974**

	Votes (percentage)	Seats Number	Seats Percentage	Votes per seat
Labour	39.2	319	50.2	35,916
Conservative	35.8	277	43.7	37,779
Liberal	18.3	13	2.0	411,289
SNP	2.9	11	1.7	76,329
Plaid Cymru	0.6	3	0.5	55,440
Others (Gt. Britain)	0.8	—	—	—
Others (N. Ireland)	2.4	12	1.9	58,508
	100.0	635	100.0	

two MPs. But none of its candidates was elected. It is evident, moreover, that in the October election a Conservative vote was worth less than a Labour vote. And a Liberal vote was worth much less than either. In previous elections, a Labour vote was worth less than a Conservative one; in 1959, for instance, Labour votes were 47,347 per seat, Conservative votes 37,671. Some votes are clearly more valuable than others and bring greater benefits to the party for which they are cast.

Considerations such as these have led to renewed demands over the past decade for the system of voting to be changed. Many of the anomalies and discrepancies already cited are directly attributable to the first-past-the-post system. Would a different system produce a more equitable result? Like all questions of electoral reform, this is an entirely political one. The Liberal party, which has suffered most from the present system, has been the staunchest advocate of change to proportional representation (PR). The Conservative party, believing above all in strong and stable government, used to oppose PR. But the electoral experience of 1974, the spectacle of becoming an opposition party with a higher percentage of votes cast than Labour, above all the conviction that the stalemate of 1974 had delivered the country into the hands of the Scottish National Party, and that the present electoral system may, therefore, foster the dismemberment of the United Kingdom, have contributed towards a change of heart. Little wonder that in May 1974 'Conservative Action for Electoral Reform' was founded. 'The real problem', its propaganda asserts, 'is not which system to choose but the political will to support change.'[51] Conservative Action has achieved a respectable following within the party. But most Conservative MPs would rather the subject of electoral reform had remained dormant. Most Labour MPs agree. 'Proportional representation', Ron Hayward, the Labour party's general secretary, said in February 1976, 'means coalition government at Westminster . . . and it is goodbye then to any dreams or aspirations for a democratic socialist Britain.'[52] Yest some Scottish Labour MPs have pointed out that, if the proposed Scottish assembly is elected on the Westminster system, the Scottish National Party could obtain a majority of seats on a minority of votes; whereas PR at Edinburgh could keep the nationalists out of power. In 1976 a Labour Study Group on Electoral Reform was launched. PR has, in short, become fashionable. The National Committee for Electoral Reform (slogan: 'More power to your vote'), formed in June 1976, has a distinguished academic, artistic, ecclesiastical and industrial membership, and covers a wide political spectrum.

Of the many electoral systems in use throughout the world, three are of particular relevance to the United Kingdom.[53] One is the Alternative Vote (AV), used in elections for the Australian House of Representatives. This method uses single-member constituencies, but the voter has as many votes as there are candidates, and marks his first preference with the figure 1, his second with a 2, and so on. A candidate securing a majority of first-preference votes is declared elected. If no absolute majority is forthcoming on the first count, the candidate with the lowest number of votes is eliminated, and the second-preference votes on his ballot papers are distributed among the other candidates. This process continues until one of the candidates achieves an absolute majority.

The AV system was actually proposed by the minority Labour government in 1930 but the bill, having passed the

House of Commons, was rejected in the Lords, and lost when the government fell. It is not a truly proportional system. It does give minorities greater representation and, in David Butler's estimation, would have increased the number of Liberal MPs, perhaps thereby lessening the decline of that party. It would not have prevented a party with less than 50 per cent of the votes from obtaining a parliamentary majority.[54] Michael Steed has shown that, under certain assumptions, had the February 1974 election been conducted under the AV system, the result might actually have given Labour a few more seats.[55]

The second system favoured by electoral reformers, and the one officially promoted by the Electoral Reform Society (founded 1884) is the Single Transferable Vote (STV). STV is based on multi-member constituencies, in which voters are able to indicate their preferencies as under AV. A quota is then established by computing the total number of valid ballot papers, and dividing that number by the number of seats in the constituency, plus one; to the resulting figure, one is added. Thus in a five-member constituency the quota would be one more than one-sixth of the number of valid ballot papers. Any candidate reaching the quota with his first-preference votes is elected. His second-preference votes, plus the second-preference votes of the candidate who comes bottom of the poll, and who is automatically eliminated, are then distributed among the other candidates. Any candidate who then reaches the quota is also elected. The process continues until all available seats have been filled.

STV is undoubtedly a complicated system, yet it has had plenty of British admirers. The Speaker's Conference of 1916–17 recommended a mixture of single- and multi-member constituencies, using AV in the former and STV in the latter. After much haggling the Commons rejected STV, in 1917, by only 7 votes. But between 1918 and 1945 STV was used for the university seats. It was used in Northern Ireland from 1921 to 1929, and Edward Heath's government thought highly enough of it to prescribe it, in the Northern Ireland Act of 1973, as the method by which the short-lived

Northern Ireland Assembly was to be elected; it was also used in the elections to the Northern Irish Convention in 1975. It is used in the Republic of Ireland, Malta, Tasmania and in the Australian Upper House (the Senate). It is the system of PR advocated by the Liberal party.

STV gives a great deal of freedom of choice to the elector, though it would be a mistake to think that much cross-voting between parties would occur if the system was adopted in this country. Political parties dominate British politics, and they would certainly take care to instruct voters, perhaps by means of dummy ballot papers, how to vote. It would, however, enable voters to choose between shades of opinion in a party, and this facility might be welcomed by constituency parties split between 'right' and 'left'.

That STV would ensure a much fairer result in terms of seats per party is beyond doubt. If applied in February 1974 it would have given Labour between 232 and 239 seats, the Conservatives between 240 and 246 seats, and the Liberals between 123 and 131 seats.[56] As these parties obtained, respectively, 31.1, 37.9, and 19.3 per cent of the total vote, the accuracy of STV is evident. But there is equally no doubt that very small parties would lose out under this system. Broadly speaking, the lower the number of seats in each constituency, the higher becomes the quota necessary to obtain a seat, and the more difficult it becomes for small parties to secure adequate representation by reaching the threshold. In 1950 the Liberals, with 9.1 per cent of the vote, returned 9 MPs, or 1.4 per cent of the seats; under STV it has been calculated that they would have obtained only 16 seats, or 2.6 per cent.[57] In 1966, with 8.5 per cent of the vote, they obtained 1.9 per cent of the seats; under STV the Liberal proportion of seats might have risen to 6.2 per cent.[58] In February 1974, minor British parties other than the nationalists obtained 0.8 per cent of the vote, giving them 0.3 per cent of the seats; STV would not have given them any seats.[59]

Beyond these statistical considerations, STV would involve other practical problems. By-elections are one. In

Malta the ballot papers of the original general election are preserved and, if a by-election becomes necessary, recounted, disregarding preferences for the deceased or retiring member. This would not, however, reflect the state of electoral opinion at the time of the by-election. Another method would be to treat a multi-member constituency, for by-election purposes, as a single-member constituency, using AV. Here the drawbacks of AV would apply with even greater force. A government with a knife-edge majority might find itself dislodged by a by-election result which did not accurately reflect a change in electoral opinion, or which apparently reflected on which had not really taken place.

The main difficulty in applying STV in the United Kingdom would lie in the problem of constituencies. STV has not, to date, been used in a country with a population approaching that of Great Britain. The minimum multi-member constituency possible under STV is a 3-member one. In an electorate of about 40 millions, with 635 seats available, this would entail constituencies with an average of about 188,000 electors. Problems of communication between MPs and constituents would be considerable. Moreover, in Scotland and Wales, and in many parts of England, where viable fourth parties exist, the fourth and, in some cases, the third parties would labour under severe disadvantages, as already outlined. So 4- or, more likely, 5-seat constituencies would probably be needed. This would necessitate huge constituencies with perhaps as many as 314,000 electors in each unless, of course, the number of MPs was drastically increased. To allow for 5-member constituencies with an average of, say, 60,000 electors in each, the House of Commons would have to accommodate about 3,330 MPs; this is impractical in the extreme. Yet, unless the number of MPs was increased, the sense of remoteness from Westminster would be intense. It is true that a very high proportion of voters would be represented by at least one MP belonging to the party they support. But the close relationship between an MP and his constituents would disappear.

Considerations such as these have led many political and academic observers to espouse a modified form of the system used for elections to the West German parliament, the Bundestag. In West Germany, half the seats are directly elected in single-member constituencies using the familiar plurality system; the other half are distributed to parties on a regional basis to achieve a high degree of overall proportionality. A party must have obtained at least 5 per cent of the total vote, or three directly-elected seats, to secure any non-directly-elected seats. In October 1975 the Hansard Society for Parliamentary Government established a Commission on Electoral Reform which, with one dissentient voice, opted for a modified form of the West German model, which it dubbed the Additional Member System (AMS).[60] Under AMS small constituencies would be retained, the House of Commons would be increased to only 640 MPs, and all candidates would stand in constituency elections. Three-quarters of the Commons would be elected on the plurality system in single-member constituencies, whose average size would thus increase from 63,000 to 83,000. The remaining 160 seats would be allocated to parties on a regional basis, a minimum of five per cent of the vote in any area of allocation being necessary to obtain any additional seats. Those of a party's candidates who failed to gain direct election would be placed in order according to the percentage of votes given them in their constituencies; additional seats won by parties would be allocated to their highest-placed candidates. By-elections for vacancies in the constituencies would take place as at present. For the additional, regional seats, vacancies would be filled by the next highest candidate, of the party in question, who is willing to serve.

It would be churlish to suppose that AMS is not complicated. The allocation of additional seats is particularly complex.[61] The drawing-up of regional boundaries would doubtless be a matter of hot dispute. But the system would not be complicated *for the voter*. The mechanics of voting would not change at all. Constituents would have directly-elected MPs to whom they could turn, as at present. They would, in addition, have regional representatives. The substantial difference would come in the way votes are treated. Minorities (though not very small parties) would be adequately represented. As with STV, rule by a party which had only a minority of the total votes cast would become a thing of the past.

Here, indeed, is the rub so far as either STV or AMS is concerned. It has been estimated that, under AMS, in 1945 the Labour party (actual majority 146 over all other parties) would have obtained 83 seats fewer, and would have had to have contented itself with forming a minority government. In 1951 Labour would have retained power, but still without an overall majority. In February 1974 the number of Conservative MPs would have been reduced (from 297 to about 250) but so would Labour's representation, and a Conservative–Liberal coalition would have been a probability. In October, Liberal representation would again have increased dramatically, from 13 to 110; Labour would have remained the largest single party, but with more than 60 seats short of an overall majority. In short, had AMS been in operation since 1945, coalition or minority governments would have been the rule rather than the exception.[62]

This is not a prospect politicians relish. Most are not accustomed to sharing power and to making the dogmatic compromises which that would involve. And too often they assume that coalition government is likely to produce weak government. The argument is therefore seen, and encouraged to be seen, as being between strong government and representative government. The first-past-the-post system, it is argued, provides strong leadership, even if the true party strengths are not accurately reflected in the Commons. A system of PR would produce a mathematically more accurate result, but would encourage politicians 'to barter for power by breaking pledges given to the electorate just days before'.[63]

It is unrealistic to see the argument in these terms. The electoral system as fashioned by the Acts of 1918, 1928 and 1948 has produced four minority governments (1924, 1929-31, March-October 1974 and since the Stechford by-election of April 1977). The coalition government of 1918-22, the National governments of 1931-40, and Churchill's wartime coalition were not even dictated by the state of the parties in the Commons; they were seen by politicians as necessary demonstrations of national unity. PR has not produced a string of unstable coalitions in the Republic of Ireland or in West Germany. In Israel, where the whole country is one constituency and seats in the Knesset are allocated proportionately to the votes cast for party lists, no election has ever produced an absolute majority for any one party; this has not paralysed the working of government. Once politicians get used to the idea of coalition, its reality is not half as grim as its prospect.[64]

One final point needs to be stressed. PR would be a leap in the dark, not merely intrinsically, by replacing one electoral system by another, but also consequentially, by its effect on voting habits. Many calculations about what might have been under PR (including those about AMS referred to above) are made on the assumption that people would have cast their votes exactly as they did under the plurality system. This is a most unlikely hypothesis. Many Liberal voters are at present deterred from voting Liberal because a Liberal vote is a wasted vote in most three-cornered contests. Under the present system, some voters in marginal constituencies put their own political preferences on one side, and vote in order to help defeat the party they most dislike. 'Tactical voting' has grown in recent years. In October 1974, about 35,000 voters in England and Wales deliberately switched parties, or voted when they would normally have abstained, in order to prevent Labour victories; this cost Labour 25 seats.[65] Voting behaviour would be very different under a PR system. The existence of such a system would be a positive inducement to voters to vote for the party they liked most. It would also be an inducement to minor parties to put up more candidates in order (particularly under AMS) to pick up as many votes as possible. The atmosphere of political debate would not be the same, and politicians would refrain from making promises they knew they would probably never be in a position to keep.

The experience of the two 1974 elections, producing indecisive results and perpetuating an election atmosphere, has swept away many of the glib assumptions about the plurality system. The prospect of devolved assemblies for Scotland and Wales has renewed interest in PR, for the Royal Commission on the Constitution (the Kilbrandon report, 1973) was unanimous in recommending STV for elections to the Scottish and Welsh assemblies.[66] The Labour government, in November 1975, rejected this view and proposed elections on the first-past-the-post system.[67] This would not ensure proper representation for minorities. It could lead to a Scottish National Party majority, in the Scottish assembly, based on a minority of votes; if the Scottish nationalists were to demand Scottish independence on that basis, a constitutional crisis of the first magnitude would result.

Direct elections to the European Parliament provide another challenge to the plurality system. In July 1976, Common Market heads of state agreed on a directly-elected 410-member European Parliament, with 81 seats each for the United Kingdom, France, West Germany and Italy. The Select Committee on Direct Elections to the European Assembly recommended that 66 seats be given to England, 8 to Scotland, 4 to Wales and 3 to Northern Ireland.[68] This proposal will result in very large constituencies, ranging from 514,000 electors per English seat to 344,000 per Northern Irish seat. And if the plurality system is persisted in, the distortions thrown up in general elections would be magnified. The Conservative and Labour parties would pick up most of the seats between them; the Liberals and other minority parties would be hard-pressed to obtain any European representation.[69] A system of PR again seems to be called for.

There is no reason why two electoral systems (PR for Europe and/or the devolved assemblies, and the plurality system for Westminster) should not exist side by side. They do so for the House of Representatives and the Senate in Australia. In Britain, single-member constituencies for Westminster coexist with multi-member constituencies for local government elections. Moreover, the elections for the

Strasbourg parliament would not be in order to choose a government of the Common Market, and thus those who argue against PR on the grounds that it does not foster strength and stability in government would have nothing to fear from an experiment with PR in the European context. Such an introduction to the mysteries of PR would perhaps ease the agony of transition to a fairer system of representation at Westminster.

One things is certain. A parliamentary democracy, such as the United Kingdom purports to be, ought to be as unlike an autocracy as possible. An electoral system which does not gurantee that the minority shall not exercise legislative power is indefensible.

Chapter Two

LEGAL CONSTRAINTS

Legal Constraints

In the preceding chapter, reference was made to the advantage possessed by a voter who finds himself in a marginal constituency, where his real ability to affect the outcome is measurably greater than that of his fellow citizen in a safe seat. A really conscientious elector might be prompted by this information to move house in order to qualify for voting in a more marginal constituency. Many students, registered to vote both in their home town and in their university residence, decide where to vote on the basis of the relative marginality of the two constituencies. They are in a privileged position. Moving house to maximize the potency of one's vote is not merely expensive but is, in any case, a dangerous exercise. Within a five-year period movements of population can turn a safe seat into a marginal one, and vice-versa. Or the boundaries of the constituency may alter with a similar result. Or an election might be fixed for a date months after the compilation of the electoral register, whose 'staleness' could affect the result. The mechanics of voting may be as important in determining the result as the voters themselves.

Universal suffrage?
The possession of a vote is, with certain qualifications, assured to all male and female British subjects (including citizens of Commonwealth countries) over 18 years of age and normally resident in the United Kingdom on 10 October of any year. Members of the armed forces and civil

servants employed outside the United Kingdom, and their wives, may also vote; so too may merchant seamen. Peers, who are represented in the upper House, may not vote, nor may traitors or felons serving a prison sentence, nor may persons convicted of corrupt or illegal practices within five years of the date of their conviction.

It is commonly supposed that lunatics are automatically disfranchised. This is not so. A person of unsound mind may nonetheless vote 'during lucid intervals', and in any case the phrase 'unsound mind' is open to a multitude of medical interpretations. In June 1976 three patients at Winwick mental hospital, in Cheshire, won an appeal against having their names deleted from the electoral register. The judge held that, though under treatment for depression, they were not suffering from mental illness and, living in detached houses in the hospital grounds, could not be regarded as patients.[1] Aliens living in the United Kingdom are disfranchised, but not if they are citizens of the Republic of Ireland; by a curious historical anomaly which no British government has dared correct, every citizen of Eire resident in the United Kingdom, and otherwise qualified to vote, may do so.

Although all adults who are not disqualifed have the right to vote, this right is not automatically bestowed. From 1832 to 1918 the duty of maintaining a register of electors fell to Poor Law overseers, who extracted names from rate-books. Those not on the register might put in a claim for inclusion, but the inclusion of any name could be challenged by party agents, and a system of registration courts was necessary to settle disputed claims. With electoral rolls of perhaps only a few hundred voters, elections were often decided by the inclusion or deletion of names; the register of electors was thus a political battleground. The Act of 1918 did away with this system. Compilation of the register is now the responsibility of the Registration Officer, who is in practice the Clerk to the Council of the local government authority within which the constituency is situated.[2] The 1918 legislation provided for the compilation of two registers a year, in the spring and autumn. On the grounds of economy the spring register was abolished in 1926; it was re-established in 1948 but, again on grounds of cost, was abandoned the following year.[3] The fact that there is now only one re-compilation annually means that it can take as long as 16 months of residence in a constituency to qualify for the vote.

The rule is that those who are resident in a constituency on the qualifying date can be included in the register of electors. The qualifying date is 10 October. Heads of households are required to enter, on forms supplied to them, the names of all residents aged 18 or over on the qualifying date, plus the names of those minors who will attain the age of 18 during the currency of the register being compiled, and the names of certain categories of absent voters, such as merchant seamen. From these replies a provisional register is compiled and open to public inspection until 16 December. Within the period of inspection (just over two weeks) those persons who think they ought to be included, but are not, may claim the vote; the claim might be on the grounds that the head of household omitted their names, or that for some reason the registration form never reached them. After mid-December the final register is compiled, and comes into force on 16 February; it remains in force until 15 February of the following year.

How accurate is the register of electors? The time taken to compile it makes for built-in obsolescence. It could never be a hundred per cent accurate. Most people do not bother to check whether they are on it, in spite of wide publicity urging them to do so. Forms are not returned, or are wrongly completed. In August 1976 the High Court reversed the result of a local by-election in the Barnes ward of Richmond Borough Council after discovering that two unqualified persons, one under 18, had been put on the voting register.[4] There is no provision for the automatic deletion of deceased voters. More serious is the fact that the register is already four months old when it comes into force. It remains valid until 16 months after the provisional compilation. Of those people who are not registered at addresses to which they have moved during the year, only a minority apply for a postal vote or travel back to their original constituencies on polling day. In 1950 the Government Social Survey found that the register was only 96 per cent accurate when compiled, and only 94 per cent accurate when published. Thereafter its accuracy diminished by one half per cent per month, so that in the last month of its life it was only 87 per cent accurate.[5] A similar study undertaken in respect of the 1966 register revealed that it was only 93 per cent accurate on publication day and only 85 per cent accurate on its last day of validity.[6]

Clearly, the effect of doing away with two registers a year has been to disfranchise between 3 and 4 per cent of eligible voters - perhaps as many as one million persons. This is a factor often overlooked. In October 1974, of the approximately 40 million registered voters, about 29 million voted, giving an apparent turnout of 72.8 per cent.[7] But not all those nominally registered actually remained in their constituencies on 10 October. Real turnout was therefore about 78 per cent.[8] The problem of the ageing register is not a minor one. Four of the ten general elections held since 1945 have taken place in October, on substantially inaccurate registers. In January 1974, in the wake of the miners' strike and the three-day week, there was talk of a snap election in early February. Had that happened, hundreds of thousands of eligible voters would have been disfranchised. Actually, polling day took place on 28 February, less than two weeks after the new register came into force. But it was still then four months old and already inaccurate.

Although it is an offence not to fill in the registration form, the accuracy of such returns depends on the honesty and intellectual ability of the head of the household. Landlords who allow their dwellings to become overcrowded with tenants will hardly wish to advertize the fact on the registration form. Many Commonwealth immigrants, especially from Asian countries, do not understand the registration procedure, or are ignorant of their rights or may suspect the motives of those who seek information, or fear the consequences of giving it. In the early 1960s probably less than half of the Commonwealth immigrants were registered.[9] A survey undertaken in Nottingham in the late 1960s revealed that 27 per cent of the immigrant respondents were unregistered.[10] Another survey, covering the October 1974 election in seven English constituencies with a high density of Afro-Caribbeans and Asians in their populations, showed that whereas only six per cent of eligible white voters were not registered, 24 per cent of eligible coloured voters were not on the register; excluding new voters and those who had lived at their addresses for less than a year, the coloured unregistered proportion rose to 30 per cent.[11]

Conversely, aliens, unless they are Irish citizens, ought not to be able to vote. Yet some find their way onto the register. This can happen at educational institutions, for instance, where the authorities in charge sometimes return the names of all students in residence without bothering to strike out the names of foreign students. During the district council elections of May 1976, it was discovered at one college campus that in a student population of 1,300, the names of 30 aliens had been entered on the electoral register. It is unlikely that any of the aliens actually voted. Some could hardly believe their good fortune in actually being on a British voting list. Nor in this instance could their votes have affected the outcome of a parliamentary election.[12] This is beside the point. Their names ought not to have been on the register in the first place.

Beyond the problems of the electoral register, there is the vexed question of absentee voting. That seamen and members of the armed forces should be able to vote by proxy or post, if they are away from home, or that people incapacitated by blindness or illness should be able to do likewise, is beyond contention. As regards other people who know that they will be away from their constituency on polling day, the law makes a curious distinction. The 1948 Act, which greatly extended the postal voting provisions, permits a vote by post to anyone whose occupation would make it impossible for him to be at home to vote in person. But those who will be away from home for other reasons, such as a holiday, are not allowed to vote by post. When the taking of an annual holiday was the exception rather than the rule, and confined to the well-to-do, this distinction was perhaps tenable. Nowadays it is not. Everyone with enough civic responsibility to want to vote, and properly qualifed, should be able to do so.

Opposition to the extension of postal voting has come more from the Labour than from the Conservative side. The 1964 Conservative election manifesto proposed the extension of postal voting to holiday-makers, and with good reason. Postal voting requires organization and initiative. A voter who thinks he may be entitled to a postal vote must put in his claim, not wait for a registration form to come through the letter-box. Conservative voters, prompted by Conservative constituency organizations, are less inhibited about staking such claims. In 1950 the postal vote enabled the Conservatives to win a dozen seats that would otherwise have been captured by Labour.[13] In 1964, the Nuffield election study estimated that, but for the postal vote, the Labour majority would have been at least 20, instead of four.[14] The 1970 Nuffield study suggests that the Conservatives owed at least six seats to the postal vote.[15] In February 1974 there were 15 cases where the number of postal votes exceeded the majority of the winning Conservative candidate; in at least 12 of these the postal vote was probably decisive.[16] In October 1974 the postal vote accounted for between eight and 11 Conservative victories.[17]

As postal ballots are not counted separately, no-one can be certain as to how they split between the parties. The general belief, confirmed by the experience of party workers, is that they divide 2:1 in favour of the Conservatives. In February 1967 the Speaker's Conference on Electoral Law reported against extending absent voting facilities to electors on holiday.[18] But in 1974 the Home Office undertook large-scale press advertising, including printed forms of application for postal votes. There was a resultant increase in the proportion of such votes from 1.9 per cent in 1966 and 2.2 per cent in 1970 to 2.9 per cent in October 1974.[19] This confirms the view of local observers that in the past the postal vote facility has not been exploited to the full by those eligible. The absence of nationwide publicity has turned the postal vote into a political weapon.

Postal voting requires personal initiative. Some of the defects of the electoral registration procedure are due to lack of initiative and common sense. These matters cannot, in the last resort, be legislated for, though better publicity would help. The annual cost of compiling the register is over £6 million.[20] In the present climate of restraint in public spending, the restoration of two registers a year is not practical politics.[21] But some procedural alterations, themselves costing very little, could be introduced to improve the accuracy of the annual register Whenever a death is certified, the deceased's name and address could be given automatically to the appropriate electoral registration officer, who could delete the name from the register at once. More importantly, a person moving house ought to be able to have his name removed from one register and added to another, without waiting for the annual recompilation; a certificate obtained from the first registration officer, and given to the second, would ensure that the system is not abused. Finally, the obligation to return the names of qualified voters ought not to be confined solely to heads of households; any qualified voter ought to be able to register him- or herself.

Free elections?

When one asks whether bribery, corruption or intimidation of electors takes place in modern United Kingdom elections, the answer must depend to some extent upon definitions. The last occasions upon which an election was declared void, and a new writ issued, because of a breach of electoral law, were Berwick-upon-Tweed (1922) and Oxford (1924); in both cases the offence was related to expenses, not corrupt practices.[22] In Great Britain there is no political bias in compiling the electoral register. Double-voting may be indulged in by unscrupulous voters who, for one reason or another, are registered in two constituencies; but, if it is, the problem is of negligible proportions. In Northern Ireland the picture is rather different. In

1951 D. G. Neill found evidence of bias in the compilation of the registers, and concluded that the practice of 'personation' of electors – the illegal exercise of the vote in the name of another (often deceased) person – was widespread.[23] Personation is, by its very nature, hard to document or quantify. The existence of intimidation in Northern Ireland is beyond doubt. The troubles there since 1969 have led to electoral violence. The headquarters of the Alliance party were blown up the day before polling in February 1974; on polling day itself, three Belfast polling stations were fired on. The violence undoubtedly deterred many people from going out to vote.[24]

But what is 'undue influence'? The law defines this as being a force, threat, restraint or fraud to compel an elector to vote or abstain. Influence, however, can be exercised in subtle ways. The spending of money by candidates during the period of a general election or by-election (ie between the issuing of the writ and the day of the poll) is strictly controlled. In 1948, the permitted expenditure per candidate in county constituencies was fixed at £450 plus 2d per elector; in borough constituencies, at £450 plus 1½d per elector. In 1969 the limit of £450 was raised to £750, plus 5p for every six electors in a county constituency, and for every eight electors in a borough one. In February 1974, three weeks before polling, a new Act increased the flat rate to £1,075, plus 6p for every six electors in counties and for every eight electors in towns. Before 1948 as much as £1,250 could be spent in a borough constituency with 60,000 electors. Allowing for inflation, therefore, the present restrictions are very severe. In 1974 the maximum amount that could be spent in a borough constituency of 60,000 electors was £1,525, and £1,675 in a county constituency of similar size.

In fact this limit is rarely reached. In the February 1974 election the average expenditure was £941 per candidate; in October it was £963. Naturally, much more than the average is spent in marginal constituencies. The conclusion of one recent study is that there is no evidence that greater local expenditure by candidates necessarily wins elections.[25]

In 1970 the Conservatives retained Heston & Isleworth for a mere £488 (45 per cent of the legal maximum); Labour held Dagenham for only £229 (24 per cent).[26] In October 1974 the Labour candidate in Norfolk South spent £1,980 trying to wipe out a Conservative majority of more than 11,000. This was only £3 below the maximum allowed. He failed.[27]

But the laws on election expenses are not all-pervasive. Firstly, the limits on expenditure apply only to money spent by candidates in their constituency campaigns; personal expenses are not included, nor are the national publicity campaigns promoted from party headquarters. In the age of mass media, the national political campaigns are of prime importance. Party labels of candidates count for a great deal. Before 1970 the ballot paper gave no indication of a candidate's party, only his or her name, address and occupation. This led to confusion, especially where two candidates in the same constituency had the same surname. It was the job of the local party to imprint the name of its candidate in the minds of the electors. The 1969 Representation of the People Act allows each candidate to add, on the ballot paper, a description of up to six words – such as 'The Labour Party Candidate'. Today, the major activity of local party is not to try and win converts but to 'get out the vote', to increase the turn-out and organize the postal vote. The packaging and selling of party policy is left to national headquarters, and the amounts spent in this way are considerable. In February 1974 the Conservative party spent £295,000 centrally on pre-election publicity, the Labour party spent £430,000; in October the respective figures were £600,000 and £500,000.[28] In each case the bulk of the funds went on advertising, broadcasting and private polls. In the October election Conservative headquarters used 80 per cent of their expenditure in this way, and the Labour party 49 per cent. A noteworthy innovation in 1974 was the use of press advertising during the campaign. In February the Liberals launched a £25,000 poster campaign (a quarter of their total campaign expenditure) in the national newspapers. The law was not invoked against them. This precedent was responsible for the increase in expenditure by the two main parties in October.

Secondly, there is no restriction on the amount of money spent by private organizations which are not themselves political parties, provided they are not seen to favour one political party as against another and provided the money is not spent in support of particular candidates. Many pressure groups are active during general elections, using the opportunity of an appeal by politicians to the electorate to exert maximum influence on them. Some such groups are covertly partisan. Thus Aims of Industry, devoted to the defence of free enterprise, spent £134,000 during the 1970 general election. Such expenditure evidently helps the Conservative rather than the Labour side. In February 1974, 155 Labour candidates were formally sponsored by trade unions. The unions made 'substantial special contributions' to local and regional Labour party funds, in addition to paying for press advertising to counter Aims of Industry advertisements.[29]

Curiously, although the law allows such groups to campaign nationally, the activities of pressure groups locally are much more heavily circumscribed, a relic of the days when all campaigns were local and national campaigns barely existed. Each candidate in a constituency is required to appoint an election agent. The agent is legally responsible for authorizing all the candidate's expenditure. An overenthusiastic supporter who voluntarily printed and distributed leaflets on the candidate's behalf, without obtaining the agent's permission, would not be thanked, especially if the candidate came top of the poll, because such expenditure would be unauthorized and would not be included in the official return of expenses. If such unauthorized expenditure came to light, other candidates in the constituency would be entitled to ask the courts to invalidate the election. The only persons entitled to act on a candidate's behalf are those whose services have been authorized by the agent.

But the reverse does not hold. It is illegal to incur unauthorized expense to *procure* the election of a candidate. It is not illegal to incur unauthorized expense to *prevent* the election of a candidate. Thus, in October 1974, the Association of Jewish Ex-Servicemen distributed leaflets giving information about National Front leaders and exhorting: 'Don't give these men a chance to get their hands on our Government!' Three members of anti-fascist organizations in the Manchester and Bolton areas distributed leaflets in more explicit terms, advising: 'Don't vote National Front, Don't Vote Fascist'. The Divisional Court dismissed the charges subsequently brought against them, and held that their activities did not constitute a breach of electoral law.[30] These precedents constitute a considerable widening of the scope for the activities of ordinary citizens locally at elections. Candidates can no longer expect voters to be insulated from all but their own entreaties.

Thirdly, none of the restrictions on expenditure apply outside the three-week period of a general election. In theory, as soon as a party chooses its 'candidate', an election contest is under way, whether or not an election has been called. In practice, local parties are careful to refer to their candidates as 'prospective' candidates until the writ for the election has been issued. In this way, none of the expenses incurred by a 'prospective' candidate in nursing his constituency can be legally chargeable to his election expenses.

This may not be so important when the gap between general elections is four or five years. But when, as happened after the stalemate of February 1974, there was a continual electioneering atmosphere for eight months, it does seem incongruous that limitations on expenditure should apply, in practice, only to the final three weeks. In spite of the fact that the trade union political levy is audited, and that company law (of 1967) now requires the public declaration of all political donations over £100, the exact sources of party finance are surrounded still by a good deal of mystery. The Labour party derives over three-quarters of its central income from trade union affiliation fees.[31] Its general election fund is very heavily dependent upon union money; in 1972 the fund received over £550,000 in this way.[32] Sources of finance for the Conservative party are more disparate. When a National Appeal was launched between the autumn of 1967 and the spring of 1969, about £750,000 came from companies – a third of the total raised by the appeal. On average, Conservative party headquarters can expect to raise about £1 million per annum from business gifts.[33] This represents about two-thirds of its annual income.

Money raised by the parties by way of subscriptions, donations, lotteries, investments, etc., can be spent, outside the election period, without restriction. To the extent that party managers and governments are much more conscious today than they were 20 years ago of the impact advertising and publicity can have, to the extent that most people in the country read one national daily newspaper and watch television, it is clear that money is, once again, a not unimportant factor in the election process. The guineas and pints of beer have gone, but only to be replaced by the persuasive hard sell and the photogenic party leader.

Two further requirements of election law deserve special mention because they too affect the framework within which elections are conducted. The first relates to the freedom to stand for election. Certain categories of persons may not be elected to the House of Commons. Although the voting age has now been lowered to 18, no person under 21 may become an MP. Anyone disqualified from voting at elections (e.g. because of a conviction for corrupt practices) is also disqualified from sitting in the Commons. Civil servants, members of the regular armed forces, full-time policemen, full-time judges and members of the boards of nationalized industries may not be elected, though some people in these categories can sit in the House of Lords. An undischarged bankrupt cannot become an MP.

Some of these exclusions are clearly reasonable. The exclusion of a person contemptuous enough of parliamentary democracy to have attempted to rig an election is reasonable. A civil servant is under the jurisdiction of the government; if such a person were to sit in the Commons, an evident clash of loyalty would result. On the other hand there is no logic in supposing, as the law now does, that a person is mature enough to elect an MP at 18, but not mature enough to be elected. More eccentric, however, is the law relating to ministers of religion. Members of the clergy of the Churches of England, Scotland, Ireland and the Roman Catholic Church cannot become MPs. Yet this restriction does not apply to nonconformist Christian ministers or to clergy of other denominations. Thus a Methodist minister may become an MP whereas a Roman Catholic priest may not. A Jewish minister of religion may sit in the Commons.[34] So may a clergyman of the disestablished Anglican Church in Wales. An ordained priest of the Church of England may not. In 1950 the Rev. J. G. Mac-Manaway, the successful Unionist candidate in West Belfast, was declared by the Commons to have been ineligible to stand for election because he was a minister of the Church of Ireland. In 1970 the Rev. Ian Paisley, founder of the Free Presbyterian Church, was elected in Antrim North without any such religious difficulty. Such anomalies, relics of the days when religion and politics were everywhere inextricably linked, are nowadays absurd.

For those not falling within any of the excluded categories, there is a right to stand for election to Parliament unfettered in theory, but in practice restricted by financial considerations. The only state aid a candidate receives is one free delivery by the Post Office to every elector in the constituency. Election addresses can be distributed free in this way. Beyond that, a candidate will need financial backing or a small army of willing volunteers, or preferably both. But no person can become a candidate unless his nomination is supported by at least 10 electors registered in the constituency for which he intends to stand. In addition he must raise a deposit of £150, which is forfeited if he does not obtain at least one-eighth of the total vote.

The deposit was introduced by the 1918 Act in an effort to stamp out freak and frivolous candidatures. The sum required has not changed since then. It can be argued that today £150 is not a great sum of money. In real terms, the amount would have to be raised to about £1,800 to maintain its original value; no-one has seriously proposed such a step. At the same time it is clear that the deposit does not prevent 'fringe' candidates from being nominated. At the October 1974 election, parties such as the Workers' Revolutionary Party, the National Front, the Communist Party, the Campaign for a More Prosperous Britain, the Gay Liberation Front, the Cornish Nationalists, and at least a dozen others all put up candidates. Though in some cases these fringe parties may have hoped to sway a result in a marginal seat, in no case could they seriously have hoped to have captured a seat for themselves.

A more dramatic illustration of the failure of the deposit to fulful its original purpose came in 1962. In June of that year Malcolm Thompson, a soldier who had been refused a discharge in order to enrol as a university student, offered himself as a candidate in the Middlesborough West by-election. Servicemen cannot become MPs, but it had been normal for servicemen seeking parliamentary election to be discharged. Malcolm Thompson came bottom of the poll but, for the cost of a forfeited deposit, secured his demobilization. This simple expedient was adopted on a large scale by other members of the armed forces. In February 1963, on the recommendation of a Select Committee of the Commons, the Home Secretary established a committee, consisting of two Queen's Counsel and six former MPs, to decide whether servicemen seeking election had genuine parliamentary ambitions. This seems to have stemmed the flood. The Rotherham by-election of March 1963 had attracted 493 requests for nomination papers. Only five servicemen applied to stand in the 1964 general election, and only one in 1966.[35]

The fact remains that at five by-elections between June and November 1962, nine servicemen actually stood for election, each paying his £150 deposit, and that hundreds more were prepared to do so. For them, raising the money was not an insuperable problem, and forfeiting it was a sacrifice they were willing, even eager, to make. More recently, in July 1976, the National Front announced that it would field 318 candidates at the next general election, in order to be in a position to demand equal television time with the main political parties. In lost deposits alone this would amount to nearly £48,000.[36] Yet the expenditure is one the party considers worth while.

The number of lost deposits varies considerably between one general election and the next. Between 1918 and October 1974 the number varied from 27 (1923) to 461 (1950), and totalled 3,136, representing a gain to the Treasury of £467,550.[37] Perhaps this is the reason why the deposit requirement is not abandoned. General elections cost a great deal of money. The election of February 1974 was estimated to have cost the Treasury about £4 million in returning officers' expenses, and the October election about £5 million, an average of £7,800 per constituency.[38] Any return on this outlay is doubtless welcomed.

Nonetheless, it is clear that the lost deposit bears hardly on the smaller less wealthy parties. In October 1974, 27 out of the 36 Plaid Cymru candidates lost their deposits, and the party thus had to pay a 'forfeit' of £4,050. Yet it can hardly be called a freak or a frivolous group. The abolition of the deposit is long overdue. Such abolition was proposed by J. F. S. Ross as long ago as 1948.[39] The Hansard Society's Commission advocated the replacement of the deposit by a 'considerable increase' in the number of supporting signatures at nomination.[40] An alternative might be to reduce the qualification for the return of the deposit from one eighth to one sixteenth of the votes cast.[41] Either of these proposals would help lessen the wealth factor which at present persists in the electoral system, and which is heavily weighted in favour of the big parties and the big spenders.

The emphasis in this section has been on money. Despite the accumulation of laws against corrupt practices, money still talks at an election. In view of the subtlety and sophistication of modern communication techniques, its talking power is substantial. The fifth report of the Speaker's Conference on Electoral Law, issued in May 1967, turned down the suggestion that candidates' expenses should be met out of public funds.[42] Since then the cost of elections has shot up. In 1970 the average expenditure per candidate, including personal expenses, stood at £798; by October 1974 it had increased by a quarter. An Exchequer grant would ensure less inequality between poor and rich parties, impecunious and wealthy candidates.

In 1975 the Labour government set up a committee, under the chairmanship of Lord Houghton of Sowerby, to examine the possibility of state subventions to political parties. Two-thirds of the committee's members recommended annual grants to the central party organizations on the basis of 5p per vote cast for each party at the previous general election, and the payment of half of each candidate's permitted expenses in parliamentary and local government elections; to qualify for a grant, a party would have had, at the previous general election, to have won at least two seats, or one seat and polled at least 150,000 votes, or to have saved its deposits in at least six constituencies; the payments towards election expenses would be made to all candidates polling at least one eighth of the votes cast, and would be payable to independent candidates as well as those belonging to a political party.[43]

These proposals, and the philosophy underlying them, bristle with difficulties. The most obvious is financial. On the basis of the October 1974 election figures, the cost to the nation in central grants would be nearly £1.5 million; the payments towards election expenses would cost about £860,000 per annum. Such expenditure would not meet with popular approval. Byond this, however, there are deep moral considerations. It is right that a Labour taxpayer should have to finance the Conservative party, and vice-versa? Or that Afro-Asian taxpayers should be obliged to subsidize parties advocating the repatriation of coloured citizens? Above all, does not the notion of state subsidies run counter to the voluntary nature of politics in the United Kingdom? There is no obligation (such as exists in Australia) to vote at an election; why should one be obliged to make, via taxation, political contributions?

Of the major political parties, only Labour welcomed the Houghton committee's proposals. National financial constraints alone seem to preclude their implementation. Yet within the existing legal framework a more logical and tic approach to the role of money in elections could be adopted; one which would, for example, recognize that money spent by the parties outside the general election period can have an important bearing on a subsequent election, and ought therefore to be subject to some supervision.

The distribution of seats

In the nineteenth century, extensions of the franchise were invariably accompanied by a redistribution of seats, usually undertaken to mollify the opinions of Conservative politicians opposed to franchise reform. An extension of the right to vote can be effectively cancelled by a redrawing of the boundaries between constituencies. Before 1832 it was possible for a handful of electors in one borough to return two MPs, but for several hundred electors in another to return the same parliamentary representation. The reform of 1832 did away with some of the worst instances of such inequality, but deliberately created others. Although the balance between industrial and agricultural areas was made less unequal, the system was still heavily weighted in favour of the rural constituencies compared with genuinely urban areas. England was still over-represented compared with Scotland and Ireland. The principle of equalizing constituencies on the basis of population was explicitly disavowed.[44] The redistribution provisions of the second Reform Act laid down some rules for the representation of boroughs; those below 5,000 population were disfranchised; those between 5,000 and 10,000 were to have one MP; the five largest boroughs were to have as many as three; 52 boroughs disappeared and 28 new county seats were created.

Only in the Redistribution Act of 1885 can one say that the Chartist demand for equal electoral districts received recognition. Wales, Scotland and the north of England were at last as equitably represented as the south of England, and for this reason alone the Liberals were the chief beneficiaries.[45] No further redistribution of seats was carried out between 1885 and 1918. The Liberals benefited from this absence of redistribution too, because they were able to count on the support of areas such as the Scottish highlands and rural Wales, which were in reality areas of declining population. The 1918 act, in general terms, redrew constituency boundaries so that most parliamentary seats had roughly the same number of electors; this ironing out of former anomalies therefore benefited the Conservatives. But no provision for further redistributions was made to enable boundaries to match population movements. Thus in 1929 Labour polled 285,808 votes fewer than the Conservatives, but won 27 more seats. By the outbreak of the second world war, the growing London suburbs had come to lack proper representation. The Redistribution Act of 1944 rectified the worst anomalies by creating 25 new seats. In the long term this favoured the Conservative party, for most of the new seats (20 of the 25 by 1959) were in outer London and became Conservative strongholds.

More importantly, the 1944 act, amended in 1946 and 1948, established four Boundary Commissions, one each for England, Wales, Scotland and Northern Ireland, to continually review and alter boundaries. Henceforth the number of qualified electors, rather than the total population, was to be the major determinant of constituency size. Each commission was to review the boundaries within its jurisdiction at intervals of between three and seven years. Each was to establish an electoral quota by dividing the total electorate by the number of seats available, and to recommend boundaries to produce constituencies with electorates as near the quota as practicable; but local government boundaries and 'localities' were to be respected and inconvenient sizes and shapes of constituency were to be avoided. Northern Ireland was to have not less than 12 seats, Scotland not less than 71, and Wales not less than 35; the total number of seats in the United Kingdom was not to be substantially greater than 625.

These constraints alone meant that the idea of equal-sized constituencies could not be attained in practice. In 1949 the electorate of the United Kingdom totalled approximately 34 million. With 625 seats to distribute each constituency ought to have had about 54,500 voters. In fact, Scotland and Wales were over-represented, their respective average constituency electorates being 47,465 and 50,061; in Northern Ireland the average size of constituency was 72,090, and in England 56,073.[46] Northern Ireland ought to have had 16 MPs at Westminster, not 12.

But the constraints facing the boundary commissioners did not end there. The drawing of boundaries is, of course, a political matter. Down to 1928, redistribution of seats could always be balanced by modification of the suffrage. After 1928, and until the lowering of the voting age became feasible in the 1960s, the option of franchise reform was not open. So boundaries became a subject of intense political argument, the more so since the last word did not rest with the commissioners. They merely recommended to the Home Secretary what boundary changes there ought, in their view, to be; it was for the government, and parliament, to give effect to their recommendations. There was also elaborate machinery for the hearing of local objections to their proposals. Constituency workers, perhaps resentful of a proposed boundary change which would force them to work with an adjacent party organization, and to alter their canvassing schedules, thus had several avenues of attack open to them.

Two boundary revisions were carried out under this scheme, in 1948 and 1954. Both aroused great controversy so far as the proposals of the English commission were concerned. In both redistributions, the commissioners proposed giving greater representation to counties than to boroughs. They had logic on their side, for the centres of many large cities were already showing signs of decay and depopulation following the ravages of the Depression and war. In most cases these city centres were Labour strongholds, and Labour backbenchers were quick to complain. The complaints became louder when, in 1948, the commissioners decided to treat rural constituencies preferentially to counterbalance the 'advantages of accessibility and convenience' enjoyed by urban voters.

So the Labour government asked the Commissioners to

allot 17 extra seats to boroughs. Even so, the average English rural constituency had more than 2,000 electors fewer than the average borough constituency. H. G. Nicholas estimated that the 1948 redistribution cost Labour between 20 and 30 seats at the 1950 general election.[47] In the 1951 general election, whilst Labour won by substantial majorities in slum areas and mining districts, the Conservatives won many suburban seats by very moderate margins. Of the 20 seats won by majorities exceeding 25,000, 17 were Labour held. In the London suburbs the Conservatives were able to win seats with majorities of between 2,000 and 5,000; overall the Conservative party polled 230,684 votes fewer than Labour, but emerged with a 26-seat majority. David Butler concluded that the relationship between votes and seats exhibited a bias of two per cent to the Conservatives — that is, they 'stood to win more seats than the Labour party even though they were as much as 2 per cent . . . behind them in the popular poll'.[48]

The second redistribution, in 1954, did not correct these imperfections. The commission's proposals were not in themselves as far-reaching as those of 1948: 172 major boundary revisions, 43 minor ones and the creation of an extra five seats. But the anger of the politicians and party workers grew at the realization that, to the burden of a general election every five years, was to be added the upheaval of a redistribution.[49] The redistribution of 1954 resulted in a net Conservative gain of between two and ten seats.[50] In 1958 a Redistribution of Seats Act released the Boundary Commissioners from the obligation to keep electorates within 25 per cent of the quota in order to respect local government boundaries; strict equality of electorates was henceforth to be subordinated to communal cohesion. The act also increased the period between general reviews to a minimum of 10 and a maximum of 15 years. The next set of redistribution proposals was not presented until 1969.

As events turned out, four general elections (1959, 1964, 1966 and 1970) were fought on the 1954 boundaries. The pro-Conservative bias persisted. In 1955 and 1959 it was estimated that Labour needed to poll 1.4 per cent more of the total vote in order to gain the same number of seats. The 1964 and 1966 elections seemed to indicate that this bias had disappeared, perhaps because of population movements. But it is equally possible that the bias persisted, masked by lower turn-outs in those two elections.[51]

The boundary proposals of 1969 were, however, rejected by the Labour Home Secretary, James Callaghan, on the pretext that a re-drawing of local-government boundaries would have to take place following publication of the Redcliffe-Maud report, but actually because the Labour party feared that the proposals would, like those of 1948, deprive Labour of city-centre seats. Instead Callaghan introduced a bill confined to rectifying a few instances of gross under-representation, and implementing the recommended changes in the boundaries of constituencies in Greater London, which was unaffected by pending local government reform. The bill was emasculated in the House of Lords and abandoned. In November, the Home Secretary fulfilled his legal obligation by laying the Boundary Commissions' proposals in full before Parliament. The Labour majority in the Commons followed his advice and rejected them. By then, as the examples in table 2:1 show, the disparities in constituency size, and hence in MPs' workloads, were considerable.

2.1 **Examples of disparities in constituency size, 1955–70**

Constituency	1955	1970
Birmingham, Ladywood	46,904	18,729
Glasgow, Kelvingrove	39,672	18,907
Manchester, Exchange	52,376	21,080
Cheadle	61,626	107,225
Hitchin	62,258	108,668
Billericay	58,872	123,121

By delaying boundary changes till after the 1970 election, it is probable that the Labour party cut the Conservative majority by about 11 seats.[52]

When the Conservatives regained power in 1970, they put into effect the 1969 boundary recommendations. The total number of seats was increased from 630 to 635; there were major boundary changes in 325 constituencies and minor ones in 90. The changes reflected the shift in population from the centres of the conurbations to the suburbs, the new towns and the commuter belts. But they did not come into operation until the general election of February 1974; until then by-elections continued to be held on the 1954 boundaries.

The Conservatives would undoubtedly have served their own interests better by postponing the new parliamentary boundaries so that they could coincide with the new local government areas. Meanwhile, revised, up-to-date electoral quotas could have been calculated. As it was, the 1974 general elections took place on boundaries over five years old. The bias towards the urban seats was still considerable. In England, 18 city-centre seats had electorates below 45,000; 29 seats, none of them in the centres of conurbations, had electorates over 85,000. Of all the English constituencies, mostly urban, with under 50,000 electors, Labour won more than two-thirds; of those (mostly covering wide agricultural areas) with over 80,000 electors they won less than a third. As an example, Edward Short, then Labour MP for Newcastle-upon-Tyne Central, had fewer than 26,000 voters on his register; John MacGregor, Conservative MP for Norfolk South, had more than 90,000 voters on his. The boundary changes of 1969, applied in 1974, produced a net gain to Labour of between 16 and 22 seats.[53] The Conservative party, for all the fuss it had made about the implementation of the 1969 proposals, found itself, in February 1974, with four fewer seats than Labour, though it had polled 226,564 votes more.

Political controversy about boundaries continues to flourish. The Boundary Commissioners have begun a new review, aming to report in 1979. Home Office figures show that, in 1976, 20 English constituencies were between 39 and 51 per cent above the provisional electoral quota of 65,753 votes; 20 constituencies were between 32 and 63 per cent below it.[54] There is, in general, gross over-representation in urban areas of declining population and under-representation of areas of population growth. Professor Peter Bromhead calculates that, even if the new review of boundaries based on 1976 populations achieves equality between urban and non-urban areas, bias in favour of urban areas will have returned by the time the first general election is held on the new boundaries.[55]

No-one expects constituency boundaries to change instantaneously with population movements. Though a computer could perform the necessary calculations and readjustments, too-frequent upheaval is clearly undesirable. It would be wrong to amalgamate wide rural mountainous regions simply to achieve strict proportionality. But the boundaries exist to serve the people, not the political activists. The quirks and foibles of local party workers ought to play no part in the delineation of boundaries. It is less edifying still that politicians should be able to delay boundary changes (as Labour backbenchers did in 1969) in order to cling to seats which are, because of their minute electorates, the modern equivalent of rotten boroughs.

In the United States of America, a series of Supreme Court decisions has curbed the power of politicians to influence electoral boundaries, and has laid down the maxim that all voters must enjoy equal political strength.[56] There is no Supreme Court in the United Kingdom. On the other hand, the Boundary Commissioners are a high-powered and extremely competent body. The Speaker of the House of Commons is ex-officio chairman of each commission and a judge is deputy-chairman. Other members are chosen for their knowledge of population matters and their independence of party politics. The Director of the Ordnance Survey is an assessor, as is the Registrar-General. The commissioners have never been seriously accused of political bias; if anything, they do their exacting work too well. There is no reason why they could not be given quasi-judicial status. Their decisions would then automatically become law, but parliament could intervene, as it can in respect of any legal judgment, by legislating to reverse a decision if it thought fit. In practice, the government of the day would have to make out a very strong case to set aside the Boundary Commissions' rulings.

But whether or not the commissioners are given such freedom of action, a minimum of ten years is too long a period between revisions. The country is now subject to rapid population changes between different areas. The longer boundaries remain unchanged, the greater is bound to be the resistance to change from party workers. Electorate figures are revised annually. Given the impact which boundaries can have on election results, it seems reasonable that boundary revisions should take place about as frequently as general elections have to – i.e. every five years. Once new boundaries are fixed they should take effect at once, not be held in abeyance till the next general election. More importantly, because new boundaries must inevitably be outdated to some extent by the time they are introduced, and in the absence of some form of PR, the commissioners should be empowered to take some account of *projected* population movements when redistributing seats. Within these guidelines, the dispensation given to the commissioners in the 1958 Act, to be able to depart from the electoral quota by more than 25 per cent, would clearly have no place; at the very least, the 25 per cent maximum leeway should be reimposed.

The problem of the apportionment of seats between England, Scotland, Wales and Northern Ireland is trickier. The Westminster representation of Northern Ireland has remained static at 12 seats since 1922.[57] The justification for this deliberate under-representation was the existence of the Stormont Parliament, created under the 1920 Government of Ireland Act, to legislate internally for the province. Stormont was dismantled in 1972; its successor, the Northern Ireland Assembly, lasted less than a year. Unless and until a devolved assembly is restored in Northern Ireland, the reasoning behind its under-representation at Westminster is untenable.

Scotland has had 71 seats (excluding university seats) since 1918. Wales was given 35 seats in 1918; the number was increased to 36 in 1948. Both countries are over-represented. Again this is deliberate, in part a concession to nationalist sentiment, in part justified by the difficulties of amalgamating mountain and island constituencies – though in fact there is nothing to prevent the Welsh and Scottish Boundary Commissioners from carrying out such amalgamations, and their failure to do so leads to over-generous representation of the rural areas of these countries compared with the towns.[58]

Table 2:2 illustrates the disparities in the parliamentary representation of the four constituent countries of the United Kingdom, based on the election results of October 1974.

2.2 **Unequal parliamentary representation in the United Kingdom**

	October 1974 Electorate	No. of MPs	No. of MPs if constituencies were equal
England	33,351,228	516	528
Scotland	3,684,791	71	58
Wales	2,008,744	36	32
N. Ireland	1,036,523	12	16
	40,081,286	635	634

The prospect of devolved assemblies in Cardiff and Edinburgh must weaken the argument for over-representation of Scotland and Wales at Westminister. But the Conservative and Labour parties both have a vested interest in maintaining the status quo. A reduction in Scottish and Welsh representation, however just, would arouse much local opposition, and this would doubtless be exploited by the nationalists. The two main parties could lose Scottish and Welsh seats as a result. The Labour party, in particular, depends heavily on its Celtic representation. In October 1974 it won 41 of the Scottish seats and 23 of the Welsh; if there had been equal constituencies, it might have won only 33 seats in Scotland and only 20 in Wales; in England it might only have gained an extra six seats to compensate, making a net loss of five seats.[59] The Conservative party might have lost three seats in Scotland and one in Wales, and gained six in England: a net gain of two seats, as table 2:3 shows.

2.3 **Party strengths, had there been equal constituencies, October 1974**

	No. of MPs returned, October 1974	No. of MPs if constituencies had been equal
Conservative	277	279
Labour	319	314
Liberal	13	13
S.N.P.	11	9
Plaid Cymru	3	3
N. Ireland	12	16
	635	634

Though the Conservative party would have been slightly better off in terms of seats, power would have been no nearer and such Scottish and Welsh seats as it retained would have been more marginal and more susceptible to nationalist propaganda. Labour, though still the largest party, would have been four seats short of an absolute majority. The Labour party is as dependent on the Celtic fringe as was the Liberal party of old. It can hardly be expected to assent to a reform in boundary delineation procedure – treating the whole of the United Kingdom on the same basis – which might deprive it of the chance of power.

It would be wrong, however, to end this discussion of boundary problems on a note of complete cynicism. Gerrymandering – the deliberate drawing of boundaries to minimize the representation of the opposition party and/or maximize the impact of one's own supporters – is unknown in the Westminister electoral system. Until pounced upon by the Supreme Court, gerrymandering was widespread in the United States; the very term is American in origin. But examples of it can be found much nearer home. One of the main complaints of the Northern Ireland Civil Rights Association from its formation early in 1967 was that local government electoral boundaries within the province were deliberately manipulated to maintain Unionist (ie Protestant) control. The Cameron Commission, appointed to inquire into the disturbances in Northern Ireland in 1969, produced convincing evidence that these allegations had been justified.

In Armagh and Omagh Urban Districts, Londonderry County Borough and County Fermanagh, Catholic majorities in the voting population had been converted into substantial Unionist majorities on the councils. In the Urban and Rural District Councils at Dungannon, small Protestant majorities in the voting population had been translated into very large majorities in the council chambers.[60] The most glaring example of gerrymandering was in Londonderry in the 1967 local elections (see table 2:4).

2.4 **Gerrymandering in Londonderry, 1967**

	Nationalist (Catholic) Voters	Unionist Voters	Seats
North Ward	2,530	3,946	8 Unionists
Waterside Ward	1,852	3,697	4 Unionists
South Ward	10,047	1,138	8 Nationalists
	14,429	8,781	20
	23,210		

The Nationalists polled 62 per cent of the votes but emerged with only 40 per cent of the seats. This extraordinary results was achieved because the ward boundaries concentrated the bulk of the Catholic voters in South Ward, allowing the Unionists to win the other wards by small majorities.[61] It is hardly surprising that such a situation should have helped fuel the fires of sectarian violence in the city. In November 1968 the Londonderry County Borough was suspended. When local government in Northern Ireland was reorganized, in 1973, elections to 26 newly-created district councils were by STV.

But the political system in Northern Ireland is *sui generis*. The rarity of such instances of gerrymandering, indeed their complete absence outside that troubled province, emphasize their uniqueness. That is their real significance for the student of British elections.

Chapter Three

POLITICS

The parties

General elections in the United Kingdom are about party political choice. Political parties do not have a monopoly of electoral politics, less still do the Labour and Conservative parties dominate the platform as they did in the 1940s and 1950s. But the abolition of the university seats saw the end of the truly independent MP, attached to no party and whose career had not been fostered by membership of a party.[1] The independent MPs elected since 1950 have of course been independent in the sense that they ploughed their own furrows in the House of Commons. But they all began in politics as members of established parties. It was on the basis of reputations built up in that context that they were able to break the party ties later on, and carry enough of their constituents with them to top the polls.

S. O. Davies, for instance, returned as the 'Independent Labour' MP for Merthyr Tydfil in 1970, had in fact been the much-respected and popular Labour MP for that constituency since 1934. Repudiated by his local party on the grounds of age (he was then 83) he stood in the 1970 election nonetheless, and won by a majority of over 7,000. Dick Taverne, Social Democratic MP for Lincoln, 1973–4, had beeen Labour MP for the town since 1962, but had broken with his party because of his support for British entry to the Common Market. It is significant that when Enoch Powell and the Conservative party parted company, he categorically rejected the suggestion that he might stand as an independent at his constituency, Wolverhampton

South-West. In a speech at Birmingham a few days before polling in February 1974, Powell called the suggestion 'a profound and dangerous misconception. . . . The elector votes not for a person, but for a party'.[2] And when he re-entered parliament, in October, it was not as an independent but as the United Ulster Unionist Council MP for South Down.

The importance of party is equally strong in the mind of the elector. In 1970 the Conservative, Labour, Liberal Communist, Scottish and Welsh nationalist and Irish parties picked up all but 0.4 per cent of the votes cast. In October 1974 these parties, plus the National Front, obtained 99.7 per cent of the total vote. Though few electors become deeply involved in party work, the vast majority think of political choice in party terms, mainly because the party is the most tangible link they have with government and control (whether real or supposed) over it. Sixty per cent of Butler & Stokes' 1963 sample felt that the competitive party and electoral system provided them with some influence over government activities.[3] As long ago as 1908 Graham Wallas characterized the party as 'the most effective political entity in the modern national State . . . something which can be loved and trusted, and which can be recognised at successive elections as being the same thing that was loved and trusted before'.[4] These words ring true today. Little wonder, therefore, that even the most ambitious and well-known politicians regard attachment to a party as an essential prerequisite to the pursuit of their careers. And it is the salience of party which is partly responsible for the paradox that, while all have votes, not all votes count.

Though it is tempting, and not entirely false, to see modern British parties as the descendants of the loose registration societies established after 1832, their world was a very different one from that ushered in by the arrival of mass electorates. Two hundred years ago, Burke told his readers that 'Party is a body of men united for promoting by their joint endeavours the national interest upon some particular principle in which they are all agreed'.[5] This may have implied propaganda, of a sort, but it did not imply organization at constituency level, less still the discipline of the whips at Westminster. In 1832 Burke's concept of a party still held good, in 1868 less so, and by 1918 not at all. Some of the changes that took place have already been mentioned in previous chapters; others, such as the growth of party discipline, are beyond the scope of the present work.[6] What is relevant is the way political parties organize themselves for the purpose of conducting and winning elections.

Modern political parties are parties of mass membership. They are also extremely oligarchic in structure. Membership figures for the Labour and Conservative parties have been falling significantly, but they are still substantial. Individual constituency (as distinct from 'affiliated', mostly trade union) membership of the Labour party fell from over a million in 1952 to 665,000 in 1973.[7] In 1953 the Conservative party claimed to have a membership of about 2,805,000; in 1970 it was not more than about 1½ million.[8] Together with the youth sections of these parties, and membership of minor parties, the total number of subscribers to British political parties is probably about 2,750,000; even including members of the Labour party affiliated through trade unions and socialist and co-operative societies, the figure approaches only about eight million, or 20 per cent of the electorate. Of these only a fraction are involved in constituency work. Studies of Greenwich and Glossop in the 1950s suggested that not more than 5 per cent of the electorate were then willing to undertake voluntary work during elections.[9] The Butler & Stokes panel included 3 per cent who took part in active campaigning during general elections.[10] These surveys suggest that the number of local party activists is not more than about 1,600,000, or 2,500 per constituency.

It is this small band of people who control the destinies of the parties at constituency level. They provide the elbow grease to make the constituency parties function. They organize the dances and the whist drives to raise local funds between elections. They distribute leaflets and canvass voters when elections come. They are the ones who turn up to branch meetings, and they jealously guard the positions of local prominence which party membership gives them. 'Some [local] parties don't want new members', Ron Hayward, the Labour party's general secretary, said in April 1972; 'They have got a nice little comfortable clique, and they don't want new faces to upset them.'[11] From such activists are drawn the constituency leaders who, inter alia, choose the party candidates.[12]

In general the social structure of party membership lists does not, except in one important respect, differ markedly from the social structure of the electorates from which the party draws its support. Labour party members are overwhelmingly manual workers. Local conservative associations, however, rarely contain their due quota of working-class Conservatives; they are dominated by people from the non-manual middle-class groups. Party activists tend, on average, to be older than electors. Women do not swamp local Conservative parties, and men predominate on the Labour side. Surveys of Conservative party members in Glossop and Newcastle-under-Lyme suggest that local Conservative members are not extreme right-wing in their views; they mirror the views of Conservative electors.[13] On the other hand, there is evidence, stretching over a period of 20 years or more, that Labour party members are more left-wing than Labour electors. In Glossop, a majority of party members favoured the nationalization of many industries at a time when state ownership was not popular with Labour voters. The Newcastle-under-Lyme Labour party was found to contain many supporters of unilateral nuclear disarmament. Recent cases of sitting Labour MPs being refused readoption at the next general election (e.g. Eddie Griffiths at Sheffield, Brightside, September 1974, Reg Prentice at Newham North-East, July 1975, and Frank Tomney at Hammersmith North, July 1976) have all involved some measure of hostility by left-wing-dominated constituency parties to middle-of-the-road MPs.

Curiously, however, the local *leaderships* of both parties are much more middle-class than the memberships.[14]

Within Conservative parties this squeezes out the manual workers almost completely from the leadership circle. Those who dominate the leadership are business and professional people, or lower middle-class groups, such as shopkeepers. The middle classes also loom large in the leadership of local Labour parties. In Glossop, only one-third of the leadership was drawn from manual workers, in Newcastle-under-Lyme about one-half.[15] On the Labour side, the middle-class leaders tend to be drawn largely from the ranks of the managerial classes and the teachers – i.e. the 'white-collar' workers and the 'intelligentsia'. It is easy to see why middle-class groups should predominate in both parties. They are politically aware and ideologically motivated. They are likely to have the spare time to devote to constituency work. Their jobs are the sort which give them the necessary literary training and organizational ability. They are likely to be better at handling people and at being articulate in public.

Choosing candidates

The ways in which the Conservative and Labour parties go about selecting candidates are also remarkably similar. In each case the national party headquarters has a built-in say in who should be selected. In each case the last word rests, theoretically, with a large representative committee of the local constituency party. In each case the actual choice rests with a small caucus of local officials who, constitutionally, are merely the executive arm of the representative committee, but who are often its master.

All Conservative candidates must be approved by the party leadership, a condition dating from 1874.[16] The selection procedure is laid down by the Standing Advisory Committee on Candidates (SACC) which also maintains a list of approved candidates. A local association is not confined to this list, but the SACC has a power of veto over anyone selected. The officers of the local association are elected at an annual general meeting which all local members of the party may attend. The elected officers, with the addition of representatives of the wards or polling district branches, Young Conservative groups and Conservative Clubs, form the Executive Council of the local association. When a parliamentary vacancy arises in the constituency, a small selection committee will be chosen from this Executive Council to go through the applications, interview the likely runners, and send the names of the two or three most probable back to a special meeting of the Council. It is the Executive Council which, after further interviews, votes by secret ballot to choose the candidate, whose nomination must then be ratified by a general meeting of the association.

Until 1948 it was possible for a prospective candidate to offer to pay his own election expenses and to make a contribution to constituency funds. This made it easy for the wealthier aspirants to buy their way into parliament. Nowadays constituency Conservative associations have to meet all their election expenses out of subscriptions and fund-raising activities. A candidate may not contribute more than £25 per annum to the funds of his association, an MP no more than £50. Nor must such donations be made a condition of selection.

The theoretical framework therefore gives much power into the hands of the constituency association, but actually into the hands of the constituency leadership. When a candidate is being selected there is much conferring with Conservative Central Office. The choice is not confined to those who apply. The Vice-Chairman of the party, who is specially responsible for the selection of candidates, will suggest names to be added to the list of those already nominated. Prominent or capable, but seatless, politicians have to be found seats; those in highly vulnerable seats must be moved to higher ground. For its part, the local leadership may be flattered to find itself being courted in this fashion.

Once chosen by the selection committee, a Conservative candidate is relatively safe. In 1951 Central Office objected to the adoption proposal of the Newcastle North Conservative Association because it wished to oppose Major Gwilym

Lloyd George, the National Liberal & Conservative candidate favoured by many local Conservatives. The Major stood with the support of an officially-recognized secessionist Conservative group and a letter of support from Winston Churchill, and had an easy victory. The seceders subsequently became the official Conservative association in the constituency.[17] In 1952 a general meeting of the Southport Conservative association rejected the choice of its Executive Council and chose one of the other candidates instead.[18]

Such rebuffs for the local leadership are very rare. Between 1945 and 1964, Professor Austin Ranney has calculated that there were 18 known attempts to enforce the retirement of Conservative MPs; 12 of the attempts succeeded.[19] Three of the 'anti-Suez' rebels (Nigel Nicolson, Sir Frank Medlicott and Colonel Cyril Banks) who abstained from the vote of confidence on 8 November 1956 were not readopted by their constituencies.[20] Fifty-eight right-wing Conservative MPs who voted against oil sanctions against Rhodesia did so in defiance of the party line, but did not encounter local admonition.[21] Sixteen Conservatives voted with Labour against the embargo on arms shipments to Israel in October 1973, but suffered no ill effects; some, particularly in London, were warmly supported by their constituency associations. Indeed, in 1959 Sir David Robertson, MP for Caithness & Sutherland, retained the support of his constituency association even though he had taken the extreme step of resigning the Conservative whip; Central Office did not put up a candidate against him.

In sum, if a Conservative candidate or MP has the support of his local association, he is in a very strong position vis-a-vis the national leadership; if not, he may find himself in grave difficulty. Between 1970 and 1974 Central Office did its best to induce local associations to remove candidates who were known supporters of Enoch Powell. A few attempts succeeded, but the exercise produced a predictable backlash. At Plymouth, Drake, the selected candidate was turned down at his formal adoption meeting because of his *anti*-Powellite remarks about the Ugandan Asians.[22] Since

1945 there has only been one case of a locally-adopted Conservative candidate being directly vetoed by the SACC.[23]

In the Labour party a similar scenario may be detected. The rules date from 1929-30, and give the power of selection into the hands of the General Management Committee (GMC) of each constituency party. This committee is made up of delegates from the ward parties, affiliated trade unions, women's sections, Young Socialist branches and a miscellany of other affiliated organizations. The size of the GMC varies widely between constituencies; it may contain as many as 200 delegates, though average membership is around 120. The GMC elects annually an Executive Committee, and it is this committee which draws up a short list of applicants from which, by secret ballot, the GMC selects a new candidate should a vacancy arise.[24]

The role of the GMC is thus similar to that of the Conservative Executive Council. The National Executive Committee of the Labour party plays a part in the selection process and has certain residual powers. It must approve the short list of names and, naturally, the final choice. It maintains two lists of candidates. List A contains the names of those candidates nominated by affiliated trade unions, whom the unions are willing to sponsor and whom the National Executive has approved. List B contains the names of individuals who are not sponsored, but whom the National Executive has also approved. A constituency party is not bound to confine itself to either list. But unlisted individuals need to be nominated by a body affiliated to the constituency party and, of course, to be approved by the National Executive.

In two important respects Labour party candidate selection is less democratic than Conservative procedure. Firstly, the choice of the Labour GMC does not have to be ratified by a general meeting of the members of the local party. This gives the local leadership greater freedom to choose, say, a candidate of the left who might not be acceptable to the membership as a whole. Secondly, the knowledge that an applicant has trade-union sponsorship can be a powerful determining factor. An individual candidate may only contribute £50 per annum to constituency party funds. But a sponsoring union may contribute up to £350 towards the running costs of a borough constituency party or £420 in a country constituency, plus 80 per cent of the candidate's election expenses and 65 per cent of the salary of an agent. The sponsored applicant thus has a decided advantage. The promise of union money must not be made a condition of selection. Financial matters must not be discussed at the selection conference. But members of the GMC know who is on list A. Past experience may tell them what to expect in the way of financial support from a particular union. If the seat is not marginal and if, therefore, the personality of the candidate is not thought to be of much electoral advantage, the attraction of choosing a sponsored candidate is bound to be considerable.

Since 1945 the number of candidates so sponsored has been about one-fifth to one-quarter of all Labour candidates, and the number elected has represented well over a third of all Labour MPs. But since the second world war there has never been a general election at which less than 70 per cent of union-sponsored candidates have been successful at the polls; in 1970 the proportion was over 96 per cent, and in October 1974 over 91 per cent.[25] Trade unions do not like financing campaigns likely to end in failure. The largest unions, pre-eminently the Transport & General Workers' Union, the Amalgamated Union of Engineering Workers, the National Union of Mineworkers and the National Union of General & Municipal Workers, alone account for over half the sponsored candidates who are successful. Some constituencies are said to 'belong' to certain unions, whose right to nominate the candidates in them is unquestioned; even if it were, the payment of 'delegation' fees enables them to pack selection conferences and sweep all before them.[26] And whether or not a sponsored candidate is successful, the constituency party adopting him is likely to have reaped some financial benefit. Between 1945 and 1959, 220 constituencies received grants from unions, and 45 from co-operative movements.[27] In an average year the grants total about £295,000 and represent seven per cent of constituency party income.[28]

As with the Conservative party, the Labour party's headquarters, through the National Executive Committee, possesses certain residual powers of interference with local candidate selection procedure. But the powers are rarely used. The main tasks of headquarters is to keep off the lists those candidates suspected of having political sympathies proscribed by the party. Between 1945 and 1964 headquarters vetoed at least ten locally-adopted candidates in this way, on the grounds that they were politically too far to the left.[29]

Labour headquarters is uncompromising in cases where an MP has been expelled from the party. In the parliament of 1945-50, five MPs were so expelled. One, Konni Zilliacus, MP for Gateshead, was renominated by his own local party in 1950, but was opposed by an official Labour candidate and defeated. In 1955 the local party at Liverpool, Exchange, dominated by the extreme left, decided not to renominate their MP, Mrs E. M. Braddock. The National Executive Committee threatened to expel any party member in the constituency who voted against her renomination, which was thus carried into effect. Pressure was also exerted to secure the readoption of Miss E. Burton, at Coventry South, in the same election.[30]

Mrs Braddock was fortunate because she was a much-loved and highly popular MP. Such forceful interventions by the National Executive are very much the exception, if only because too much interference with a local party machine can weaken its effectiveness, perhaps fatally. After 1948 two Labour ministers, A. Creech Jones (Colonial Secretary) and Lewis Silkin (Town & Country Planning) searched for new seats to replace their own, which had disappeared through boundary changes. But they searched in vain; no local party was willing to adopt them. In 1958 the constituency Labour party at St Helens passed over the name of Tom Driberg, at that time chairman of the Labour party. The following year Morgan Phillips, the general secretary, was rejected by the constituency party of Derbyshire North-East. All the left-wing MPs from whom the whip was withdrawn in 1954 and 1961 continued to enjoy the support of their local parties. In all, between 1945 and 1964, 16 known attempts were made locally to force the retirement of Labour MPs; 12 attempts were successful.[31]

At the beginning of 1965 the policy of non-interference by Labour headquarters was reversed. The party needed to find a seat for the Foreign Secretary, Patrick Gordon Walker, who had been defeated at Smethwick in the general election the previous autumn. The Rev. R. W. Sorensen, the Labour MP at Leyton, was persuaded to accept a peerage, and Gordon Walker was foisted onto the local party as the Labour candidate. The move was not popular. There was much local ill-feeling with what was felt to be an unwarranted intrusion into the constituency by the party bosses. At the by-election a Labour majority of 7,926 was turned into a Conservative one of 205.

Since then the National Executive Committee has maintained a low profile. There were no threats of expulsion against members of the Merthyr Tydfil constituency party who refused to renominate S. O. Davies in 1970, or against the party at Clapham for not renominating Mrs M. McKay in the same general election. Dick Taverne was not rescued by the National Executive when he broke with the party at Lincoln in 1973, nor was E. J. Milne, MP for Blyth since 1960, who was rejected by his constituency Labour party in February 1974.

At Merthyr and Clapham, as at Lincoln and Blyth, Labour was defeated at the subsequent general elections.[32] After the events of 1970 the Labour party conference created a right of appeal for dismissed MPs to the National Executive. Yet the right of appeal is only on matters of maladministration. Has the correct procedure been followed? Were those who voted against the renomination entitled to do so? 'There is', Frank Tomney told the National Executive sub-committee hearing his case, 'nothing for loyalty, nothing for service, nothing for principle, nothing for dedication.'[33]

If therefore it is true that Conservative constituency

associations can be run, and the candidates selected, by a small group of influential leaders, it is doubly true in the case of the Labour party. The General Management Committee decides on the candidate, but only from a short list presented to it by the Executive Committee, perhaps as few as 20 people. Since 1945 the National Executive has withheld approval from only five candidates adopted by constituency parties.[34] An MP or candidate faced with dismissal has little leverage at his command; he has no personal right to examine local party records to see if his detractors are properly qualified, by membership and residence, to sit in judgment on him. The National Executive used to publish a list of proscribed organizations; it no longer does so, thus making it easier still for left-wing groups to infiltrate constituency parties.[35] Even a Labour Cabinet Minister, as the case of Reg Prentice shows, will find his status and position of little use if his General Management Committee are determined to be rid of him.

The same narrow base of selection can be detected in the minor parties, though in their case friction is not so great because the first priority is to win seats, not examine the inner recesses of a candidate's credentials. Sometimes, where membership of the party is small, the number of suitable candidates is necessarily diminished, and the national committee of such a party is likely to have a much greater say in selection discussions. But often a minor party is happy to get volunteers to stand at elections and put up a respectable fight. The Liberal party is a case in point. There exists an officially approved list of candidates drawn up by the party secretary and a sub-committee of the Liberal Party Organisation. But constituencies are not limited to this list, nor does the party headquarters possess a veto over a local choice. Liberal candidates are in short supply, so local activists are given a free hand in finding a suitable person. There is no limit to the amount of money a Liberal candidate can give towards his election expenses or donate to his constituency party, though large contributions are unlikely to be a frequent occurrence.

Headline-making clashes between constituency Labour

parties and Labour headquarters, or between Conservative Central Office and local Conservative associations, are not everyday occurrences. For most constituency parties, most of the time, relations with head office are cordial, with due deference paid on either side. There are many local parties which have never had a cross word with the national organizers, on whom they have come to rely for advice on a wide variety of matters, including candidate selection. This is especially so when by-elections crop up and publicity focussed on a single constituency is intense. Then headquarters will draft in workers from other areas and generally take a much closer interest in the conduct of the campaign. The Labour party has special powers of supervision over selection procedure when a by-election is due. At by-elections or general elections, it is the party headquarters that produces much of the propaganda material on which candidates rely. But this policy of tact on both sides should not lead an observer to suppose that national headquarters and national leaders call the tune. They do not, and if they attempt to do so they generally end up with egg on their faces. As Dr Michael Rush concludes in his study of selection procedures, 'local autonomy over selection is the price which the national parties must pay for adequate local organization'.[36]

The power which constituency parties have over the candidates they choose, and the realization that the choosing is done by a very small group which is often not representative of all the shades of opinion within the party membership locally, has from time to time led to demands for an institutionalized widening of the selection procedure. The obvious example to follow is the United States of America, where the ordinary voters may take part in choosing Congressional candidates through primary elections. In a 'closed' primary, a voter must register as, say, a Republican; he can then vote to choose the Republican candidate, but cannot take part in the Democratic primary. In an 'open' primary, a voter can take part in both Republican and Democratic primaries. Both types of primary have their drawbacks. An open primary allows, perhaps invites, wrecking tactics: Republicans support the worst Democratic candidate, and vice-versa. A closed primary lends itself to the objection that the mere taking part in it is a public advertisement of political support, and to some extent this must militate against the safeguards of the secret ballot. In addition, any type of primary must increase the cost of elections and hence the influence of wealth.

It is doubtful if the open primary would ever find much support in Great Britain. The general feeling is that only those with sufficient commitment to join a party should have the right to select that party's candidate. This leaves the possibility of a closed primary, and there have in fact been a number of closed primaries in Britain over the past three decades, all to settle disputes about Conservative candidatures.

At Hampstead, in 1949, a ballot of the Conservative association's 7,500 subscribing members was held to choose between the incumbent MP, Charles Challen, and his most-favoured replacement, Henry Brooke. Brooke won by 714 votes to 449. In 1965, 1,000 of the 2,300 paid-up members of the Brighton, Kemptown, Conservative association balloted to choose a new candidate following the loss of the seat by seven votes the previous year. On the second ballot, the ex-MP was defeated by 346 votes to 253.[37] The most celebrated primary was at Bournemouth East, where Conservative Central Office arranged a postal ballot following the repudiation of the MP, Nigel Nicolson, by the local association. Nicolson, elected in 1955, had displeased the local party on a number of occasions, especially by his vote in favour of the abolition of capital punishment in February 1956, and by his abstention on a vote of confidence on the Conservative government's Suez policy the following November. He lost the ballot by 91 votes in a poll of 7,433 and agreed not to stand at the next election.[38] Most recently, Conservatives in the Lambeth Vauxhall constituency were invited to choose between three contenders shortlisted from 31 original applicants. In a total membership of 500, only 36 bothered to vote; the constituency chairman declared that the low poll was the result of apathy and the

Grand National horse-race on television.[39] Yet even the Bournemouth primary did not turn out as the democratic affair it was dressed up to be, for those who participated in it represented only 76 per cent of the local Conservative membership. Nigel Nicolson was in fact rejected by the votes of a mere 39 per cent of the membership of this constituency party.

The Hansard Society's Commission on Electoral Reform recommended that all registered members of a constituency party be given the opportunity to vote by secret ballot (preferably postal) on the choice of candidate, and that the readoption of a sitting MP be taken to a ballot where at least 20 per cent of the paid-up members sign a declaration to this effect; the cost of the postal ballot would be publicly financed.[40]

Such a reform would constitute a novel departure in candidate selection, diluting the influence of local leaderships and of militant well-organized cliques. It would require legislative interference with the internal workings of political parties, and might be resisted on these grounds alone. But it would not, in all probability, amount to a revolution. It can hardly be supposed that the name of every person who applied for nomination would appear on the ballot paper. An initial selection procedure would have to take place and the constituency party members presented with the names of three or four for their final choice. In practice, the types of candidate selected would probably not differ markedly from the present patterns.

The end result of candidate selection, the MPs elected to Westminister, will be considered in the final chapter. Here it is worth noting some well-defined traits arising from the selection process. The first is the small proportion of women candidates adopted, and the falling proportion of women elected, as table 3:1 shows.

This picture must to some extent be modified by reference to the two major parties (see table 3:2). Women have a better chance of being selected by Labour than by Conservative constituency parties, but in both parties their chance of being selected for winnable seats has declined:

3.1 Women candidates and MPs, 1964–October 1974

Election	Total	%	Number elected	%	Proportion of total MPs (%)
1964	90	5.1	29	32.2	4.6
1966	81	4.7	26	32.1	4.1
1970	99	5.4	26	26.3	4.1
1974 (Feb)	143	6.7	23	16.1	3.6
1974 (Oct)	161	7.1	27	16.8	4.3

3.2 Women candidates in the Conservative and Labour parties, 1964–October 1974

	Conservative				Labour			
Election	Total	%	Elected	%	Total	%	Elected	%
1964	24	3.8	11	45.8	33	5.3	18	54.5
1966	21	3.3	7	33.3	30	4.8	19	63.3
1970	26	4.1	15	57.7	29	4.6	10	34.5
1974 (Feb)	33	5.3	9	27.3	40	6.4	13	32.5
1974 (Oct)	30	4.8	7	23.3	50	8.0	18	36.0

It is clear that women, in spite of the hard work they put in at constituency level, are not adopted as candidates in anything approaching their proportion of the electorate. Is this deliberate? To some extent it is not. Fewer women offer themselves for parliamentary honours, and this is bound to be reflected in the number of female candidates. But there is evidence that prejudice exists against women, and that this prejudice is stronger in the Conservative party than in the Labour ranks. In the 1950s it was widely believed that voters were less likely to vote for a woman than for a man. This feeling appears to have lingered on, even though exhaustive analysis of election results has found that the statistical basis for this superstition is diminishing. The results of the 1955 and 1959 elections show that where a Conservative man replaced a Conservative woman candidate, he could have expected to pick up about 300 extra votes. In the case of Labour candidates there was no difference at all. The 1964 and 1966 results showed again that Conservative women candidates did worse than men, but that Labour women did somewhat better than men.[41] In the 1970s it is clear that anti-female bias among Conservative voters has disappeared. The recent Nuffield election studies declare that there is no clear evidence that the sex of the candidate affected voting.[42] The superstition persists nonetheless.

Another Conservative idiosyncracy is the decided reluctance to adopt working-class candidates. Since 1966 no more than six such candidates have been adopted at any one general election; in February 1974 the figure was four. Most of these stood in hopeless seats. No more than two were elected: Ray Mawby (Totnes since 1955), an electrician and trade union official, and Sir Edward Brown (Bath since 1964), a former member of the Association of Supervisory Staffs, Executives & Technicians. Various initiatives from Conservative party headquarters to get local associations to adopt working-class people have fallen on deaf ears; a strange omission for a party that relies so heavily on working-class votes. Sir Edward Brown went before 29 constituency selection committees between 1954 and 1963 before finding a reasonably safe seat.[43]

Religious prejudice in the selection of Conservative candidates is, however, diminishing. There is no evidence nowadays of the anti-Catholic prejudice which was widespread at the turn of the century. Though Jews encounter prejudice in some areas, this too is diminishing. In 1951 not one Jewish Conservative candidate (there were seven in all) managed to get adopted for a winnable seat; in February 1974, out of 21 Jewish Conservatives who were adopted, no less than 12 were elected, the highest Jewish Conservative contingent ever in the Commons. Out of 38 Jewish Labour candidates in the same election no less than 33 were elected. Outside Northern Ireland, in fact, religious background of candidates is in general not a factor of importance. But it is a factor nonetheless. In some constituencies on Merseyside and in Glasgow, Labour nominees who are Roman Catholic have an advantage.[44] Nonconformists do better in the Labour party than in the Conservative; in 1966 about a quarter of Labour candidates were from nonconformist religious groups, but only about one eighth of Conservative candidates.[45]

Labour candidates as a whole are no more a mirror of their party's supporters than are the Conservatives of theirs. The substantial sponsorship by trade unions does lead to a surfeit of working-class candidates. One reason is that unions have difficulty in finding men and women of the right calibre from amongst their own ranks. The Amalgamated Union of Engineering Workers requires all its potential sponsored candidates to pass a series of tests in public speaking and knowledge of politics.[46] The National Union of Public Employees requires its sponsored MPs to submit to a test of their 'political fitness' by writing a 1,000-word essay on trade union power.[47] The best union brains tend to be directed towards full-time union administration. Partly as a result, the number of working-class Labour candidates in recent years has been less than a quarter of the total: 17 per cent in 1970, 21 per cent and 24 per cent in 1974. Sponsorship of university-trained professional men is now not uncommon.[48] The Transport & General Workers' Union sponsored Peter Shore (Cambridge) and Dr Jeremy Bray (Cambridge and Harvard); the National Union of General & Municipal Workers' sponsored William Rodgers (Oxford).

For both parties, in fact, the preference is now to choose as candidates people with professional backgrounds. For the Labour party the development is highly significant. For the Conservative party the significance lies in the growth of the teaching and journalistic contingents at the expense of the law and the armed services. The trend over the past decade is traced in table 3:3.

In October 1974, 62 per cent of all Conservative candidates had been to a public school; 38 per cent had been to Oxford or Cambridge. The comparable Labour percentages were 17 per cent and 20 per cent.[49] A Labour candidate is more likely to have gone to a secondary school and a redbrick university. But this is still, of course, a startling contrast to the educational background of the mass of the population, whom only three per cent are educated at

3.3 Conservative & Labour Candidates, 1966–1974: socio-economic background*

1966

	Conservative (%) Elected	Conservative (%) Defeated	Labour (%) Elected	Labour (%) Defeated
Professional	47	48	43	50
Business	29	38	9	17
Miscellaneous	23	12	18	24
Workers	1	2	30	9
	100	100	100	100

1970

Professional	45	48	48	54
Business	30	38	10	14
Miscellaneous	24	13	16	22
Workers	1	1	26	10
	100	100	100	100

October 1974

Professional	46	46	49	55
Business	32	40	8	14
Miscellaneous	21	13	15	18
Workers	1	1	28	13
	100	100	100	100

*These calculations are based on information in the Nuffield election studies

public schools and of whom less than six per cent attend a university of any sort. A distinction needs to be drawn also between Conservative and Labour businessmen; many of the latter are small businessmen rather than substantial pany directors. Nevertheless the overall picture is one in which well over half the candidates, defeated and elected, of the two major parties are drawn from the ranks of the professions and the world of commerce. This is bound to colour heavily the composition of the House of Commons.

Election by the few

The role of the constituency parties in choosing candidates is crucial because in many cases, to all intents and purposes, choice of candidate is tantamount to choice of MP. This is because at any general election only a proportion of the seats change hands or are likely to do so: the so-called 'marginal' seats. In a 'safe' seat the incumbent party is sure of success; the lucky candidate of that party knows that he possesses a through-ticket to Westminster.

Politicians have for long known that some seats are winnable, others dead certainties or dead losses. Those which were considered dead losses were often not contested; the expense and effort were simply not worth while. Today this philosophy no longer holds. The Conservative and Labour parties contest every seat in Great Britain, the Scottish National Party every Scottish seat, Plaid Cymru every seat in Wales. In October 1974 the Liberals left only four British seats uncontested.[50] This is to some extent a matter of honour. It would not do to be seen abandoning a part of the battlefield. It is also a matter of expediency, to pin down opposing party workers and force the opposition to spend money and effort where it would otherwise have the easiest of victories. For minor parties there may also be a tactical consideration in the fighting of hopeless seats: to attract publicity, to gain time on radio and television, or even to put pressure on one of the main contenders by threatening to draw off much-needed support. In the last resort, however, and so long as the first-past-the-post system prevails, general election results are decided by the number of marginal seats which change hands. In safe seats MPs are chosen by the constituency parties. In marginals the voter really does come into his own. But the number of marginals can be very small indeed.

In popular mythology the definition of a marginal seat is simple. It is a seat which is vulnerable, and may fall to the opposition, when the nationwide 'swing' against the incumbent party is as great as or greater than the swing needed for the seat to fall. On the eve of general elections many newspapers print lists of marginal seats, indicating what swing would be needed for each to change hands. But obviously the degree of marginality depends on the mood of the electorate. Where the movement of opinion between one general election and the next is small, the number of seats which can reasonably be expected to change hands is small also. Where there are violent fluctuations of electoral opinion, or where support for third parties increases, the number of safe seats is bound to diminish.

A digression is necessary here to deal with the over-used and much-abused term 'swing'. The most commonly used method of determining swing, known as 'conventional swing', is to average one major party's percentage gain in votes cast and the other's percentage loss, as compared with the previous election, according to the following formula:

$$\text{Swing} = \frac{(L \text{ minus } L^1) \text{ minus } (C \text{ minus } C^1)}{2}$$

L is the present Labour percentage, C is the present Conservative percentage, and L^1 and C^1 are, respectively, the previous Labour and previous Conservative percen- If the result is positive, the swing is to Labour; if negative, to the Conservatives. An example will illustrate the formula in action. In 1970 the Conservative percentage vote in Wednesbury was 46.2; in 1966 it had been 41.2. The Labour percentage was 53.7; it had been 58.8. Here, therefore, the swing was:

$$\frac{(53.7 - 58.8) - (46.2 - 41.2)}{2} \text{ per cent}$$

$$= \frac{(-5.1) - (+5.0)}{2} \text{ per cent}$$

$= -5.1$ per cent (to the nearest decimal point)

i.e. a swing of 5.1 per cent to the Conservatives.

Where there is a straight fight between the two major parties, (as most elections were in the 1950s and early 1960s, when the notion of swing was popularized) swing is a useful shorthand way of expressing net shifts in voting behaviour. To say that in Wednesbury, in 1970, there was a swing of 5.1 per cent to the Conservative does *not* mean that there was a simple switch of that percentage of voters from one party to the other. Abstentions, deaths, new voters might all have played a part. But where third parties intervene, and especially where such a party benefits substantially at the expense of one of the major ones, swing can turn out to be meaningless. At Preston North, in 1970, the Conservatives obtained 50.6 per cent of the votes, Labour 43.2 per cent, and the Liberals 6.2 per cent; in February 1974 the percentages were: Conservatives, 40.9, Labour 41.5, Liberals 17.5. There had been no boundary change. So the swing was:

$$\frac{(-1.7)-(-9.7)}{2} \text{ per cent}$$

i.e. 4.0 per cent to Labour

This calculation says nothing about the origins of the Liberal vote, which had almost trebled. Not even the voting figures would reveal that; at the most they would only suggest possible explanations. Labour gained Preston North in February 1974 even though their total vote *fell* by over 300. The Conservative vote fell by over 3,500. The probability is that Labour won the seat through Conservatives abstaining or switching to the Liberals. To say that there was a swing of 4.0 per cent to Labour is highly misleading.

But where a third party intervenes with disastrous results for the other two, swing becomes a nonsense. On 2 November 1967 Labour lost one of its safest Scottish seats, Hamilton, to the Scottish National Party. The nationalists polled 46.0 per cent of the votes, Labour 41.5 per cent, and the Conservatives a paltry 12.5 per cent. At the general election the previous year, when the nationalists had not contested the seat, Labour polled 71.2 per cent and the Conservatives 28.8 per cent. So, using the formula given above, the swing in 1967 was:

$$\frac{(-29.7)-(-16.3)}{2} \text{ per cent}$$

i.e. 6.7 per cent to the Conservatives

In fact, the Conservative candidate came bottom of the poll and lost his deposit. It is likely that the Conservative defection to the Scottish National Party was less than the Labour switch to that party – hence the theoretical pro-Conservative swing. But the calculation, in a case such as this, is devoid of real meaning.

The intervention of third parties is now the rule rather than the exception. In 1951 the combined Conservative and Labour share of the total votes cast was 96.8 per cent; in 1970 it was 89.5 per cent, and in October 1974 only 75.0 per cent. Moreover, swing is not uniform over the whole country, as table 3:4 indicates.

3.4 **Variations in swing, February and October 1974**

	United Kingdom	England	Scotland	Wales
February	1.3% to Lab.	1.2% to Lab.	1.4% to Con.	1.5% to Con.
October	2.1% to Lab.	1.9% to Lab.	4.0% to Lab.	2.4% to Lab.

The pro-Conservative swings in Scotland and Wales in February 1974 mask the nationalist success; the English figures mask the Liberal impact. In short, because of the large slice of the vote now taken by other parties, excessive use of the term 'swing' is doubly dangerous. The term is a mathematical abstraction, useful up to a point but concealing much more than it reveals. It grew up with the two-party system in mind. It has never explained the behaviour of individual voters; a swing of 0.0 per cent in a straight fight might in fact conceal many voting patterns. Swing purports to compare the behaviour of the electorate over a period of time in which electorates are bound to change in composition. Where there are many boundary changes (as in February 1974) swing cannot be calculated for the new constituencies. It is, at most, a convenient but crude measure of one party's net gain against another's net loss.[51]

Swing, then, is no substitute for looking at the voting figures. But it has a limited use in arriving at some estimate of the degree of marginality of a seat, because the swing needed for the seat to change hands can be computed, bearing in mind that third parties may upset the calculation. In 1970, at Wednesbury, it would have needed a swing of 8.8 per cent for the Conservatives to have captured the seat. The national swing in 1966 had been 2.7 per cent to Labour, so Wednesbury was not considered a marginal. But after 1970 it would have needed a swing of only 3.8 per cent for Wednesbury to change hands. Since this was much less than the national swing in Great Britain in 1970 of 4.7 per cent to the Conservatives, the seat had become marginal (but in fact disappeared in the subsequent boundary alterations).

Marginality is, therefore, a relative concept and must be understood not merely in terms of swing, but also in terms of the turnover of seats at each election, as table 3:5 indicates:

3.5 **Swing and turnover of seats, 1950–74**

Year	National (U.K.) Swing	Number of seats changing hands
1950	2.9% to Con.	18
1951	0.9% to Con.	28
1955	2.0% to Con.	15*
1959	1.0% to Con.	35
1964	3.0% to Lab.	70
1966	2.7% to Lab.	54
1970	4.7% to Con.	89
1974 (Feb)	1.3% to Lab.	30*
1974 (Oct)	2.1% to Lab.	29

*Boundary changes

Practically identical swings in 1950 and 1964 produced very different numbers of seats changing hands. In 1950, although the swing was nearly 3 per cent, only 18 seats changed hands. In 1951, 1955 and 1959 the average swing was a mere 1.3 per cent; the number of marginals was still small, and an MP with a lead of 5 per cent over his opponent – say a majority of 3,000 – could feel safe. In those three general elections, only four seats ever changed hands with swings of 5 per cent or more. As the electorate has become more volatile, this margin of safety no longer gives adequate protection. Writing in the late 1960s, R . L. Leonard could say that 'any constituency with a majority of . . . about 14 per cent of the votes cast' was 'unlikely to change hands at a general election'; indeed, between 1945 and 1966 only three had done so.[52] Yet in the 1970 election no less than 12 seats changed hands with swings of more than 7 per cent; the highest swing was 11 per cent to the Conservative at Cannock, in a straight fight.[53] In 1970, therefore, a constituency with a majority of less than 4,000 was considered unsafe; Labour in fact lost 70 seats out of about 90 that were vulnerable. The cumulative effect of the erosion of comfortable majorities has been to increase the number of marginals. In the general elections of 1974 about 80 seats were considered to belong to this category.[54]

The conclusion must therefore be that in about 555 constituencies the MPs are chosen by probably less than 1,600,000 party members. In the remaining 80 constituencies the choice is made, not by all the voters, but by those of them (who they are will be discussed in chapter five) who are not died-in-the-wool supporters of one party or another, plus those who die and those who come of age, perhaps as few as a quarter of a million persons in all. This is an improvement on the situation a couple of decades ago, when 600 or so constituencies were 'safe' and the choice in the remaining 30 was made by less than 100,000 voters. But it is a far cry from Aristotle's vision of a democracy in which 'the people are in the majority, and a resolution passed by a majority is paramount'.[55]

Campaigning

The use of the term 'swing', especially by broadcasters and journalists, not only oversimplifies results but also lends an air of impersonality to voting behaviour and tends to dehumanize the voter. Furthermore it exaggerates the importance of party in plotting and explaining election results. This is perhaps inevitable given the 'nationalization' of party propaganda and the reliance which most candidates place on the national party effort and the pull of the leaders. In fact, a crucial distinction must be drawn between the *real* issues of an election, those which most exercise the minds of the voters – especially in marginal constituencies – and the issues which the politicians would prefer the election to be about, and which, indeed, they stress and reinforce with every weapon at their disposal. The confusion of these two elements, the real issues and the contrived, is less intense at a by-election, when there is no national campaign; at a general election such confusion is widespread, because the media and the party workers stress the national campaign above all else.

The aim of the politicians, and of the national campaign which party headquarters direct, is to simplify as much as possible, to concentrate on a few issues which are regarded as vote-winners. Justifying his appeal to the people in February 1974 Edward Heath asked:

> Do you want Parliament and the elected Government to continue to fight strenuously against inflation? Or do you want them to abandon the struggle against rising prices under pressure from one particular group of workers?[56]

Such an appeal sounded eminently reasonable, almost beyond argument. Harold Wilson attacked it the following day. The election, he said, was not about the power of the unions, or the miners' strike, but about the collapse of the house-building programme, mortgage rates, Heath's refusal to consult the electorate over the Common Market and, in general, the 'disastrous failure' of the Conservative government.[57] In the 20 days that followed these opening salvos, the issues were narrowed down: on the Conservative side, 'who governs?', the unions or the government; on the Labour side, rising prices and excessive profits by commercial undertakings. The leadership on both sides brought in sympathetic experts to put forward campaign ideas and answer questions from anxious candidates. Daily press conferences were held, as in previous elections, to rebut the charges made by the other side the previous day or in the morning papers. Both sides commissioned their own private opinion polls to enable them to assess, day by day, the reaction to their propaganda and to modify it accordingly. There was also feedback to headquarters from local canvassing.[58] Party headquarters once again produced a mass of publicity material for local distribution, even though the impact hardly justified the expense. In 1970 only 53 per cent of the electorate, according to a Gallup survey, claimed to have read so much as one election address; in February 1974 the figure was 51 per cent. In 1970 ten per cent claimed to have displayed a window bill; in February 1974, only 9 per cent.[59]

Above all, there was little effort to project the idea of collective leadership in a political party. Growing concentration upon the leader has been a feature of post-war British electoral politics, and with good reason. The party leaders are the most exposed figures in their parties. It is rare indeed for their subordinates to match their degree of public exposure and attraction: the prominence achieved by Ernest Bevin and Enoch Powell are really the exceptions which prove the rule. A *Sunday Times* survey in 1962 showed that the majority of those interviewed could not name a single political figure in either party other than the leaders.[60] Attitudes to party leaders do, moreover, have some impact upon electoral choice. Butler & Stokes found that between 1966 and 1970 attitudes towards the leaders made a small but distinct contribution to the improvement in the position of the Conservative party.[61] A party whose popularity is improving is likely to gain an additional advantage from having a leader whose public image is improving too. But a good, even a great leader will not help a party which is clearly out of public favour. In 1945 the Conservatives hoped Winston Churchill would win the election for them; in fact they lost it for him. Churchill was projected strongly, to better effect, in 1950 and 1951.

It is much easier to project the image of a single person, and much easier to argue that your party will provide strong leadership, if it is seen to have a strong person at the helm. Harold Wilson was projected in this way in 1964 and 1966. In 1970 Edward Heath appeared by himself at his early press conferences. The Labour party's publicity leaflets talked about 'Labour's winning team', and on no less than three occasions Wilson left the running of the Labour Press conference to his colleagues.[62] But in its totality the Labour campaign centred around him, and was directed by him to a greater extent than ever before. In retrospect this was felt to be a mistake. In February 1974 the Labour campaign really was much more of a team effort.[63] Nonetheless, it was Wilson's face that appeared most frequently on the television screen, and Wilson's pronouncements received more publicity than those of other Labour leaders.

For the lesser parties the need to concentrate on the leader is even greater, for they have far fewer figures of national prominence. The Liberal campaign of February 1974 was almost exclusively concentrated on Jeremy Thorpe, the leader, even though he was 200 miles away, in North Devon, defending a majority of 369. At a cost of £16,000, a colour television link was set up between Barnstaple and London, enabling him to conduct the London press conferences.[64] The Liberals were thus able to present themselves as being above, or at least away from, the mud-slinging of the metropolis, but at the cost of isolating and elevating their own leader to a peculiar degree.

These features of the campaign are mirrored at constituency level. Labour candidates tend to follow very closely the themes of the national campaign; Conservatives somewhat less so. In February 1974 the Labour party's secretary urged candidates to fight 'a synchronised campaign with the accent on Labour's *positive* proposals – *taken straight from our Manifesto*'. Over 80 per cent of Labour candidates emphasized the manifesto 'a great deal'; only two-thirds of Conservative candidates did so. Over twice as many Labour as Conservative candidates paid attention to what party headquarters had to say, and close attention to the national campaign was much greater on the Labour than on the Conservative side.[65] This does not mean that Conservatives ignore the campaign issues, but it does reflect a conscious desire in the Labour party to produce the impression of a well-disciplined army, united in the targets it has selected for attack. For all except the most individualistic (of whom there were a few on the Conservative side in 1974), the manifesto remains the basis of their appeal; in October 1974 Conservative emphasis on the manifesto actually increased.[66]

When the authors of the Nuffield studies asked candidates in 1974 which national issues were most frequently raised by voters during the campaign, the replies merely reflected the issues the candidates themselves were stressing (prices, inflation, the unions, housing) in their speeches and election addresses. The nationwide recipe was perhaps varied slightly to suit particular local conditions (for instance, housing might be linked to local immigration pressures, nationalization to local job prospects), but the ingredients were essentially the same.

Often, indeed, candidates are quite put out when other issues, not nationally promoted, are injected into local campaigns. In Scotland and Wales this attack, from the nationalists, is to be expected. In Scotland no seat is 'safe' for either of the major parties. Candidates thus have to fight the Scottish National Party on grounds of its own choosing: mainly self-government and the control of North Sea oil revenues. In Wales Plaid Cymru's impact has been to force other candidates to deal with its demand for Welsh control of Welsh affairs and resources; London-inspired leaflets are re-vamped with a (not-always-convincing) Welsh dimension, which in practice means concentration on local issues in a way not attempted by the Conservative and Labour parties in English constituencies.[67] Efforts by Liberal candidates to exploit 'community politics' and local grievances at national elections are frowned upon by other parties. When other pressure groups weigh in, particularly by introducing issues which are embarrassing for the main parties, and on which they do not have a ready-made policy, and would be split if they did, the response is one of anger. The activities of the 'abortion lobby' in one constituency in October 1974 were, one candidate said, 'a confounded nuisance, and . . . quite ruined my hope to campaign on other issues'.[68] For the same reasons, the Common Market has been deliberately played down. In 1970, two-thirds of the candidates made no mention at all in their election addresses of British entry into the Common Market; in 1974 the proportion was even higher. The situation in Northern Ireland, which has rarely been out of the headlines since 1969, was not mentioned in any Labour address in February 1974; only 9 per cent of Conservative addresses mentioned it then, and only 7 per cent in October.[69] Immigration did not fare much better.

Are the issues which the politicians stress the ones which the electors want them to stress? To some extent, of course, they are, they have to be. The economy, housing, education, the social services are all staple issues of British politics, and have been since the end of the second world war. But there are undoubtedly some issues upon which the electorate feels strongly, but on which most politicians are unwilling to base their appeal. Real electoral choice is narrowed as a result. In 1959 Trenaman & McQuail compared the content of the party political broadcasts with those of other broadcast programmes and the press. Two subjects – nationalization and industrial relations – figured very little in the party broadcasts but were quite prominent elsewhere. The theme of 'prosperity' got twice as much attention elsewhere than on the party broadcasts.[70] In the 1960s capital punishment was a burning topic, one of intense national concern. Opinion polls in 1960 and 1961 showed about three-quarters of the voters in favour of its retention.[71] An independent who stood against the Labour MP Sydney Silverman, the chief abolitionist, in the 1966 election, obtained 13.7 per cent of the vote – enough to save his deposit and to demonstrate that many people in the constituency felt strongly on this issue. Yet neither the parties nor the media were willing to give this issue the national coverage it deserved.

Immigration is another and more obvious topic which would probably be swept under the carpet were it not for the intervention of third parties. It has been an issue in British politics for over a decade. Resentment at coloured immigration was responsible for Conservative victories at Eton & Slough and Smethwick in 1964, and for pro-Conservative swings in other constituencies.[72] The defeat of the Labour candidate Dr (now Lord) David Pitt at Clapham in 1970 was party attributable to his colour. The only politician of national repute to have campaigned on the issue of immigration is Enoch Powell. An examination of unpublished opinion poll data for the 1970 election shows that Powell was a Conservative vote-winner, even though the Conservative leadership had disowned him.[73] The only political party to have made an issue out of immigration is the National Front. In 1970 an attitude of 'enlightened self-interest', according to the Nuffield study, led Labour and Conservative parties in sensitive immigrant areas to play down the issue. The National Front fielded 10 candidates and averaged 3.6 per cent of the votes; it 'probably prevented' Huddersfield West from going Conservative.[74] In February 1974, with 54 candidates, the Front polled an average of 3.3 per cent, and in October, with 90 candidates, 3.1 per cent. This may or may not be evidence of a National Front decline, but it is certainly proof that many voters care passionately about the immigration issue. In 13 Labour strongholds in the East End of London in October 1974, it polled 6.2 per cent of the vote.[75] The Butler & Stokes survey found that between 1963 and 1970 immigration, as a problem perceived to be facing the government, rose from eighth place, in the estimation of the panel, to fifth, displacing education and transport.[76] Yet the Labour manifesto of October 1974 devoted barely three lines to the subject of immigration; only two per cent of Labour candidates bothered to mention it in their election addresses.[77]

What is true of immigration is true of other issues which can in no sense be called 'local'. Ulster, for instance, was not mentioned in the February 1974 Labour manifesto or in Labour candidates' addresses,[78] yet Ulster politics have important consequences, financial and otherwise, for voters outside the province. Foreign policy is consciously played down. Yet the evidence is that for some sections of the population, such as Jews in relation to the Middle East, and immigrants from the Indian sub-continent in relation to Bangladesh, the foreign policies of the parties and candidates are regarded as important. The Conservative victory at Bradford West in 1970 was at least partly due to the identification of the Labour party there with the Bangladesh movement, for the origins of the Pakistani community in

Bradford are predominantly in West Pakistan. The campaign in Hendon North in February 1974 was largely not about the miners or the three-day week, but about support for Israel, which became a major election topic because of the large Jewish electorate in the constituency.[79]

Thus issues which are not 'national' may nonetheless emerge in isolated constituencies as the most salient features of the campaign. It is often the case that when seats swing against the national trend, local issues are the explanation. In 1959 there were pro-Labour swings in parts of Lancashire and Scotland; the explanation probably lay in the depressed state of the cotton and shipbuilding industries in these areas. In October 1974 there was a pro-Conservative swing in Brent North, presumably because of local disenchantment with comprehensive education, a feeeling shared by the outspoken Conservative MP for the constituency, Dr. Rhodes Boyson. There is, in fact, no guarantee that the issues on which the parties nationally would like to appeal to the electors are the same ones in which the electors are most interested, less still the ones on the basis of which they will make their choice on polling day.

What, then, do campaigns achieve, and why do political parties attach so much importance to them? Here, again, a distinction must be drawn between the safe seats and the marginals. To the extent that campaigns do concentrate on issues in which voters are interested, the political parties are well advised to campaign vigorously in marginal seats. They do so with studied seriousness. Both the Conservative and Labour parties maintain lists of marginal seats, which they revise in the light of local and by-election results, boundary changes, etc. At election time professional help is concentrated in the most marginal seats. In February 1974 over half Labour's professional agents were in seats the party considered marginal; most Conservative marginals also had a professional agent.[80] Special grants are made for extra secretarial help, workers to organize the postal vote, and the buying of advertizing space. Marginals are also given much attention by prominent national leaders – the front-bench spokesmen – who can be relied upon to draw large audiences and attract column-inches in the local press. A voter in a marginal constituency is more likely than one in a safe seat to receive personal visits from the main contestants, and to be offered a motorized conveyance to the poll.

These efforts appear to bear some fruit. In marginal seats, turnout is likely to be better. Between 1964 and 1966, turnout in the United Kingdom as a whole dropped by 1.3 per cent; in marginal seats it rose by 1.4 per cent, and in the most marginal Conservative seats by 2.3 per cent.[81] Between February and October 1974 turnout dropped by 6.0 per cent, but in marginals only by about 5 per cent, and in the most marginal by less than 4 per cent.[82] The importance of postal-voting in marginal seats has already been noted.[83]

It appears, therefore, that the concentration of the national party effort in the critical seats leads to more voters being persuaded into voting. But it would be wrong to suppose that this public relations effort will necessarily influence the way they vote. In 1970 there was a national swing of 4.7 per cent to the Conservatives; in the 100 seats where the 1966 Labour majority had been narrowest, the swing to the Conservatives was only 4.4 per cent.[84] Prior to the 1970 election, Conservative Central Office had mounted an exercise to determine which Labour- or Liberal-held marginals they needed to win to have a working majority at Westminister: the so-called 'critical seats' exercise. There were 68 seats in all, and upon them, from as far back as September 1969, was lavished all manner of extra luxuries – more money, more advertising, more professional help, more front-bench speakers. During the general election campaign itself, the Conservative boast was that their performance in these seats would be better than over the country as a whole.

In fact it was worse. In the 68 'criticals', the pro-Conservative swing was only 4.1 per cent. As if to add insult to injury, in 16 seats not on the 'critical' list, the Conservatives 'achieved' an average swing of 5.8 per cent, and won ten of them.[85] In October 1974 the rewards were somewhat better. Forty-seven criticals were selected for special treatment; the average swing against the Conservatives in them was 1.5 per cent, less than the anti-Conservative swing nationally.[86] Four seats which Labour might have gained (Brentford & Isleworth, Upminster, Northampton South and Norfolk North-West) were saved, and a further two (Hazel Grove and Bodmin) were captured from the Liberals. But pro-Conservative swings were achieved in seats not on this list.[87] It may be significant that the average swing against the Conservatives in seats they were defending (1.0 per cent) was lower than in seats they were attacking (1.8 per cent); an incumbent MP might, on this basis, be said to have a built-in advantage, perhaps based on his or her local reputation, over other candidates not so well-known in the constituency.[88] If so, credit for this must go to the MP, or even just the 'system', not to any elaborate propaganda exercise to win votes.

So far, this discussion has concentrated on the marginals, the winnable seats. The parties simply dare not risk ignoring them. The party organizers may know, deep down, that there will be little, if anything, to show for their effort. But to ignore the marginals, or to give them less attention than the news media say they deserve, would be tantamount to raising the white flag, and would certainly damage party morale. That is important. The safe seats are generally left to their own devices. That can be dangerous.

In 1970 Labour lost nine seats to the Conservatives at swings of over 7 per cent. There is no obvious factor connecting these results. The constituencies were widely separated. Three (Bolton East, Bolton West and Rossendale) conformed to a remarkable and unexpected pattern of anti-Labour swings in the Lancashire textile towns. Cannock and Leek may have been part of a similar anti-Labour pattern in the west Midlands. Clapham was probably lost as a result of colour prejudice. A sharp fall in the Liberal vote may have helped the Conservatives to win Gloucester, and the decision of the Liberals not to fight Bosworth may have give that seat to the Conservatives too. The loss of Pembroke was certainly due to the defection from the

Labour party of its member, Desmond Donnelly, who nonetheless fought the seat under his own colours and so split the Labour vote. These nine results worried Labour supporters less because of the loss of seats than because they were losses without a simple, blanket explanation, without a common cause, a fault which could be put right. It is normal for marginals lost at one election to be won back next time round. But of these nine seats, only three returned to Labour in the elections of 1974.[89] So much for taking 'safe' seats for granted.

There is, then, no correlation between local campaigning effort and electoral performance. A strenuous campaign may be followed by a good result; if so, the probability is that local or regional factors, the personality of the candidate, or just plain luck, will have been the root cause. No campaign at all, or rather a campaign which relies heavily on what the party nationally is doing, is just as likely to produce a good result. Conversely, a bad result ought not to be blamed on the local campaigners. This prompts two further questions. Why are campaigns undertaken at all? And what motivates voters to vote as they do? The following chapters seek, *inter alia*, to provide some answers.

Chapter Four

RITUAL

In previous chapters, I have tried to show that a gulf exists between the theories which are commonly supposed to enshrine the British electoral system, and the actual consequences of that system. The system is supposed to give equal weight to every elector's vote; actually some electors are far more powerful than others. The system is supposed to ensure the representation of electors at Westminster; actually only a small minority of electors do the choosing, and the representatives they choose in no way accurately reflect the state of opinion in the country as a whole. When general elections take place, the issues the politicians talk about are not necessarily those most dear to the hearts of the constituents. Nor is the success a party achieves necessarily commensurate with the efforts it puts into the campaign. The astute observer might be forgiven at this point for asking whether all the time, effort and money put into elections are really justified; indeed, why hold elections at all?

The answer is twofold. Campaigns and elections are not entirely irrelevant. Some issues do get discussed. Some voters are persuaded; voters who are canvassed by a party are more likely to switch their votes to that party, and though the precise impact of canvassing cannot be calculated, it clearly cannot be discounted.[1] Some aspects of the campaign – such as the postal vote – are obviously important. And if parliament is not a faithful reflection of nationwide political preferences, it is not a complete negation of the views of the electors either. The abolition of the death penalty for murder was not a democratic act of the legislature. The Commonwealth Immigration Act of 1968 clearly was. A government with a comfortable majority, or a parliament with a long life ahead of it, will often treat with impunity the known wishes of the electorate. A government on a knife-edge, or a parliament in an electioneering atmosphere, is less inclined to do so.

From this point of view, the parliament of March-October 1974 was one of the most democratic of recent times. Everyone knew another election was not far off. The minority Labour government did not want to spoil its chance of electoral victory. Backbenchers had one eye continually on their electors. The government was defeated 18 times in the Commons. There were frequent backbench revolts. Though the February election was over, the stalemate result enabled the shadow of the electorate to hover about the Palace of Westminster in a way which many MPs found uncongenial and irritating.[2] The trouble is that minority governments and stalemate parliaments cannot be elected to order. The result of the February 1974 general election was an accident. Even if every elector had voted, or abstained, in October as in February, the result would probably not have been the same, because some electors had died in the interval, and young electors had become enfranchised. Unless the electoral system is changed, the only guarantee that future governments will be minority ones lies in an increase of support for third parties, and for runners-up in marginal constituencies. Nonetheless, the experience of 1974 suggests that the electoral process can, even if accidentally, bring dividends for the voters.

But even if elections do not decide who governs, or determine what measures the government shall take, they fulfil certain important functions which are essentially ritualistic and non-rational. For they possess dramatic and social attributes, a therapeutic dimension which can often be overlooked in the welter of facts and figures which are the meat and drink of the election pundits.

The legitimation of government

The problem of how to reconcile men to good government, even though it may not be the form of government they most desire, has attracted the attention of political writers through the ages. Plato, turning his back on the democracy of the Greek city-state, advocated a form of rule by specialists – 'philosophers' – who would frame laws according to the light of pure reason, but who would themselves be above the law. In order to cajole the masses into accepting the edicts of the 'philosopher-kings', Plato advocated the use of a myth, a piece of propaganda which would give a veneer of divinity to the philosophers' pronouncements and so make them acceptable to all.[3] In nineteenth-century England the problem of making government acceptable to people who had no part in choosing it was similarly felt. Walter Bagehot, who did so much to illuminate the real centres of power in his day, and to cut the monarch down to size, nevertheless defended the institution of monarchy on the grounds that it was 'an intelligible government'.[4] The masses of mid-Victorian England may not have understood the intricacies of parliamentary procedure and of the Cabinet. But they understood and knew about Queen Victoria, in whose name all acts of government were carried out, and to whom obedience was owed by every citizen. The monarchy gave to government a sense of awe, mystery and reverence. That alone was a sufficient *raison d'être* for it.

But the monarchy, though still extremely popular, no longer has this sort of hold over people's imaginations. The monarchy may still be regarded as a way of maintaining traditional values, and of removing the headship of state from the realm of politics.[5] But its value as political cement is diminishing. In 1963, 63 per cent of the Butler & Stokes sample thought that the Queen and Royal Family were 'very important' to Britain; in 1970, only 55 per cent.[6] Nothing has quite replaced the monarchy in this respect, certainly not the Prime Minister or his Cabinet colleagues.

Until recently the Cabinet could have been said to have contained within itself a residue of awe, mystery and reverence. Those privy to its proceedings were a select few; if they had not been annointed as the monarch had been, they still derived their authority and seals of office from Her, via the Prime Minister. A number of developments have served to undermine this feeling of reverence. It has now become commonplace for retiring ministers to publish accounts of their public life. In consequence, much more is known about the way the Cabinet works, especially since Cabinet records over 30 years old are available for public inspection. The posthumous publication of the late R. H. S. Crossman's account of his day-to-day life as a Cabinet minister under Harold Wilson, and the clumsy attempt of Wilson's government in 1975 to have the first volume banned (thereby giving it much more publicity) has laid bare the workings of a Cabinet within the recent recollection of the electors.[7] In June 1976 the proceedings of the Cabinet relating to child benefit allowances the previous month were leaked to the magazine *New Society*.[8] Cabinets are seen to be composed of fallible and gullible men and women, more often concerned with scoring points off their rivals than with advancing the public good, and not averse to lying and cheating when it suits them.[9] Cabinet ministers fall a good deal short of Plato's concept of philosopher-kings; and they are not above the law.

As the role of the monarch and the Cabinet as legitimating influences have declined, the electoral process has stepped into the breach. Before the advent of universal suffrage this could hardly have been so. Since then, the appeal to the people has developed about it the air of drama and finality, notwithstanding the inequities under which that appeal is conducted. The electorate does not draw up the manifestos, or decide who the contestants shall be. Usually its role is merely to select between policies and candidates chosen by others. Yet the mechanics of modern elections give the appearance of participation. The election itself is a legitimating ritual, a means by which the policies of politicians are purified (or rendered unclean) by means of the trial by ordeal through the ballot box.

To the extent that general elections are inquests upon the

record of the party in power, this notion has some definite reality, provided it is interpreted in a reasonable fashion. The turning out of the Labour government in 1951 did not imply a green light for the incoming Conservative administration to reverse all the acts of nationalization of the Attlee governments, or to dismantle the National Health Service. But it did give the Conservatives the right to stop such further instalments of nationalization as they reasonably could; the fact that Labour's share of the vote was higher than the Conservatives', and was indeed higher in 1951 than it had been in 1945, was irrelevant in this context. The Conservatives had been returned to power with a majority in the Commons. Their election manifesto, *Britain Strong and Free*, had promised to reverse the nationalization of the iron and steel industry, and road haulage. Attlee opposed these measures on the grounds that it was apparently a general principle of British politics that incoming governments do not seek to reverse major actions of a preceding government. Such an argument is spurious and contrived. It was not heeded by Churchill, the incoming Prime Minister, and has not been followed by other Labour leaders. Thus in 1966 the Wilson government renationalized the iron and steel industry; the measure had been included in Labour's election manifesto in March of that year, and was therefore presumed to have the sanction of the electorate. In 1974 Labour repealed the Conservative Industrial Relations Act of 1971 on the grounds that the repeal had been included in the February 1974 Labour manifesto and that, though Labour itself was in a minority in the Commons, the repudiation of Edward Heath at the polls had signalled the electorate's rejection of Conservative industrial relations policy – as indeed it had.

Parties which lose elections recognize that the blessing of the electors has not been forthcoming. They go back to the drawing-board to devise new policies, not on the basis of whether such policies will meet particular national problems, but with an eye to the acceptability of the policies to the electorate. The real aim is of course to win power by pandering to whatever the electors are thought to fancy most. The politicians, in fact, seek to flatter the electors by endowing *them*, as it were, with the virtues of the philosopher-kings. If the electors reject a policy, that policy must somehow be illegitimate and 'wrong'. The controversy within the Labour party after its 1959 electoral defeat illustrates this line of argument. While the left wing of the party urged that the electoral popularity of the party was less important than sticking to first principles and putting forward radical policies, Hugh Gaitskell and the revisionists urged that the third defeat in a row for the party meant that its policies – especially on public ownership - were out of tune with the electorate. They pointed to the survey evidence of Abrams & Rose that the image of the party was 'one which is increasingly obsolete in terms of contemporary Britain'.[10] By the time of the 1964 election, the revisionist philosophy had won through. The Labour manifesto, *The New Britain*, played down the old ideology, and stressed instead the new one of growth, technological improvement, domestic reform, and tax changes to stimulate enterprise and initiative. It was avowedly voter-orientated.

It will of course be objected that all appeals to the electorate have to be voter-orientated. Politicians are not in business to be in perpetual opposition. Electors are not, in a free society, going to legitimate policies they heartily dislike. But the notion of the election as a legitimating ritual has certain limitations which, as they become more apparent, create a gnawing uncertainty that the rules of the game are equally applicable in all circumstances, that what is legitimate for the goose is also legitimate for the gander. The notion, if it is to continue to have real force, demands that all will consent to the results of the election and hence to the decisions, approved in parliament, of the elected government. But what if this consent is not forthcoming, or if the amount of popular support for the government is demonstrably so small as to deprive it of national appeal? Then the notion of legitimacy is in grave danger of collapse, and the election decides nothing.

There are signs that this is precisely what is happening in

the United Kingdom of the 1970s. Even when the result of an election is clear-cut, it is no longer universally acceptable. In 1965 Professor Rose wrote: 'Today, there is no sizeable political group in England that would challenge the legitimacy of decisions made by a freshly elected government'.[11] In 1971 this is exactly what happened when the Conservative government, true to its election pledge the previous year, passed the Industrial Relations Act to 'lay down what is lawful and what is not lawful in the conduct of industrial disputes'.[12] The electoral authority for the passage of this measure was clear-cut. But the Trades Union Congress instructed member unions to have nothing to do with the machinery of the act, and in September 1972 expelled all unions that registered under it. Several unions which were brought before the Industrial Relations Court refused to recognize its jurisdiction or to pay fines imposed by the court for contempt. This was a stark contrast with the attitude of the Amalgamated Society of Railway Servants 70 years before, when the judgment of the courts against it in the Taff Vale case had been accepted, and the damages paid without demur. Those who had voted Conservative in 1970 because they had been attracted by its industrial relations policy thus found themselves robbed of the fruits of their victory. The industrial relations legislation may have been a major plank in the 1970 Conservative election platform; the Conservative victory in no way legitimated that policy.

A second example, from local government, illustrates the same point, that electoral verdicts are no longer regarded as sufficient authority for carrying out policies put before the electors. In May 1976 the Conservatives gained control of Tameside Metropolitan Borough Council. One issue in the election had been whether or not Tameside should adopt a system of comprehensive education. Conservative election leaflets had made it clear that the local party was pledged to the preservation of the non-comprehensive system. Having gained control of the council, Conservative councillors felt themselves justified in putting this policy into effect, and there followed a legal battle with Fred Mulley, the Labour

Secretary of State for Education, who tried through the courts to block the implementation of Conservative policy, but who was eventually defeated by the Law Lords.

The importance of this controversy lies less in the merits and demerits of comprehensive schools than in the attitude adopted in certain important and responsible quarters towards the meaning of the Conservative victory in Tameside. The Education Secretary, backed by the Cabinet and the Labour party, refused to accept the verdict of the electors until forced to do so by the highest court in the land. A leading national newspaper tried to argue that, because the Conservative share of the vote in Tameside was only 49.8 per cent, giving the party a total of 29 seats out of 54 against Labour's 22, this 'could not by any stretch of political rhetoric be called an overwhelming mandate to do anything'.[13] It maintained a discrete silence over the fact that the Labour government, which was at that time legislating to enforce comprehensive education everywhere, had been returned with only 39.2 per cent of the vote. When the matter of Tameside was first debated in parliament, Labour MP Roderick MacFarquhar proferred the view that the Conservatives there had made 'a totally irresponsible election promise'; Jeremy Thorpe, who had recently resigned as leader of the Liberal party, went further:

> It is an extremely difficult judgment on the one hand to ensure that elected councillors can carry out pledges on which they were elected weighed against the welfare and interests of the children. *If there is conflict between these two considerations the welfare of the children must prevail.*[14]

In other words, electors may elect, but they must not be so bold as to think that those whom they elect will be allowed to carry out the pledges on the basis of which they were elected. Clearly the concept of the election as a means of giving legitimacy to government is not as strong as it once was. A freely elected majority party can no longer expect its authority to go unquestioned.

But if elections are not quite the final court of political arbitration of former days, as participatory dramas they have grown in stature. The fact that turnout has fallen over the past two decades, from an average of 80.5 per cent in the 1950s to 74.5 per cent in the 1970s, must in no sense be taken as an indication that people are less interested in elections than they once where. Non-voters are not apathetic, disenchanted with politics. Some of those who do not vote are prevented from doing so by circumstances over which they have no control. Others abstain deliberately. Those who insist they are not interested in politics may nonetheless be prompted to vote in a general election. The British election Study at the University of Essex, in an examination of non-voting in the four general elections of 1966–74, found that among those declaring no interest at all in politics, 90 per cent voted at least once and 80 per cent at least twice.[15] There are, in fact, very few people who never vote at all; non-voters in one election are not the same non-voters in the next. At the same time, the phenomenon of tactical voting may be an indication that the voter is thinking more about the way in which he uses his vote. Abstention is a legitimate means of political expression, and a potent one; it must not be confused with apathy. In 1964, Butler & Stokes found that 77 per cent of their sample voted in the general election, but 92 per cent followed the campaign in some way; 15 per cent, therefore, were prevented from voting or decided not to vote.[16] By 1970 the proportion of the sample voting had fallen by 5 per cent; the proportion following the campaign had fallen by a mere 1 per cent.[17]

Some voters may indeed be too interested in politics to feel that a visit to the polling booth suffices. The excitement of the campaign affects them more than the partisan appeal of party rhetoric. They enjoy watching the race. They follow the opinion polls. A large number place bets on the result, just as they would at a horse race or a dog track. Ladbrokes began taking bets on general election forecasts in 1964; in 1970 the voting public spent £1,300,000 with the firm.[18] William Hill have taken more money through betting on the general election than on any individual horse race, including the Derby and the Grand National; although the actual number of bets is considerably fewer than those placed on these particular horse races, the average investment is very much higher.[19]

The very existence of an election campaign heightens people's awareness of political issues. The coverage of elections by the media forces people to ask themselves what the campaign is about, and who are the contenders. In the summer of 1963, only 55 per cent of the Butler & Stokes sample could name their MP, and in the summer of 1969 only 49 per cent. But immediately after the 1964 election, the proportion rose to 85 per cent; this degree of awareness evaporated as the memory of the election receded in people's minds.[20] For most people, voting in or following the course of a general election is the only form of political activity they will ever undertake. The gulf between turnout at general elections and at local elections reinforces this point. If 50 per cent of the electorate votes in a local election, the turnout is considered a good one; the figure is likely to be 40 per cent, and turnout figures much lower are not uncommon. To anyone familiar with the relationship between central and local government, these figures will come as no surprise. Ultimate power does not reside in the town hall. The media do not sustain the importance of local elections in the way they elevate a general election. Few people, regardless of degree of political commitment, are bored or put out by the general election atmosphere.[21]

For local party workers, and those candidates who know they have no hope of winning a seat, the campaign fulfils an important additional social function. It gives them a sense of belonging, and reinforces their partisan identification.[22] Winning an electoral contest is not the only reason why people stand for parliament; if it were, safe seats would never be contested. The vast majority of candidates know they must lose. Yet they enjoy being a centre of attraction for three weeks, seeing their names in the national and local newspapers, perhaps being interviewed or making broadcasts. Perversely, perhaps, the replies to a survey conducted immediately after the 1966 general election indicated that the worse the result, the more likely a candidate was to express a favourable view of campaigning.[23] A candidate fighting a hopeless cause against a national figure can attract a great deal of publicity, which may help his or her career, or open up new avenues of opportunity, or the possibility of a safe, or winnable, seat next time. For many candidates, the ignorance or hostility of the electorate comes as a shock. Few cherish the hope that they may actually be able to change voters' minds, though this possibility can never be discounted. They see their main tasks as getting regular supporters to vote, and making themselves known.[24]

For candidates, as for electors, an election can be an educational experience in itself. For the party workers, even in safe seats, electoral activity is a means of political expression. Those who are committed enough in politics to bother to join a party need to be encouraged in their diligence and need to have their enthusiasm kept alive. Their work in an election campaign bolsters their ego by bringing them into contact with the machinery of government and with the men and women who control it. No politician is an island, and few can claim to have achieved electoral success by their own unaided efforts. They are beholden to the volunteers, and both they and the party faithful know it. Participation in constituency work is therefore part of the process of legitimation of government, and an important facet of the ritual aspect of election politics.

The myth of the media

The impact of the mass media on election campaigns is without doubt the most powerful single force that has shaped the approach of politicians and voters to electioneering since the second world war. It is largely because of the mass media that 'national' campaigns exist at all; without the media, elections would revert to being local contests locally reported, thus reducing the influence of party headquarters and the parliamentary leadership. It is the media which give to elections much of their entertainment value, which give electors far more easily-digestable political information than they would otherwise be able or want to absorb, and which give politicians the opportunity to put over their message, instantaneously, to audiences of millions. Access to the media is crucial for the parties. For the readers, viewers and listeners, the media provide the best, indeed probably the only means by which they can participate in the election process outside the polling booth. The media are thus part of the legitimating ritual. But their effect on the outcome of the polls is less certain.

The Press
As with all innovations, politicians were slow to come to terms with the press, and resented its latent power. In the nineteenth century, newspapers depended financially upon the political parties. They were partisan because they had to be. Ostrogorski referred to the press as 'the organs of the parties, which . . . [they] . . . consider as their most valuable auxiliaries'.[26] The newspapers imparted political information and made the right political noises; they did not seek to mould the political judgment of their readers. Ostrogorski explained that the number of newspapers a party had at its disposal bore no relation to its success at the polls. The job of the newspaper was to keep voters loyal to the party: 'if the voter does not take his politics from the paper, it confirms him in his party preferences or prejudices'.[27]

This pattern was broken by the Harmsworth brothers, who used advertising revenue to become masters of their own editorial content. Alfred Harmsworth (Lord Northcliffe) founded the *Daily Mail* in 1896; it was the first daily paper in which the public could buy shares. Later he and his brother, Lord Rothermere, controlled the *Daily Mirror*, which had been founded in 1903. So began the rule of the press lords, amongst whom were also Lord Beaverbrook, who acquired control of the *Daily Express* in 1915, and Lords Kemsley, Camrose and Iliffe, who bought the *Daily Telegraph* in 1928. These newspapers, and others which developed mass circulations after the First World War, were not controlled by party politicians. But they contrived to influence political event in ways which sometimes drove politicians to indignation or despair. The establishment of newspapers as public companies, and the development of rival media, has led to a diminution in circulation and in partisan bias. Nonetheless most national daily newspapers are identified with a political cause, and their combined circulation, though falling significantly, is still impressive.

4.1 **Circulation of national daily newspapers 1951–74***

	Circulation in thousands		
	1951	1964	1974
Popular Press			
Daily Express	4,192	4,224	3,226
Daily Herald/Sun[1]	2,072	1,301	3,302
Daily Mail	2,245	2,479	1,768
Daily Mirror	4,566	4,630	4,192
Daily Sketch/ Daily Graphic[2]	777	922	—
News Chronicle[3]	1,582	—	—
Quality Press			
Daily Telegraph	975	1,315	1,427
[Manchester] Guardian[4]	140	266	364
The Times	253	254	351
	16,802	15,391	14,630

*Source: *Newspaper Press Directory*
[1] Became *Sun* in 1964, and relaunched
[2] Became *Daily Sketch* in 1952; amalgamated with *Daily Mail* in 1971
[3] Ceased publication in 1960
[4] *Manchester Guardian* until 1959

The *Daily Herald* (1912–64) came closest to being a party newspaper. Founded by George Lansbury, it was owned and controlled by the Labour party between 1922 and 1929; thereafter the Trades Union Congress held 49 per cent of the shares, the remaining 51 per cent being owned by Odhams Press; but only the directors appointed by the Trades Union Congress were allowed to vote on the political policy of the paper. This link was broken in 1962 when

Odhams was taken over by the Mirror group. Since then, although both the *Sun* and the *Daily Mirror* generally support Labour policies, the Labour party has had no national newspaper to call its own.

This has always been the case with the Conservative party. Informal and historic links, however, ensure for the Conservatives favourable treatment, if not unflinching loyalty, from at least three dailies: the *Daily Express, Daily Mail* and *Daily Telegraph*; the *Daily Sketch* was also, until its demise, a strong Conservative paper. The Liberal party comes off worst. The *News Chronicle*, formed in 1930 by an amalgamation of two staunchly Liberal papers, the *Daily News* (controlled by the Liberal Cadbury family) and the *Daily Chronicle*, went out of business in 1960. The *Guardian*, though committed to taking a radical line, is no longer the Liberal organ it was in the Manchester days of C. P. Scott. The *Times* is Conservative *sui generis*. The only national newspaper to survive into the 1970s with strong political links is the *Morning Star*, successor, in 1966, of the *Daily Worker* and, like it, under the control (though not the ownership) of the Communist party; but it cannot be called a newspaper of mass circulation.

The advantage possessed by the Conservative party in terms of press coverage would in fact appear to be greater than mere partisan labels would suggest. [28] At no general election since 1945 have the *Express* or *Telegraph* (or, for that matter, the *Sketch* or *Graphic*) failed to support the Conservative cause; only once has the *Mail* failed to do so, when it declared itself in favour of a Conservative-Liberal coalition in October 1974. The *Times* flirted with Labour in 1945, but supported the Conservatives from 1950 to 1964 inclusive, and since then has appeared to favour Conservative-Liberal alliances. Only in the elections of 1945, 1950 and October 1974 did the *Guardian* support the Liberal party uncompromisingly; at other times it has sometimes favoured Conservative-Liberal alliances, sometimes Labour-Liberal alliances, in 1964 the Labour party and in February 1974 an all-party alliance. The *News Chronicle*, by contrast, was always loyal to the Liberal camp. The *Daily Heralid* and *Sun* were loyal to Labour until 1970; in February 1974 the *Sun* came out in support of the Conservatives, and in October it supported an all-party alliance. The *Mirror* is now the only newspaper on whom the Labour party can rely with any degree of certainty at elections. Put simply, therefore, at no time since 1945 have newspapers supporting Labour, totally or partially, commanded more than half the circulation of the leading national dailies; in 1974 the 'Labour' circulation was only about 30 per cent.

But whether this numerical advantage is actually worth votes is another matter. Available evidence suggests that, while readers are extremely loyal to their papers, and continue buying the same one year after year, the influence which the newspapers have on their readers is not one of conversion.

Many readers buy the newspaper which most accurately reflects their own political partisanship.[29] The readership of the *Express* and *Telegraph* is largely Conservative, that of the *Mirror* and *Sun* largely Labour. Even when a paper changes its political line, as the *Guardian* did in the late 1950s, it is most unlikely to carry its readers with it; it may attract new readers of a different political persuasion, but its veteran readers (in this case Liberal) remain unconvinced. Some readers loyal to one party do buy a newspaper inclined to favour another; in 1963 Butler & Stokes found that more than a fifth of Labour supporters read a Conservative paper, though only a tenth of Conservative supporters read a Labour paper. Newspaper readers are on the whole discriminating in their interpretation of what they read. They recognize partisan bias but are not persuaded by it. By matching what was known about the family background of their respondents with the respondents' own partisan support and the newspapers they read, Butler & Stokes were able to show that in general people acquired their political preference first, and then bought a paper to match it; if the paper they bought did not match their partisanship, neither did it alter it.[30] The most likely effect of reading a newspaper is to bolster and reinforce the reader's own partisan support, whether the newspaper's own political bias is in accord with that of the reader or not.

The scope which the press gives itself to influence people's judgment is circumscribed by its own political content. Only newspapers of the extreme left and the extreme right slavishly follow the party line. Since 1945 there has been a noticeable decline in the unambiguous partisanship of the press, in an unquestioning loyalty to one party and an unadulterated political orthodoxy. In the years immediately after the second world war, the *Herald* and the *Telegraph* exemplified this tradition. The *Herald* was geared to the organisation of a Labour victory and 'judged its news by the test of whether it would help the party'.[31] The *Telegraph* regarded it as a duty to hold the Conservative banner high. During the 1950s, however, newspapers of all persuasions became less partisan in their approach. In 1955 the *Mail*, *Mirror* and *News Chronicle* all devoted some space to the views of political opponents.[32] Since then the practice has grown of inviting articles from a wide spectrum of political opinion. In October 1974, for instance, one Liberal MP, David Steel, wrote articles for the *Mail* and *Telegraph* and another, Clement Freud, continued writing for the *Express*. Winifred Ewing, of the Scottish National Party, also wrote for the *Telegraph*. Enoch Powell and Ken Gill, a communist and a member of the General Council of the Trades Union Congress, wrote for the *Times*. The *Mail* invited one MP from each of the Labour, Liberal and Conservative parties to state their case.

Beyond this, no serious newspaper can ignore the views of its opponents, less still ignore criticisms made on radio and television, or the evidence of opinion polls. For a fortnight during the 1959 election campaign, three Conservative newspapers had to report increases in Labour support; in 1966 the same papers had to give space to evidence of a spectacular Labour lead.[33] The growth of other mass media has deprived the papers of their near-monopoly of news dissemination; they no longer address a voting public in isolation. Editors, moreover, know much more than formerly about their readers' habits and preferences. It is known, for instance, that the number of people who buy a newspaper with a political bias different from their own is growing; between 1967 and 1970 the number of Conservative readers of the *Express* fell from 54 per cent to 47 per cent, and of the *Mail* from 62 per cent to 56 per cent, while the Labour readership of the *Sun* fell from 69 per cent to 60 per cent during the same period.[34] And even in relation to those people who do read newspapers whose politics correspond to their own, it is very doubtful whether the newspapers are read primarily on political grounds; entertainment and general approach to news and sports coverage are more likely criteria.

In their leader columns, the papers may well continue to pour forth political dogma. In their news coverage their approach is much less unbalanced. Between election periods the papers have no qualms about criticising the party they normally support. In the spring of 1963 some of the most strident criticism of the Conservative government came from the *Daily Express*; in the late 1960s the Labour government came under attack from the *Mirror*. Within the election period some papers make a habit of setting out the pros and cons of each party's appeal, providing their readers with the information but letting them draw their own conclusions. For local newspapers, which cannot afford to be too partisan, this is a staple of election coverage. Some nationals appear to give this 'service' to increase circulation, just as they produce election-night guides and charts. Reading a newspaper, therefore, is no more likely to make a political recruit than reading party literature, hearing election broadcasts, or talking to one's family and friends. There is no evidence that a voter will be swayed by the way in which a newspaper says he ought to cast his vote.

This particular myth about press power is of long standing, and has a peculiar hold on Labour politicians. It originated in the general election of October 1924, when the *Daily Mail* published, five days before polling, what it alleged was a letter from Grigory Zinoviev, President of the Communist International, to the British Communist party, instructing that party to stir up revolution amongst the British proletariat. Ramsay MacDonald, the Labour Prime

Minister, had pursued a policy of friendship and conciliation towards the Soviet regime. The Conservative press therefore used the Zinoviev letter to urge voters not to support the Labour government. In 1945 the Conservative press tried to use the same tactics over two pronouncements made by Harold Laski, chairman of the Labour party. One pronouncement asserted that Labour's National Executive Committee was the ultimate arbiter of the party's foreign policy, and that a future Labour government would be subordinate to it in this respect; the other declared that the Labour party might have to use violence to achieve a socialist state. Once again the Conservative newspapers engaged in scaremongering. The *Express*, in particular, exploited 'Gauleiter Laski' to the full.

These episodes did the Labour party nothing but good. Labour won the 1945 election handsomely. Although they lost that of 1924, emerging 40 seats poorer, their total vote actually increased by over one million. The Zinoviev letter may not have won recruits for Labour, but it did not lose them votes; the Laski affair was undoubtedly overplayed, and may well have rebounded on the Conservative camp. Churchill blamed the *Express*, and Beaverbrook, for his 1945 defeat. Labour, less justly but no less significantly, blamed the Zinoviev letter for their 1924 defeat. Both these episodes were used as excuses, and that is their real importance. Since 1945 comparable press campaigns during an election have not been repeated.

There is some evidence that a voter who deserts his party for another is more likely to read a newspaper of a different political partisanship to his own, and to espouse the partisanship of that paper, and that a voter who is uncommitted is likely to end up voting for the party favoured by the newspaper he reads.[35] But none of the 'blame' for this can be laid at the door of the newspapers themselves. A voter who is uncommitted does not have a mind which is a political vacuum; if, on polling day, he supports the party favoured by his newspaper, this is probably because his own inclinations were leading him in that direction anyway. By comparing the move towards a party preference among uncommitted voters in the period 1959-66 with the partisanship of the papers read by those voters, Butler & Stokes contrived to conclude that the eventual preferences 'tended to follow the party bias of the reader's paper; those who ended . . . in a major party camp, but who began . . . outside either camp, were more likely to have joined the Conservatives if they read a Tory paper, Labour if they read a Labour paper'.[36] This sort of argument is a classic instance of putting the cart before the horse. The effect of a Conservative paper in inducing its uncommitted readers to vote Conservative, or the success of a Labour paper in winning converts for the Labour party is nowhere demonstrated. Butler & Stokes themselves found that 44 per cent of their respondents, though aware of their newspaper's party bias, nonetheless did not agree with it.[37] And the point needs to be stressed again that readers of newspapers are attracted to them for many reasons, of which political content is but one.[38] Moreover, the newspapers themselves form, nowadays, only one channel through which political information reaches the electors.

Radio and television
One reason why politicians distrust the press, and are ready to blame it for so much, is that it is largely uncontrolled by them. The content of a newspaper is governed only by the official secrets legislation and the law of libel. Politically, it can be as partisan as it likes, in or out of an election season. This is not so with radio and television. As election broadcasting has grown, the political content of what is broadcast during the election period has come under greater political scrutiny.

Radio was first used during a British election campaign in 1924. Before the second world war, however, the political impact of radio was restricted firstly by the small number of households owning a receiver and then, in the 1930s, by the growing attraction of the cinema. Neville Chamberlain was the first politician in the United Kingdom to popularize and exploit the visual media. He used the cinema newsreels to great effect to explain his budgets when Chancellor of the Exchequer in the National Government and, prompted by his success, Prime Minister Stanley Baldwin used the newsreels during the 1935 general election. Baldwin gave a polished performance. Attlee, the newly-elected Labour leader, performed badly, and was clearly an amateur in front of the cine-cameras. This helped the Conservative leadership to press home their point that Labour was not fit to govern.

But the newsreels had grave limitations. People went to the cinema to be entertained, not to be confronted with political banter. Though not subject to formal censorship, newsreel editors were constrained by a formidable array of social and political forces. When one newsreel interviewed prominent critics of the Munich agreement, the Foreign Office contacted the American government, who persuaded the parent company to withdraw that particular item. In any case, real political debate could never be conducted within the newsreel format; the reporting of events as they happened lay with the newspapers and, increasingly so, with the broadcasters.[39]

Radio was an important feature of the 1945 election, by which time there were over nine-and-a-half million licences in an electorate of 33 million. The Conservative and Labour parties had ten broadcasts each, the Liberals four; the Communist and Commonwealth parties, because they each had more than 20 candidates, were allowed one broadcast apiece. It was on the radio that Churchill made his 'Gestapo' charge against Labour, declaring that the erection of a socialist system would require the service of a political police. It was on the radio that Attlee accused Beaverbrook of being the brains behind Churchill's wild accusations. These exchanges, which may well have damaged Churchill's reputation in the eyes of the electors, were one of the most memorable features of the campaign.[40]

Television, which had a brief history of broadcasting between 1936 and 1939, recommenced in 1946. It was not used in the election of 1950. In 1951, on the initiative of the BBC, each party was given one 15-minute programme.[41] As the number of households owning a television set increased, television rapidly overhauled radio as the main broadcasting medium. In 1950, ten per cent of households owned a television set; by 1970 the proportion was 95 per cent.[42] In 1959, for the first time, the total amount of time allotted to party broadcasts on television was greater than on radio. 1959 was, in more ways than one, 'the first television election'. The Conservative and Labour parties had five broadcasts each, the Liberal party two. Audiences for the television broadcasts averaged 21 per cent, as against three per cent for radio, and, in all, 61 per cent of the electorate claimed to have viewed at least one election broadcast.[43] In 1959 television became the prime medium of political communication. It has remained so ever since.

The 1959 election was a watershed for television in other ways too. Before then, there had been no reference to elections, not even in news bulletins; any programme which might have had the merest trace of a political flavour about it was cancelled for the duration of the campaign. The BBC was required to be impartial in its presentation of political news and was, indeed, supposed to have no opinion of its own on current affairs at all. The Representation of the People Act of 1949, section 63, specifically excluded the press from the prohibition of unauthorized spending with a view to promoting the election of a candidate. Broadcasting was not give this privilege; *prima facie*, therefore, a candidate could be charged with the costs of a broadcast in which he appeared, and the BBC might have laid itself open to prosecution under the act. When commercial television was set up under the terms of the Television Act of 1954, the same restrictions were applied to the Independent Television Authority (ITV, now the Independent Broadcasting Authority – IBA), and the regional companies working under its aegis. The 1954 act in fact went further, by laying down that all political broadcasts on the ITV network, other than party broadcasts, had to be in the form of properly balanced discussions or debates. This seemed to close the door to news coverage of election meetings, for instance, or interviews with single politicians.[44]

As for the party broadcasts, these were arranged by a

committee representing the Labour, Liberal and Conservative parties and the broadcasting authorities. In general, the amount of time allotted to each party was, and is, based upon the number of votes gained by the party at the previous general election. But it was agreed also that a party nominating at least 50 candidates could qualify for one broadcast. Between 1951 and 1964 this effectively barred other parties from access to the broadcasting media, and added another dimension to the importance of wealth in elections. The party broadcasts themselves were provided, without legal obligation, free of charge. The control of the politicians over the broadcasting media in a non-authoritarian society could hardly have been more complete; in the 1950s it was not at all uncommon for politicians interviewed on television to demand to know, in advance, what questions they were going to be asked, and some even tried to draft the questions themselves.

Two developments undermined this cosy arrangement. As television, particularly commercial television, demonstrated its ability to persuade people and mould opinions, the politicians themselves became aware of its potential. But such potential could only be fully realized by allowing the networks to break out of the stylistic straitjacket in which they had been confined. For their part, the television networks chaffed at the bit. In March 1958 Granada, the commercial company operating in the north of England, decided to report in full the progress of the Rochdale by-election. The triviality, gimmickry and superficiality which pessimists said would result from allowing this sort of thing on the air did not materialize. The public interest was beyond doubt. It soon became normal practice for by-elections to be reported, and to broadcast debates between the candidates, provided all of them agreed to appear.[45]

Early in 1959 the broadcasting committee agreed that the same approach would be adopted at the next general election. Political balance had to be maintained. Party spokesmen did not mention their constituencies in political broadcasts of a general character. But the 1959 election was fully reported by both BBC and ITV news services; in addition, there were a number of special election programmes, sedate and heavily structured, with no opportunity for people other than party nominees to state their views or ask questions of the politicians. Still, the election broadcasts were a breakthrough.[46] Since then, the scope and extent of television election coverage has grown by leaps and bounds. Television now outstrips the press as the most important medium through which people follow election campaigns.[47] It is no exaggeration to say that, for the vast majority of electors, the campaign means primarily the campaign on and as reported through the television networks.

The way in which the campaign is covered by the networks has changed out of all recognition. In 1959 the BBC put on two 40-minute *Hustings* programmes in all its regions except Ulster. Spokesmen for the three main parties answered questions put by 'audiences' hand-picked by the parties themselves; in Wales a candidate representing Plaid Cymru also took part. Granada put on *Election Marathon*, in which every candidate in the Granada area was allowed to make a short speech. Of the 348 candidates eligible only 231 took part, because a number of those invited refused to appear, and Granada took the view that if one candidate in a constituency refused, his opponents should not be allowed to broadcast. Other current affairs programmes, such as BBC's *Gallery* and ITV's *This Week* were taken off the air.

By the time of the 1964 election such caution had disappeared. The BBC launched *Election Forum*, in which the three party leaders were given half an hour each to answer genuine questions sent in by the public. Each leader got through between 21 and 28 questions, and the programmes attracted audiences ranging from 5 to 8 millions; they were 'a significant political event'.[48] Meanwhile, the popular current affairs programmes continued. What is more, they provided wide campaign coverage and searching analyses of the campaign issues and the opinion polls. For the first time, the television coverage of the election approximated to that of the press.

Between 1964 and 1970 control of television election presentation by the major parties was somewhat reduced. Following the 1964 election, the Communist candidate who had opposed the then Conservative Prime Minister, Sir Alec Douglas-Home, asked the courts to declare Sir Alec's election void, on the grounds that the Communist claim for equal broadcasting time had been refused. The Communist party, having fielded only 36 candidates, had not been allowed to make any election broadcasts; yet the Conservative Prime Minister had appeared frequently and for long periods on television during the campaign. But the Communist petition was refused. It was held that the dominant motive of the television companies was to give information to the public, not to promote Sir Alec's election. The judgment thus left the companies free to present programmes in which front-bench spokesmen appeared, so long as no reference was made to their own particular constituencies. In 1966 party control over spokesmen, which in 1964 had enabled the politicians to veto programmes they disliked, was much reduced.[49] The Representation of the People Act of 1969 gave to the television networks a freedom as regards campaign coverage which more nearly approaches that enjoyed by the press, defined their ability to include candidates in any items which did not concern the constituency or electoral area, and enabled candidates who did not intend to appear in a 'constituency item' to consent to the programme continuing without them.

Political influence over the way elections are treated on radio and television is still strong. The parties do not like 'live audiences' – i.e. unrehearsed confrontations between politicians and members of the public. In 1959 Selwyn Lloyd and Barbara Castle were brought face to face with a live audience in Granada's *Last Debate*. There was a shouting match and the audience won. Since then the parties' allergy to live audiences has flourished. In 1970 plans to have selected live audiences on both radio and television were vetoed.[50] The proposal thereafter, to at least allow voters a chance to question politicians directly, was less easily brushed aside. In February 1974 there were two significant developments. Some IBA networks were able to induce politicians to appear before live audiences, usually carefully selected. On Radio 4, the BBC's *Election Call*, a daily 55-minute phone-in, allowed listeners to question a different politician each day. The programmes were expertly chaired by Robin Day. The questions, mostly from genuine callers, were incisive and highly relevant. The politicians were courteous. The success of the programme was immediate, and helped re-establish radio as an important campaign medium. By bringing politicians into contact with live but remote audiences, it may perhaps have helped weaken their resistance to the live audience concept.

Programme producers are naturally anxious to avoid outraging the politicians. Throughout the 1950s and 1960s, the politicians had insisted on no Sunday programmes, and this wish was faithfully followed. The political parties like to know what constituencies are to be featured in programme surveys. There is a great deal of consultation between the parties and the networks. There is, still, a great deal of suspicion on both sides. There is, on both sides, a concern with 'balance' which, though commendable in moderation, sometimes borders on the obsessional. It is as impossible to achieve balance on a spontaneous phone-in programme as it is to achieve balance when a candidate knocks spontaneously on the doors of his constituents. Politicians who recoil at the prospect of facing blunt, perhaps embarrassing questions on the air, ought to ask themselves whether they are in the right job. An interviewer who persists in putting the ruthless searching question to the national leader is, after all, doing so on behalf of the millions of viewers and listeners who have no such opportunity. The only fair alternative would be to scrap campaign coverage altogether, including party broadcasts, which are a privilege not a right. This would hardly be in the interests of anyone.

The effects and consequences of election coverage on radio and television have been profound. People are no longer interested in reading party propaganda. During the 1895 election campaign, the central Liberal Organisation distributed more than 23 million leaflets, or more than three per elector.[51] In 1951 Conservative Central Office produced less than 19 million copies of leaflets, manifestos, and broadsheets, even though the electorate had increased fivefold. Between 1951 and 1970 the number of copies produced of the Conservative manifesto, both in its full and in its popular versions, fell by three-quarters, though the electorate grew by 14 per cent.[52] The fact that television is now the foremost medium through which electors follow the campaign means that the campaign, at least nationally, is to some extent moulded and defined by that medium. Programme producers can, in this way, force to the fore issues which the politicians would prefer to avoid, such as the Common Market in the 1966 election.[53] Election programmes nowadays do much more than simply report speeches and party manifestos. By exploring issues and discussing grievances, they themselves become part of the election, a factor which campaigners must take into account. The Labour party's anger at the behaviour of the BBC in this respect in 1966 was vented by Harold Wilson, who, after the result, agreed to be interviewed only for ITV.[54] Politicians have had to alter their style of electioneering to suit the demands and constraints of the television cameras. Speeches are timed and written with an eye to easy inclusion in evening news bulletins. The ritualistic morning press conferences, established on the initiative of the Labour party in 1959, are orchestrated wholly for the benefit of the media, and for obtaining maximum advantage from them. Instead of conducting a dialogue with each other, the party spokesmen converse with the cameras and microphones.

There are dangers in these developments. Election broadcasting inevitably focusses the mind of the viewer and listener upon the party leaders. In 1970, Edward Heath and Harold Wilson took up 53 per cent of all news coverage of politicians, in February 1974 59 per cent, and 51 per cent in October.[55] In this way, campaigns are given a presidential character, and a photogenic leader with a good broadcasting style, as Harold Wilson certainly was in the 1960s, is at an obvious advantage. A leader who performs badly in front of the cameras may depress party morale and lose the party some of its support. In 1964, Sir Alec Douglas-Home's performance on *Election Forum* 'increased the feeling among some campaign planners and the wider public that he was a liability'.[56] In 1966 Edward Heath's poor television ratings 'had a discernible impact on morale in the party organisation'.[57] Consequently, broadcasting potential is now a factor in the choice of party leaders.

Another frequently-heard criticism of election broadcasting in the 1950s and 1960s was that it 'nationalized' the election; that is, by concentrating on the national leaders and the national issues, it demoted the importance of the constituency campaign and the strengths and weaknesses of local feeling. In the pioneering days of election broadcasting this was undoubtedly so. There were few television channels, few experienced interviewers, few cameras and camera-crews. Coverage of the election had to revolve around the campaign nationally if there was to be any coverage at all.

Today this criticism is less just. There is a great deal of constituency and regional reporting. In February 1974, for example, Granada ran a series entitled *Let The People Speak*, in which a random sample of Preston electors, helped by a panel of experts, discussed various election issues. In October, the BBC's *Campaign Special* sent a reporter to the highly marginal constituency of Keighley to explain the reaction of its voters to the election issues; the programme also had special editions on Wales, Scotland and Northern Ireland. The network of local radio stations, too, has done much to restore the importance of the constituency. These instances also illustrate how the broadcasting media have switched the emphasis from the parties to the voters. If politicians will not meet the voters face to face in front of the camera, at least the voters can be asked what they think about the things politicians are saying. On television, panels of voters are asked for their views. On radio, phone-in programmes enable voters miles apart to 'talk' to each other, or at least discuss each other's views, instead of relying on party propaganda and what the papers say. These voter-orientated programmes themselves make election news. It used to be said that television trivialized politics. It would be truer to say that television and radio cut the politicians down to size, treating them more as the public servants which they really are, or ought to be.

Are the broadcasting media fair to the politicians and the political parties? Do they give reasonable and equitable coverage of the issues being discussed and the people discussing them? At the outset it is as well to realize that there are no absolute standards by which such questions can be answered, and that often the media are not the final arbiters of these matters. The vexed question of differential access to the mèdia, for instance, and its relevance to the position of nationalist and small parties, is one which is to some extent beyond the control of the broadcasting authorities. Until October 1974 only the Conservative, Labour and Liberal parties were represented on the Committee on Political Broadcasting. In the 1950s and 1960s, the nationalist parties were badly served. They were allotted no political broadcasts, and were poorly reported on news bulletins and election programmes. Since 1966, Plaid Cymru and the Scottish National Party have been allowed television time, though only on local Welsh and Scottish transmitters, in spite of the fact that their policies vitally affect the whole of the United Kingdom. In the case of the Welsh party, the 50-candidate rule has been dispensed with. It remains in force for other minor parties. Thus in both 1974 elections the National Front qualified for five-minutes worth of broadcasting time, the Communist party did not. The Scottish National Party and Plaid Cymru were allotted 10 minutes each on local transmitters; the Conservative, Labour and Liberal parties allotted themselves a number of 10-minute broadcasts, in the ratio 5:5:3 (in October 5:5:4), including separate Scottish and Welsh versions.[58]

The ratio of broadcasts in Scotland and Wales is clearly unjust. On the basis of the 1974 results the Scottish National Party ought to have more Scottish broadcasting time than the Conservative party; in Wales Plaid Cymru ought to have more time on the air than the Liberals. The exclusion of minor parties from the Committee on Political Broacasting is also hard to justify. After the February 1974 election the Scottish National Party was admitted to the committee, with the implicit task of watching over the interests of all the minor parties; Plaid Cymru are now also represented on it. Curiously, the committee contains no independent 'consumer' voice. If it did, the party broadcasts might be scrapped, for they are far from popular and achieve audience ratings as high as 26 per cent only because there is generally nothing else to switch to.[59] They are convenient tea or coffee breaks for the viewing public.

More contentious than the number of party broadcasts is their timing. In 1970 the BBC and ITV decided to shift the television broadcasts from 9.10 p.m. to 10.00 p.m. This was greeted with dismay by the parties, for it meant smaller audiences. In February 1974 there was a row following the decision of the television authorities to bring forward the Plaid Cymru and Scottish National Party broadcasts from the final Tuesday of the campaign to the previous Saturday. Plaid Cymru invoked the law courts to prevent such a rearrangement.[60] There is a convention that the final round of party broadcasts is in the order Liberal, Opposition, Government. Since there is no Sunday or eve-of-poll (i.e. Wednesday) party broadcast, this means that the Liberals make their last appeal to the electorate the Saturday before polling. A tidier arrangement might be to allow all the parties eligible for broadcasting time a final fling on the Tuesday evening.

The broadcasting authorities can, however, be acquitted of accusations of gross and intentional bias. Producers have been increasingly keen to concentrate on issues which politicians find embarrassing, and to promote confrontations between party spokesmen. In 1966 this approach did not accord with Labour's campaign strategy. Labour wanted a low-key campaign. The BBC television's *Campaign Report*, in which there were 22 confrontations in 13 programmes, hardly helped. Accusations of bias inevitably followed, though the supposition of the politicians that the media are under an obligation to foster and project the sort of campaign they want is a typical piece of impertinence.[61]

When the only election broadcasts were those of the parties, bias was easily controlled through the amount of time each party was allowed. Once television producers were permitted to put their own election programmes on the air, partisanship became more difficult to measure. After the October 1974 result, Ron Hayward, the General Secretary of the Labour party, accused the BBC of 'trivialisation which amounted to cynicism' and of being largely responsible for the lower turnout which, he alleged, lost seats for the party.[62] Hayward persuaded the National Executive Committee of the party to sponsor an inquiry into the BBC's coverage. The investigation, undertaken by a Labour political scientist, Anthony Barker, gave the BBC a clean bill of health.[63] In a manner curiously reminiscent of the Zinoviev letter, the charges of bias against the BBC were not, of course, an explanation for Labour's failure, but an excuse.

The impact of the media

The need to come to terms with the media has been a powerful incentive to the development of a more professional approach to campaign management. Private surveys are commissioned to tell the parties who their supporters are and, more importantly, what their potential supporters like most. Politicians no longer trust their own intuitive judgment to tell them what the electorate is thinking, or how best to communicate with the voters. Public relations firms are now a valuable campaign weapon. The firm of Colman, Prentis & Varley was called in by the Conservatives between 1949 and 1951. In the period 1957–9 its services were used more extensively to plan a newspaper and poster onslaught to refurbish the Conservative image. The result was a brilliant publicity campaign, stressing the Conservative penchant for prosperity and Labour's obsession with class.[64] The Conservatives spent £468,000 in the 1958–9 pre-election period on publicity of this sort; Labour spent £103,000.[65]

Because the Labour party did not have access to more money to match the Conservative campaign, Labour politicians attacked the exercise as a denigration of rational persuasion and an attempt to commercialize politics. The Prime Minister, Richard Crossman complained, was being sold 'as though he were a detergent'. When a group of advertising men with Labour sympathies offered the party their services, they were firmly refused.[66] This display of puritanism did not survive Labour's 1959 defeat. In the early 1960s the party paid much closer attention to what public relations experts and professional journalists had to say. Between 1962 and 1964 Dr Mark Abrams, of Research Services, conducted surveys into voter attitudes in marginal constituencies, identifying the 'target voters' and the issues they regarded as important. Labour's 1964 campaign was much influenced by the conviction that the 'hard sell' pays off; the private polls, one Labour official subsequently remarked, 'were prodigiously influential'.[67] In the 1966 campaign the Conservatives intended to make much of their opposition to comprehensive schools; when a survey revealed that *their* target voters were actually in favour of comprehensives, the idea was dropped.[68]

Party television broadcasts now also reflect more intensive professional preparation. The parties employ professional television producers and call on the services of famous and politically-sympathetic film-makers. In 1970, for instance, the Conservative party received advice from the film actor and director Bryan Forbes; in 1974 the Labour party turned to the late Stanley Baker.[69] MPs, candidates and journalists with broadcasting experience are also much in demand at election time. The party broadcasts themselves have broken away from the old straight-to-the-camera approach. In style they hover somewhere between feature films and television commercials. They are concerned less with arguing party dogma and answering the challenges of opponents (such challenges are usually ignored) than with building up an image and putting across an attitude. 'By themselves', Professor Martin Harrison wrote of the 1970 campaign, 'the party [television] broadcasts would have given an odd idea of what the parties stood for, and what they might achieve in office. It needed the autonomous current affairs programmes to tackle the unstated issues and to fill in the vacuum in the parties' discussion of the future.'[70]

The impact of the media on voter attitudes is not straightforward. The 1959 Conservative campaign, characterized by the slogan 'Life's better with the Conservatives. Don't let Labour ruin it', would not have been a success if there had been an economic recession, with the standard of living palpably on the decline. No amount of projection of the leader will compensate for basic unpopularity. In the first four months of 1964 the Conservative party spent nearly half a million pounds trying to popularize Sir Alec Douglas-Home; his popularity as measured by one opinion poll during that period fell by 10 per cent.[71] Labour might have done just as well in 1964 without any of the lavish surveys and public relations exercises which they undertook. The attempt to project Edward Heath, then Leader of the Opposition, in 1970, did not pay off either. His popularity rating was lower than Harold Wilson's, as indeed it had been almost continuously for the previous four years. Yet this did not affect the fortunes of the Conservative party in the 1970 election.[72] The notion of the voter being persuaded to change his party because of public relations campaign techniques, as he might be persuaded to change his brand of petrol, or his soup, is a complete myth.

How can this essentially negative impact be squared with the undoubted salience of the media as avenues of political information? Butler & Stokes found that 92 per cent of their sample claimed to have followed the 1964 campaign through one or other of the mass media. Yet most electors said they had made up their minds how they intended to vote before the campaign began; in 1964 and 1966 Butler & Stokes found this proportion to be 89 per cent, and National Opinion Polls, by re-interviewing people they had contacted earlier in the campaign, found the proportion whose views did not change during the election period to be about 82 per cent in 1964 and 86 per cent in 1966.[73]

On the bulk of the electorate, therefore, the campaign has no simple persuasive impact. But it does have an important didactic role, in which the media play a pre-eminent part. Whatever understanding the mass of the voting public has of the issues in an election, and whatever familiarity the bulk of the public acquires with the main contenders, derive almost exclusively from the media, above all from television.[74] On a very mundane level, most voters nowadays know what the party leaders look like, their speech, their mannerisms, their style. When Anthony Eden made the first ever Conservative election broadcast on television, in 1951, the Nuffield study, reflecting on the novelty of vast numbers of people seeing him 'in the flesh' for the first time, declared it to be 'compelling electioneering'.[75]

The mass media also have a strong tendency to concentrate on issues defined in simple terms. The press, in particular, leans heavily on the manifestos as the authoritative statements of party policy. The manifestos are printed in full in the 'quality' dailies, and given much prominence in the popular tabloids. Statements by political leaders are reduced to pronouncements short enough to fit into a couple of headlines. Since the media have a preference for variety, constantly searching for new 'angles', they are unwilling to sustain the same issue day after day. This may force politicians to veer off topics they think important and to play down subjects they would like to keep before the public eye. Explaining the reluctance of the Conservatives in 1966 to press the Common Market issue harder, one party member commented that 'the press was already getting bored'.[76]

Conversely, news stories which have little relevance to the party battle may be given extensive media coverage, and become election issues thereby. Press concentration on the affairs of the Jasper group of property companies in 1959, and on the 'trial' of eight BMC employees by their colleagues at Cowley, in 1966, for failing to join an unofficial strike, are cases in point.[77] It was only because of the media that such stories became part of the campaign. There are obvious dangers in such tendencies, but there are also some advantages. Politicians no longer have exclusive control over the shape and direction of the election. It may be objected that control has merely shifted from them to the journalists and the television producers. The difference is that the latter are more dependent than the former on the day-to-day whims and fancies of the public. A politician only prostrates himself before his electors during the election period. For the media, audience feedback and programme ratings are a constant presence; the media dare not serve the public unpopular election diets. If this means, as it sometimes does, pandering to instincts of sensationalism, the defence must be that that is what the public wants, and that giving the public what it wants is a not unimportant characteristic of a democratic society. It should also be said that sensationalism is much less evident on television and radio than in the press. The general level of election coverage on the broadcasting media is remarkably high. There is, if anything, too much of it. The proportion of the electorate who thought that there was 'far too much' coverage rose from 31 per cent in February 1974 to 40 per cent in October.[78]

The very large proportion of voters who are not influenced by the campaign still leaves a small but no less important section (11 per cent according to Butler & Stokes, perhaps as much as 18 per cent according to National Opinion Polls) for whom the final choice is one left until the campaign period.[79] As was argued in Chapter 3, the impact of the party political propaganda on these voters is open to serious doubt. But, to the extent that the media concentrate people's minds upon the election – even simply upon the fact that there *is* an election – the impact of the media might be highly significant. The relationship is not simple. One must, in particular, beware of confusing the claims that the media, especially the press, make for themselves with their actual effect. In 1959 the *Mirror*, in an effort to win over uncertain Labour supporters, proclaimed on the day of the poll 'Only A Dope Will Be A Don't Know Today', and advised 'To Hell With The Telly Until We've All Voted'.[80] As the Labour vote fell by 189,082, this advice must be presumed to have been largely ignored. The broadcasting authorities do not issue such advice to voters. Yet the wider impact of the mass media ought not therefore to be discounted entirely. The media present the election as a battle for votes (even though there are few votes to battle over) or a clash of opposing ideologies (no matter how little ideological differences may mean in the practical task of running the country). The media abhor whatever is insignificant and unexciting. They can give to an election an importance that it would not otherwise possess in the eyes of the voting public. By thus stirring people's minds they may help counter voter apathy. They may not be directly responsible for straight switching of voting allegiance; but they have an effect, positive or negative, not quantifiable but important nonetheless, on turnout and abstention. That effect could be an important component of the final result.

Minor parties, in particular, have everything to gain and nothing to lose from continuous exposure in the media. Neither the press nor broadcasting are responsible for, say, persuading more Scottish voters to support the Scottish National Party, or more English voters to support the Liberal party. But the coverage given to these parties in and between elections cannot but help fix an image of them in the voters' minds. The strength of that image, whether it is or is not a favourable one, is itself a measure of the media's impact.[81]

Opinion polls
There are few aspects of a general election which arouse more public interest, and for the popularity of which the media are more responsible, than the business of forecasting the results. The polls of public opinion which appear in the newspapers are avidly followed by the politicians, for whom they are an invaluable barometer of the state of the public mind. The papers report, not merely their own results, but those published by their rivals. The results form the subject of many of the lead stories at election time. They are also picked up by the broadcasters, who incorporate them in their news bulletins and election features. The polls

have, in short, become an essential ingredient of the jamboree of the campaign, a staple supporting act to the main entertainment provided by the parties.

The first poll appeared in the *News Chronicle* in 1938, and was conducted by the British Institute of Public Opinion, an offshoot of the American Gallup Poll. The British Gallup Poll findings continued to appear in the *Chronicle* until that paper's demise; now they appear in the *Daily Telegraph* and the *Sunday Telegraph*. National Opinion Polls (NOP) was founded in 1957 as a subsidiary of Associated Newspapers, and its findings appear in the *Daily Mail*. The findings of Opinion Research Centre (ORC) appear in the *Times*, the *Sunday Times* and the London *Evening Standard*. The *Daily Express* at one time published its own Poll of Public Opinion, but now reports the findings of Louis Harris Research. Marplan, which used to have its findings reported in the *Times*, is now reported in the *News of the World* and the *Sun*. The findings of Business Decisions appear in the *Observer*. The television networks sometimes employ the polling organizations to carry out specific surveys, and the services of the pollsters are also used by the political parties.

There are two principal methods by which opinion polls are conducted. In a systematic random sample, every Nth name (perhaps every hundredth or every thousandth) on the electoral register of the constituency or area being surveyed is listed, and the voters so chosen are visited in their own homes. Provided the starting point on the register is itself randomly selected, every voter in the area has the same probability of being selected. In a random sample, therefore, the interviewers must interview only those voters chosen by the random method. In a quota sample, each interviewer is told to interview a number of voters of each sex, each particular age group, occupation, social class and so on, based on the proportions of the population in the area being surveyed known to fall within each of these groupings. Whom the interviewer interviews is immaterial, so long as the proportions of people interviewed in each of the specific sub-divisions conform to the quotas laid down.

The random method often involves several visits to a particular dwelling to secure an interview with a single voter. The quota method does not, but its success does depend much more on the skill and sense of responsibility of the interviewer; it is therefore cheaper than random sampling, but less reliable. Gallup uses both methods for general election work. NOP switched from quota to random sampling in 1963. Neither method gives a perfect sample, but it is possible to calculate statistically that margin of error which arises from the sampling procedure itself.[82] A poll perfectly conducted, which uses a random sample of 2,500 voters, is as likely as not to be 1.3 per cent inaccurate in one direction or the other; such a poll *could* be more than 5.1 per cent wrong. The smaller the sample, the greater the margin of error; a random sample of 1,000 could be over 8 per cent wrong simply on account of intrinsic statistical inaccuracy.[83] In practice, few election polls are based on samples of more than 2,000, and the polling organizations habitually allow themselves a 3 per cent sampling error.

These factors need to be born in mind when judging the success of the pollsters. It must also be remembered that what the polling organizations are really predicting are people's voting intentions, not the number of seats each party will obtain at Westminster. The record of the pollsters is set out in table 4:2. The record is generally a good one. In 1945 most newspapers were speaking in terms of a Conservative landslide. Little attention was paid to the Gallup prediction, which came within a very acceptable margin of error in forecasting a Labour victory. From then until the 1966 election the opinion polls maintained a satisfactory record. In 1951 none of them forecast that Labour would obtain more votes than the Conservatives, though the Gallup and *Daily Express* results, allowing for error, could be taken as evidence of a knife-edge situation; all the polls were correct in picking the Conservatives to form the next government. In the period 1945–66 the average error of all the polls was only 1.5 per cent.

In 1970 the pollsters came unstuck. Four out of five predicted a Labour victory; Gallup and Marplan predicted

4.2 Opinion poll forecasts 1945–74
Percentage gap of total votes cast between major parties
(Great Britain only)

Election	Result	Poll	Forecast	Error*	Average Error*
1945	Lab. 9.4	Gallup	Lab. 6.0	−3.4	−3.4
1950	Lab. 2.6	Gallup	Lab. 1.5	−1.1	0.5
		D. Express	Con. 0.5	2.1	
1951	Lab. 0.8[1]	Gallup	Con. 2.5	3.3	
		D. Express	Con. 4.0	4.8	5.3
		R. Services	Con. 7.0	7.8	
1955	Con. 3.3	Gallup	Con. 3.5	0.2	
		D. Express	Con. 2.7	−0.6	−0.2
1959	Con. 4.2	Gallup	Con. 2.0	−2.2	
		D. Express	Con. 3.7	−0.5	−1.0
		NOP	Con. 3.9	−0.3	
1964	Lab. 1.9	Gallup	Lab. 2.0	0.1	
		D. Express	Con. 0.8	2.7	0.8
		R. Service	Lab. 1.0	−0.9	
		NOP	Lab. 3.1	1.2	
1966	Lab. 7.3	Gallup	Lab. 11.0	3.7	
		D. Express	Lab. 16.9	9.6	4.0
		R. Services	Lab. 8.1	0.8	
		NOP	Lab. 9.0	1.7	
1970	Con. 2.4	Gallup	Lab. 7.0	9.4	
		NOP	Lab. 4.1	6.5	
		Harris	Lab. 2.0	4.4	6.0
		ORC	Con. 1.0	−1.4	
		Marplan	Lab. 8.7	11.1	
1974 (Feb.)	Con. 0.8[2]	Gallup	Con. 2.0	1.2	
		NOP	Con. 4.0	3.2	
		Harris	Con. 8.0	7.2	
		ORC	Con. 3.8	3.0	3.1
		Marplan	Con. 7.0	6.2	
		Business Decisions	Lab. 1.5	−2.3	
1974 (Oct.)	Lab. 3.5	Gallup	Lab. 5.5	2.0	
		NOP	Lab. 14.5	11.0	
		Harris	Lab. 8.4	4.9	
		ORC	Lab. 7.4	3.9	4.8
		Marplan	Lab. 9.7	6.2	
		Business Decisions	Lab. 4.5	1.0	

*positive = overestimate; negative = underestimate
[1] Conservatives obtained a majority of seats in the Commons
[2] Labour emerged the largest single party in the Commons

an overwhelming Labour victory. There are a number of possible explanations. Sampling error is not one of them. NOP, Marplan and Louis Harris used random sampling; Gallup and ORC used the quota method. During the election period, 16 of the 18 polls conducted showed Labour leads, often very substantial; although a single poll in an election can be expected to make an error of such proportions, the chances of 16 doing so through sampling deficiencies are very slim. The impact of the postal vote offers a partial explanation. Random sampling, by its very nature, misses those people who have moved away from a constituency, but who vote there by post. The postal vote favours the Conservatives. Failure to account for it could have led to a one per cent error between the pollsters' forecasts and the final result. Differential abstention – i.e. more potential Labour supporters abstaining than Conservatives – could also have resulted in a margin of error, but again only of about one per cent; in any case, the Conservative victory of 1970 cannot be explained on the grounds of differential abstention alone.[84]

The most likely explanation, and the one favoured by the pollsters in their election post-mortem, was the phenomenon of 'late swing', in this case a shift to the Conservatives in the final stages of the campaign. There is a great deal of circumstatial evidence in favour of this scenario. Trade figures published three days before polling were bad, and depressed the Labour campaign as much as they breathed new life into the Conservative effort. Enoch Powell's election speeches helped the Conservatives in spite of Edward Heath's rift with him. ORC re-interviewed a sub-sample of 257 electors who had originally been interviewed during the final weekend of the campaign. On the basis of the re-interviews, and of evidence of differential abstention, ORC adjusted its findings to show, instead of a Labour lead of four per cent, a Conservative lead of one per cent. ORC was, in fact, the only poll to predict a Conservative victory. Post-mortems carried out by NOP and Marplan also revealed evidence of a 'late swing' to the Conservatives of about 1.5 per cent net.

The failure of the opinion polls in 1970 damaged their reputation for reliability, which is important for them since they earn their money mainly through commercial market research. They were therefore anxious to take to heart the lessons of that election, and in February 1974 went on interviewing as near as possible to polling day. Their findings in February 1974 were more respectable; four out of five predicted a Conservative lead in terms of votes, and the Gallup, NOP and ORC results were well within accepted margins of error. Ironically so was the prediction of Business Decisions, which completed its interviews a week before the election. In October 1974 only the NOP result was wildly inaccurate. All the polls predicted a Labour lead, and all predicted the size of the Liberal vote (actually 18.3 per cent) to within 1.7 per cent.[85]

As with other aspects of mass media election coverage, the effect of the polls is only imperfectly understood, and a great many (sometimes intentional) myths are spread about them by the politicians, for whom they are often a convenient scapegoat. One is that they have a 'bandwagon' effect. According to this view, everyone likes to back a certainty, and voters who see the polls predicting, say, a Conservative victory will be lured into voting Conservative to be sure of coming out on the winning side. The experience of 1970 has dealt this theory a devastating blow, but has also added substance to another, that of the 'boomerang'. The possibility of a boomerang effect cannot be dismissed. The pure version of this theory, that electors who see one party, the party they would normally support, soaring ahead in the polls will change sides and vote for the underdog, has no substance. For the theory to be correct the opinion polls themselves would have to be consistently over-estimating the leading party's margin. In fact only on six occasions since 1945 (1951, 1964, 1966, 1970, February and October 1974) has the general trend of the poll forecasts proved to be an overestimate of the winning party's margin. Only in 1951, 1966 and October 1974 did all the polls agree in overestimating Labour's lead; in 1964 and February 1974 the forecasts, taking sampling error into account, were no different from the actual results. It would clearly be unfair to find the pollsters guilty of creating a boomerang effect at general elections on the basis of the 1970 result alone.[86]

There are, however, variants of the boomerang theory with more substance to them. According to one, apathetic voters who see their party well ahead in the polls will be less bothered about voting; Labour spokesmen alleged that this happened in 1970 though, if it did, it did not affect the result. The same allegation was made after the October 1974 result. William Molloy, Labour MP for North Ealing, estimated that one in four of the voters in his constituency who announced they were not going to vote did so because they considered Labour was destined to have an easy victory.[87] A more sophisticated version of this theory bases itself on the eminently plausible view that some voters, wishing to do what they could to prevent the emergency of a majority government at Westminster, saw the Labour lead in the opinion polls and voted tactically to reduce it on polling day. T. F. Thompson, chairman of ORC, 'believed people had voted tactically in the light of the polls, and that having seen the large Labour majority [predicted], decided not to vote Labour. While he thought it might infuriate the Labour party, he believed the polls could have cost it its predicted majority.'[88]

If this is what happened, it is a tribute to the intelligence of the voting public. Of course it does infuriate the politicians. Two Conservative MPs, Aidan Crawley in 1962 and R. Gresham Cooke in 1966, called for polls to be made illegal.[89] The all-party Speaker's Conference on Electoral Law, of 1965-8, recommended banning the publication of opinion polls during the period of 72 hours before the close of voting.[90] William Molloy called for the ban to be imposed during the final ten days of the campaign.

Any ban on publication would, as Professor Stacey has said, 'be intolerable in a democratic society'.[91] It would not only amount to a curb on freedom of expression, which, important at all times, is crucial during an election period. It would deny the elector access to vital information – viz.

what his fellow electors are thinking. If a voter talks to his friends and neighbours during the election and, apprehensive because they are heavily supporting one party, decides himself to counteract this tendency by voting for another, that is something the political parties must put up with. Following the findings of opinion polls is merely another and more accurate way of going about the same exercise.

The main criticism which could be levelled at the pollsters was that they did not, in the past, give enough information about the way in which their data was collected, nor did the newspapers who published their results alert their readers to the sampling errors involved. Shortly before the 1970 election the main polling organizations agreed on a code of practice, one proviso of which is that every poll report now mentions the sample size, method and timing; in September 1974 a further clause was added, that election predictions should only be in terms of votes, not seats.[92] The pollsters also exercise greater superintendence over the headlines accompanying poll results in the newspapers with which they are connected. More, however, could be done to make readers aware of the pitfalls of interpreting poll results too glibly; perhaps by adding a prominent rider warning them about statistical error and pointing out that votes cast and seats won are two different things.

The polls exist, and they are an important feature of the election circus, a side-show admittedly, but one which is very popular with the voting public. In a post-election poll in 1970, NOP found that 56 per cent of people claimed to have noticed the polls during the election.[93] They are, therefore, more popular than the party broadcasts, and their salience alone marks them out as a channel through which the electorate is informed about the progress of the election. The polls, like the phone-in programmes, are a means by which voters 'talk back' to the politicians. They enhance the feeling of involvement and, in their way, help to legitimate the election process.

For the politicians they pose major problems. The party which is leading in the polls worries about complacency among its workers and supporters. The party which is trailing is prone to depression and loss of morale. In 1951 Morgan Phillips, the Labour party's General Secretary, castigated the polls as 'a new technique of propaganda . . . calculated to sow the seeds of depression in the ranks of the Labour movement'.[94] Yet adverse polls can spur a party to greater activity and force it to modify its campaign techniques, as the Conservatives successfully did in 1959, to try and recoup lost ground.[95] Party spokesmen would prefer not to have to react publicly to poll results; as Leader of the Labour party, Harold Wilson was steadfast in his refusal to comment on the polls.

Since the débâcle of 1970 it has obviously been easier for politicians to brush aside the findings of the pollsters as meaningless gimickry. In 1974 a few spokesmen even suggested that they were not seriously or fairly conducted. This is a slur on the integrity of the polling organizations, who need to maintain a reputation for accurate forecasting to attract commercial business. It is, moreover, an opinion which politicians do not hold in private. The parties started to commission their own private polls as early as 1950; in February 1974 both the Labour and Conservative parties invested, for the first time, in daily private polling.[96] These polls are more concerned with consumer reaction to issues than with voting intention, and their findings are jealously guarded from the public view. The authors of the October 1974 Nuffield study report that they cost each of the two major parties about £30,000.[97]

The politicians, whatever they may say in public, obviously believe that opinion polls give them value for money. As Tom Forester, a journalist and a member of the Labour party, wrote candidly in the *New Statesman* on 4 October 1974: 'Despite the unfortunate experience of the last two elections . . . many of us remain secretly fascinated by the pollsters and eagerly await their latest batch of tempting percentages'.[98]

Chapter Five

RESULTS

Voters are individuals. In the welter of information which is now available concerning the voting habits of the British electorate, it is as well to bear this simple fact in mind. The inevitable tendency of the many studies which have been made of electoral behaviour is to stress the degree to which the voters under examination do or do not conform to rules or hypotheses. The opinion polls predict on the basis of the views of a very small section of the electorate; the electorate as a whole is deemed to be bound to follow the tendencies of the carefully-chosen sample. Politicians address themselves to mass audiences on the basis of national issues.

None of these approaches is invalid. But all of them, cumulatively, tend to de-humanize voting behaviour, and to give the impression that voting preferences are determined by whatever issues are dominant at the time. Class is a good example of this tendency. The pre-eminence of class divisions, in social and economic terms, since the Great War has led political scientists to look for class divisions in voting behaviour also. The questionnaires they use in their surveys are often designed to focus upon the class background of the respondent. The salience of class in their results is thus a self-fulfilling prophecy.

The most frequent offenders in this respect are the psephologists, who (especially on election night) talk about swings as if the swing determined the constituency result, rather than the reverse. There is also, it must be said, a remarkable resilience about received wisdom on voting behaviour, reinforced partly by politicians who are unwilling or unable to change their electioneering style to suit different audiences in different circumstances at different times, and partly by authors of textbooks, for whom the task of rewriting whole sections is too daunting. In these conditions, myths and misconceptions about the origins of voting behaviour flourish in abundance. The present author, before he begins his analysis of what makes people vote the way they do, would like to stress that the conclusions at which he has arrived, though he believes them to be true at the time of writing, are in no sense put forward as a prediction of or guide to future voting trends.

Politics and class

The extension of the franchise in the nineteenth century brought about a definite correlation between social class and party support. The term 'Tory' was revived and made respectable at the time of the Napoleonic wars and the rapid industrialization of the country. The Tory party of Lord Liverpool and the Duke of Wellington stood for the preservation of the unreformed constitution, the union of Church and State, and the repression of what were termed seditious organizations and dangerous beliefs. The party also manifested an antipathy towards the upstart bourgeoisie, and looked back nostalgically to a not-entirely-mythical golden age before the coming of the factory. It championed the cause of agriculture and its protection. Persuaded by Peel to accept and come to terms with the new order in society, the Conservative party (as it came to be known) was nonetheless the party of the land and the church, dedicated to the preservation of as much as possible of the old order without, however, threatening by its obstinacy to bring that order crushing down about its ears, as had almost happened in 1831. Age, for the nineteenth-century Conservative party, implied resilience; an exceedingly good case had to be made for interfering with institutions which had survived the scourge of time. The object of the party was, in Lord Salisbury's words, 'the administration of public affairs . . . in the spirit of the old constitution which held the nation together as a whole'.[1]

The bourgeoisie did not, at first, find much of a welcome in the Conservative ranks. It was to the Whig connection that they had to turn for help in their struggle for political equality with the landed aristocracy. The Whig/Liberal party thus became the party of industrial capital and nonconformity. The political division of the country into a party of the Land and the Church, and a party of the Factory and the Chapel, is of course at variance with classic Marxist ideology, and was never clear-cut or complete. Nevertheless, its basic reality is borne out by an examination of the poll books and an analysis of the social composition of the nineteenth-century House of Commons. In the Leicester election of 1847, for instance, the 'gentlemen' of the borough voted about two to one in favour of the Conservative candidate; the Anglican clergy voted Conservative to a man; the dissenting clergy voted six to one for the Liberals; and the manufacturers supported the Liberal candidates in the proportion of about five to one.[2] In the Cambridge election of 1868 the Conservative vote among the gentlemen and farmers was one-and-a-half times as great as the Liberal vote; the businessmen's support for the Liberal candidates, by contrast, was nearly twice as great as for the Conservatives.[3] In the House of Commons elected in 1847 the landed interest was a third greater in the ranks of the Conservative party as in the ranks of the Liberals; in 1868 the manufacturing interests, hardly discernible in the Conservative ranks in the Commons, formed a large and growing section of the Liberal parliamentary party.[4]

This amounted to a political division along class lines, but also along religious lines. The connection between the Liberal party and Dissent was particularly strong.[5] But it could not be said that the class division was between Labour and Capital. Labourers were more likely to vote Conservative than Liberal, and this was as true of urban as of rural constituencies.[6] Shopkeepers and craftsmen were more likely to vote Liberal than Conservative; this too was equally true of market towns as of industrial centres.[7] The class division was between different types of Labour and different types of Capital. No party had a monopoly of support from either side.

This pattern broke down in the later Victorian period. A number of factors were at work in the process. The gradual enfranchisement of more poor unskilled working men brought within the voting population segments of society for whom religious observance, if it meant anything at all, meant very little beyond hearing the Salvation Army band on a Sunday morning; the dogma of the early socialist societies meant nothing at all. The Conservative party, as refashioned by Disraeli, lost its chance to become the party of the manual working classes when, after the turn of the century, it turned its back on them. It did this primarily because it had become the party of Capital, industrial as well as landed. And this happened because of a rift in the Liberal party.

The Liberal party had always been an uneasy coalition of Whig aristocrats, middle-class industrialists, and radicals. After 1868 the alliance between property and radicalism became increasingly uncongenial to both. As early as 1877 contemporaries looked forward to the period 'more or less remote, when the two great sections of Liberalism should fall definitely apart, and fuse on the one side with the great Radical body . . . [and] on the other, with its natural opposite, the Conservatism of the time'.[8] This was precisely what happened. Frightened by the campaign against property inspired by the radicals, the bulk of the Whigs and then the industrialists left the Liberal party. Gladstone's Irish policy (with its incessant attacks upon the rights of property and the sanctity of contract) came as the last straw. By 1900 the Conservative MPs and their new allies, the Liberal Unionists, formed not merely the overwhelming majority of landowners in the House of Commons, but the overwhelming majority of merchants and industrialists as well.[9]

The Liberal party, for its part, was to find a new ally in the Labour party, which, prior to 1918, was reformist without being socialist. In the constituencies the correlation between class and party became much more distinct. Between 1885 and 1918, the 56 most affluent English constituencies were predominantly Conservative and Unionist, with an average Conservative or Unionist poll of 58.6 per cent. The 89 most working-class constituencies had an average Liberal or Liberal-plus-Labour vote of 53.2 per cent; the 15 English constituencies in which the mining vote was over 40 per cent had an average Liberal poll of 61.9 per cent.[10] In London the 18 most middle-class constituencies polled an average Conservative vote of 63.9 per cent, the 24 most working-class ones polled an average Liberal or Liberal-plus-Labour vote of 52 per cent.[11]

These figures make clear, however, that the correlation between class and party, though stronger than formerly, was far from complete. The mining constituencies were by no means overwhelmingly Liberal, nor were the cotton and wool towns of Lancashire and Yorkshire. Issues such as Ireland, religion, anti-alienism and tariff reform prevented political divisions along purely class lines. So did the longevity of the Liberal party. Some of these issues disappeared, or became less explosive, after the First World War. By 1924 Liberalism was visibly in decline; by 1935, when its total vote fell to under 1½ million, and only 21 Liberal MPs were elected, it had lost all claim to be the chief alternative to the Conservatives. That mantle had fallen upon the Labour party. Since 1945, and until very recently, the electoral battle has been exclusively between the Conservative and Labour camps. After 1945 the correlation between class and party seemed complete.

Before examining and testing this hypothesis, the terminology of class merits closer definition.[12] The Victorian 'upper classes' were persons of the highest 'rank'; they belonged to a social rather than an economic group, the titled, hereditary aristocracy. Their power and influence derived as much from the respect paid to them as from their wealth, which was landed wealth. Today they exist as a very small residual group, less wealthy than a hundred years ago, and generally less respected.

The term 'middle classes' came into general usage in the early nineteenth century. Originally it denoted merely the next rank in the hierarchy below the upper classes. But in the reaction against the power of the aristocracy the term acquired an economic dimension: the 'industrious classes', those who used their capital in a productive manner. John Stuart Mill talked about the 'three classes' of 'landlords, capitalists and labourers', and Karl Marx talked in much the same terms about the three 'great social classes . . . wage labourers, capitalists and landlords'. The term 'middle classes', which was thus originally social in its implication, became an economic term, and one moreover which denoted not merely a certain kind of wealth, but also a certain economic relationship (that of employer) with those – the 'working classes' – whose only wealth lay in the labour they sold to their employers in return for wages. In the later nineteenth century there developed an important distinction between those who earned their livelihood by means of a wage, those who drew a salary, and those (such as doctors) who relied on fees. Wage-earners belonged to the working classes, fee-earners to the middle classes. Salary earners ought, properly speaking, to have been included in the working classes, and legally they often were. But the social position of many salary-earners (such as bank managers) made this highly incongruous. So gradually the salaried sections of the population crept into the middle classes, even though they were employees.

Today the term 'middle class' is, indeed, social rather than economic. All who work as employees ought to be called working-class people, but they are not. Surgeons and dentists employed by the National Health Service are not thought of as, nor do they think of themselves as belonging to, the working class, even though they are (at a sophisticated level) manual labourers. Questions of educational background and cultural identification also arise. A docker may earn more than a teacher. A stockbroker may go broke. Such circumstances do not affect the class to which such people belong. In T. H. Marshall's words, 'the essence of social class is the way a man is treated by his fellows (and, reciprocally, the way he treats them), not the qualities or the possessions which cause that treatment'.[13]

'Middle' and 'working' class are not, therefore, really synonymous with non-manual and manual occupations. Political scientists and sociologists have long felt the need for some other, more objective classification, in which the subdivisions are logical and reasonably clear. The problem is that most people use the terms middle and working class when describing their own social status, and when talking about the social status of others; the needs and refinements of political sociology mean nothing to them. Most market research organizations follow a scale, used by the Institute of Practitioners in Advertising, which consists of the following categories:

 A – Professional and higher managerial
 B – Administrative and lower managerial
 C1 – Supervisory, clerical and skilled non-manual
 C2 – Skilled manual
 D – Semi-skilled and unskilled manual
 E – State pensioners and casual workers.

This is fine as a scale of occupational status, but as a measure of social class it may not differentiate finely enough between the middle and working classes. Butler & Stokes found that the C1 category included qualified local authority officers, draughtsmen and secretaries with a supervisory role, but also shop assistants, transport inspectors and lodging-house keepers. Of those at the top end of the C1 category, 60 per cent described themselves as middle class; of those at the bottom end, only 32 per cent said they were middle class. Butler & Stokes therefore further subdivided class C1 and constructed a sevenfold classification, groups I and II corresponding to classes A and B, group III corresponding to the upper end of C1 (skilled and supervisory non-manual), group IV to the lower end (lower non-manual), and groups V, VI and VII corresponding respectively to C2, D and E. If group IV is counted as middle class, the proportions of Conservative supporters in the middle class and Labour supporters in the working class were found to be remarkably similar: 77 per cent and 73 per cent respectively. But if this group is included in the working class, the proportions of Conservative supporters in the middle class and Labour supporters in the working class are considerably dissimilar: 80 per cent and 68 per cent respectively.[14]

This difference is a significant one, and could have important implications for, say, a discussion of working-class Conservatism. If group IV is reckoned as working class, the proportion of Conservatives who are working class rises from 27 per cent to 32 per cent. The people in group IV clearly believe themselves to be members of the working class. But because they are non-manual workers, other people regard them as belonging to the middle class. There are more components of class status than mere occupational level – income, education, life-style and so on – and these other components are by no means dependent solely upon occupational level. At the present time the popular wisdom is to identify the working class with manual workers and the middle class with non-manual workers. In the second edition of their book Butler & Stokes reverted to this formula.[15] Perspectives and social attitudes are, however, continually changing; there is no objective scale by which class may be measured.

That said, the relationship between class and party is undeniable. Data collected by the Gallup poll shows that middle-class support for the Conservative party has at no election between 1945 and 1966 averaged less than 68.5 per cent. Working-class support for the Labour party averaged not less than 55.5 per cent. The wealthier the middle-class sub-group under observation, the greater the degree of Conservative commitment; the poorer the working-class sub-group, the greater the adherence to the Labour party.[16] The findings of NOP at the elections of 1964, 1966 and 1970 reveal a similar pattern. At those three elections, Conservative support in the AB category averaged 75.3 per cent and in the C1 category 59.7 per cent; Labour support in the C2 category averaged 55.7 per cent, and in the DE category 60.3 per cent. Table 5.1 shows the trend over the past five general elections, as plotted by NOP and Louis Harris.

The broad pattern of class support is clear enough. But it

5.1 **Conservative and Labour party preferences by class, 1964–74**
(NOP and Louis Harris)*

	AB	C1	C2	DE
	percentage supporting the Conservative party			
1964	75	61	34	31
1966	72	59	32	26
1970	79	59	35	33
1974 (Feb.)	67	51	30	25
1974 (Oct.)	63	51	26	22
	percentage supporting the Labour party			
1964	9	25	54	59
1966	15	30	58	65
1970	10	30	55	57
1974 (Feb.)	10	21	47	54
1974 (Oct.)	12	24	49	57

*NOP data from Nuffield election studies for 1964, 1966, 1970 and February 1974;
Louis Harris data from Nuffield study for October 1974.

is no longer so clear as to warrant such sweeping assertions as 'Class is the basis of British party politics; all else is embellishment and detail',[17] or that 'the most significant division in electoral loyalties is that the well-to-do . . . predominantly vote Conservative, while those of a lower social status and a lower income group tend to vote Labour'.[18]

The first point to note is that, though a substantial proportion of the electorate vote according to their class, an important and growing minority do not do so. In 1964 a quarter of the AB class did not give its support to the Conservative party; a decade later over 30 per cent did not do so. More surprising still is the evident lack of working-class solidarity. At no election since 1945 has more than 60 per cent of the C2 class supported Labour; in 1974 the proportion fell to less than a half. Even the very poor are less solidly Labour than they used to be.

Another way of looking at this phenomenon is to ask, not what percentage within each class supports a particular party, but what are the class components of each party's total support – i.e. what proportion of each party's vote is derived from a particular social class. In 1963 Butler & Stokes found that 90 per cent of Labour's support came from occupational grades IV, V and VI, and only 10 per cent from the higher grades. In 1970 grades I–III accounted for 20 per cent of Labour's support; grades IV–VI accounted for 45 per cent of the Conservative vote.[19] Clearly the working class is more disposed to vote Conservative than is the middle class to vote Labour. But for both parties the pattern of class-dependence is very blurred, and becoming more so. The Labour party is much more dependent on the votes of the higher social classes than it used to be, or would like to admit. The Conservative party has to attract the votes of the poor and would appear, on the whole, to be doing a good job in this direction.

Working-class Conservatism has attracted a great deal more attention from political scientists than middle-class Labourism. In a country in which two-thirds of the working population is engaged in manual work, it seems highly incongruous that this section of society should give so much support to the party of Capital and of the employing classes. Even in an election marked by inflation, a three-day working week, much industrial unrest and a head-on clash between the miners and the government, as the election of February 1974 was, even in an electioneering atmosphere in which class tension was apparently higher than at any time since 1945, working-class Conservatism remained remarkably resilient. In the longer view, the coming of universal manhood suffrage in 1918 ought to have resulted in perpetual Labour governments, had the working population voted in accordance with its class. Of the 17 general elections held since then Labour has only won five.

The traditional explanation for the existence and persistence of working-class Convervatism has been couched in terms of deference. Walter Bagehot argued that this was the basis of the survival of the English construction, namely that 'the mass of the people yield obedience to a select few'.[20] According to this view (and there is plenty of contemporary evidence to give it substance),[21] the Conservative party is regarded as the natural repository of political wisdom, and its members are deemed to be those best fitted, by family background, breeding and experience, to rule the country. The often-public school education of Conservative politicians is regarded as an extra intellectual qualification. So is business prowess, the ability to make money. One working-class Conservative neatly summarized this philosophy:

> [The Conservative party] have some of the best brains in the country. They are altogether more successful and brainy than the Labour, and they have a great deal of experience behind them. They've a tradition of governing and leadership behind them for generations.[22]

This type of attitude is particularly prevalent among those working people (especially with below-average incomes) who aspire to middle-class values and life-style and who, indeed, would prefer to be regarded as members of the middle class. Working-class home-owners, and those who are buying their own home, if their income is below average, are twice as likely to vote Conservative as those working people who rent their accommodation.[23]

Deference is, however, by no means the beginning and end of working-class Conservatism. The evidence of both Butler & Stokes and McKenzie & Silver is that deference is on the decline. McKenzie & Silver found that deferential Conservatism was more prevalent in the older age-groups, those who were born before the first world war.[24] Butler & Stokes found that the percentage of Conservative voters in grades V and VI was greatest among those who had come of age before 1939.[25] Working people who acquired their political opinions between the two world wars, when Labour's record in government (1924 and 1929–31) was marked by mediocrity and failure, and when the Liberal party was tearing itself to pieces, or even before the first world war, when Labour was little more than a pressure group sheltering under the Liberal umbrella, can hardly be expected to give the Labour party automatic support. Between the wars, in fact, working-class Liberals were more likely to move over to the Conservatives than to support the new Labour party wedded to socialism.[26] And the

Conservative party took care, after 1945, not to turn its back on social reform, as it had done at the turn of the century.

People who came of age after 1945 are much less affected by Labour's early history, and the experience they have of the Labour party is one of relative success and, more important, credibility as a party of government. Deference to the Conservative party has never been part of the political education of these younger age-groups. This does not mean that younger working-class voters do not vote Conservative, only that their Conservatism is more likely to be 'secular' than deferential, that is, it is likely to be based only on the pragmatic appeal of Conservative policies, such as law and order, private enterprise, selective education. Predominant among the secular Conservatives are younger male voters with above-average wage packets.[27] Their commitment to Conservatism is practical, not emotional, and cannot be guaranteed. As the older 'deferentials' are being gradually replaced by the younger 'seculars', it is obvious that the dependibility of working-class Conservatism has been undermined. This process is an important component in the erosion of class-based partisan alignments in British political sociology.

Middle-class Labourism is more diverse in origin. Socialism has always had an intellectual appeal for certain middle-class people. The early Fabian Society, which did so much to mould the policies of the Labour movement, was overwhelmingly middle-class. More recently, a study of the Campaign for Nuclear Disarmament has delineated a group of middle-class radicals, largely educated at public and grammar schools followed by university or some other form of higher education, and working mainly for state and local authorities, universities, trade unions or in the freelance professions, who largely identified themselves with the politics of the broad left (e.g. on nationalization and immigration control) and some of whom were prepared to engage in civil disobedience.[28] A survey of university teachers, generally reckoned to be a middle-class group, has revealed that the dons distribute their support for the parties very much like the working class.[29] At the parliamentary level, the Labour party has become progressively more middle-class in composition. At a constituency level, the growing sophistication and professionalization of politics has made for the middle-class 'takeover' of the active leadership.[30]

These features of the Labour party are well known and were, indeed, to some extent endemic right from the start. More recent developments owe their origin to post-1945 social mobility and economic change. The spread of state education has given greater opportunities for children of working-class parents to proceed to higher education and so enter the professions. Though middle-class themselves, they are not thereby cut off from their Labour origins. Butler & Stokes found that not less than 12 per cent of electors with Labour parents had entered the middle class, and that 57 per cent of those middle-class Conservative or Labour electors with Labour working-class parents were themselves Labour supporters – 'a tribute to the influence of early socialization in the family'.[31] This is entirely consistent with the general discredit into which the *embourgeoisement* thesis has fallen. It is no longer believed that anything as deep-rooted as class consciousness can be overturned solely through the purchase of a range of consumer durables by a prosperous workforce.[32]

At the same time the Labour party, among others, has benefited from an erosion of middle-class Conservative support within the managerial classes. A post-election survey conducted by the British Election Study showed that in February 1974 35 per cent of those who had voted Conservative in 1970 and who switched to Labour four years later were non-manual workers.[33] This movement has contributed to the rise of a 'secular' Labour vote, prepared to judge Labour policies on their merits, but not prepared to vote Labour under any circumstances. For the Labour party, therefore, middle-class Labourism is a mixed blessing, a welcome inroad to areas of traditional Conservative strength, but unreliable in times of adversity.

The decline of class-based partisanship
The existence of working-class Conservatism and, to a

lesser degree, of middle-class Labourism, would not by itself invalidate the concept of class voting, which has never asked its admirers to believe that a person's political preference will always, under all circumstances, be determined by his occupational status. In politics all rules must incorporate exceptions. But until the mid-1960s it could be said that manual workers *in general* voted Labour and that non-manual workers *in general* voted Conservative. Electoral behaviour was marked by a lack of volatility, with the two major parties supported by those classes gathering the vast majority of votes cast. A stable two-party system, the fluctuations in which were the result of small, reasonably evenly-balanced swings of the electoral pendulum; these were the hallmarks of British elections. It is now clear that the period of stable class-based partisanship has come to an end, and that electoral volatility has increased. The crude voting figures since 1945, shown in table 5:2, paint the overall picture.

5.2 **Electoral support for the Conservative and Labour parties, 1945–74**

Election	Turnout %	Conservative + Labour share of the vote %	Conservative + Labour share of the electorate %
1945	72.8	87.6	66.0
1950	83.0	89.6	74.9
1951	82.6	96.8	79.2
1955	76.8	96.1	73.8
1959	78.7	93.2	73.4
1964	77.1	87.5	67.4
1966	75.8	90.0	68.2
1970	72.0	89.5	64.4
1974 (Feb.)	78.8	75.1	59.2
1974 (Oct.)	72.8	75.0	54.7

In the 1950s roughly eight out of ten eligible electors considered it worthwhile to bother to vote. The vast majority of these votes (on average 94 per cent) went to the Labour and Conservative parties, who obtained 99 per cent of the seats in the House of Commons. Since 1964 the trend of the turnout, though it has occasionally risen, has been unmistakeably downwards. The fall in turnout in the centres of large cities has been even more acute. In 1970 the average poll in the 42 inner-London seats was 58.4 per cent; in eight of them it was under 50 per cent. In October 1974 turnout in the 20 largest conurbations in the United Kingdom was four per cent below the national average. But turnout has remained high in those constituencies where there were third- or fourth-party interventions. The impact of the minor parties is in fact to increase turnout, absolutely or relatively.[34]

The closer the fight, the more interesting and varied the contest, the greater the desire to register a vote. Faced with a choice between the two major parties, many voters simply abstain. The total share of the electorate willing to support the Conservative and Labour parties has fallen almost without respite since 1951. Abstention and minor-party support have seriously eroded the popularity of the major parties. In sharp contrast to the elections of the 1950s, those of the early 1970s have displayed, not movements of opinion between the major parties, but withdrawal of support from both of them.

This evidence of increasing electoral volatility is reinforced by the results of by-elections and the findings of public opinion polls. It is natural for governments in midterm to be less popular than they were immediately after the general election which brought them to power. In the 1950s it was rare for anti-government swings at by-elections to be above 10 per cent; between 1950 and 1966 there were only nine such cases in 187 contested by-elections. In the parliament of 1966-70 there were 16 in 38 contests. In 1976 there were five out of nine with this characteristic. The fall in the government's share of the vote at by-elections has become increasingly severe, as table 5:3 shows.

It is now commonplace for governments to lose seats in by-election contests. Between 1945 and 1959 governments lost only six seats in by-elections; between 1959 and February 1974 they lost 28. The Conservative and Labour parties, even if they win a general election, must now live

5.3 **Performance of the government at by-elections, 1950-77**

Parliament	No. of contested by-elections	No. in which government share of the vote fell by over 10 per cent
1950–51	15	1
1951–55	45	0
1955–59	52	12
1959–64	62	37
1964–66	13	1
1966–70	38	33
1970–74	30	20
1974	1	0
1974–77	17	11

with the fact that they could see their parliamentary majority seriously eroded through by-election defeats. The majority of 30 which the Conservatives had in 1970 had shrunk by a third by February 1974. The implications of such a trend for a government's ability to manage its parliamentary business are obvious, especially where its majority is paper-thin to begin with. In October 1974 the Labour government's majority over all other parties was three; its loss to the Conservatives of West Woolwich the following year, and of Workington and Walsall North in November 1976, seriously intensifed its parliamentary difficulties and its ability to push legislation through parliament.

Opinion poll data confirms this picture of volatility and disenchantment with the two major parties. Table 5:4 shows the average monthly percentage lead of one of the two major parties over the other, as recorded by the Gallup poll, for seven periods since 1947.

5.4 **Fluctuations in the Gallup Poll, 1947–74***

Period	Average percentage lead per month
1947–50	2.7
1950–55	3.1
1955–59	3.0
1959–64	5.0
1964–66	4.4
1966–70	7.8
1970–74	5.3

*Based on the Gallup findings in D. Butler & A. Sloman, *British Political Facts*

It can be seen that since the late 1960s the major party lead has fluctuated nearly twice as much as in the 1950s; since many voters deserted both major parties for a third party, actual electoral volatility was certainly greater than table 5:4 suggests. Of those voters who remained loyal to Labour in 1970, the year of its defeat, over a quarter deserted the party in February 1974; of those who had voted Conservative in 1966 *and* 1970, nearly a quarter deserted four years later.[35] That such massive defections of support occurred in elections which, *prima facie*, had all the traditional characteristics of class appeal, must itself raise doubts about the stability of the two-party system and its validity in the eyes of the electorate.

The roots of this weakening of political identification by class lie in the erosion of partisanship in the British voting population. In 1964, 81 per cent of the electorate identified themselves with the Labour or Conservative parties; 40 per cent had a 'very strong' identification. In October 1974 only 24 per cent identified 'very strongly'. Until 1970 this erosion among the strong identifiers was hardly noticeable. Thereafter it proceeded so rapidly that the organizers of the British Election Study at the University of Essex have likened the election of February 1974 to a 'critical' or 'realigning' election, perhaps marking a permanent alteration in the partisan allegiance of the electorate.[36] Partisan commitment is not the same thing as party identification. Although in October 1974 only 24 per cent of the electorate were strong identifiers, 59 per cent voted Labour or Conservative. The habit of voting for one of the two major parties is still deeply ingrained. But the proportion of 'secular' Labour or Conservative voters has clearly increased. Those who automatically support either of these parties are members of a diminishing fraternity.

In the long term, the election of February 1974 may well turn out to have been 'critical', even cataclysmic, as that of 1924 was in relation to support for the Labour party. For the moment, contemporary observers must act with prudence and suspend judgment on explanations of this sort. One clue to the diminution of partisan commitment over so short a period since 1970 certainly lies in the attitude of the young voters. The hardening of partisanship with age (discussed below) is now a well-known and well-defined process. It is among the young electors that party attachments are weakest. The influence of the family and the home is less pervasive than formerly, the mass media provide alternative standards, there are more opportunities for travel. 1970 was the first election in which the voting age was lowered to 18. It is therefore possible that the newest generation of electors has repudiated the two-party system.

The Essex study gives some supporting evidence, for it shows that between 1964 and October 1974 there was a marked diminution of partisan commitment among successive age-groups. During this period the partisan strength of the youngest group of voters (aged between 20 and 27 in 1964), measured on a scale ranging from 0 for non-identifiers to 3 for very strong identifiers, declined from 1.97 to 1.82; for those who were aged between 28 and 35 in 1964 the decline was only from 1.98 to 1.88. This indicates that the rate of partisan weakening has been somewhat greater in the younger group of voters.[37] But it also shows that the dilution of partisan commitment is by no means confined to this group. It is, in fact, a phenomenon general to the electorate as a whole, and from which no age-group has been exempt.[38]

Too little research has as yet been carried out into the erosion of partisanship to permit of any definite conclusion as to its origin or extent of penetration within successive age-groups and within different occupational grades. Nonetheless, there is enough qualitative evidence to suggest ways by which the erosion has progressed.

To begin with, the electorate is better educated. There is a growing refusal on the part of electors to believe in or take much notice of the shibboleths of class politics. On the Labour side, creeping affluence among manual workers has not led to *embourgeoisement* and the espousal of Conservatism. But it has led to rejection of the socialist ethic of class warfare, and must be counted among the reasons – possibly the chief reason – for the above-average drop in turnout in industrial constituencies, noted earlier.[39] The Labour party developed upon the foundations of the heavy industries – coal, engineering, shipbuilding, the railways, etc. – in which the workforce struggled to make ends meet. Class warfare actually existed, even in a physical sense. This is no longer the case. The trade unions have in general won the fight for recognition. The working classes no longer live at subsistence level. The hard grind which characterized the life of working people before 1939, and which sustained their support for the Labour party, has gone. It is not a socialist society which has given the working classes the consumer durables they enjoy; it is a capitalist society, or at best a 'mixed economy'. In 1906 the trade unions needed the support of the Labour party; today the reverse is true.

In their survey of working-class attitudes, carried out between 1958 and 1963, McKenzie & Silver noted that when Labour supporters described their party, there was 'an almost complete absence of any reference to "socialism" or a "new social order"'. The support for Labour was not ideological, but economic; what respondents hoped to derive from a Labour government was not a socialist state, but a better standard of living. As one young lower working-class respondent put it:

> It's not politics that make me vote Labour – it's a case of the one that helps you most. Only wish I was in the position to vote Conservative.[40]

McKenzie & Silver also found that even in a period of Conservative unpopularity, Conservative working-class voters were more loyal to their party than were Labour working-class voters to theirs; 82 per cent of the Conservatives were moderately or very pro-Conservative; only 46 per cent of Labour voters were moderately or very pro-Labour.[41] The clear inference from this evidence is that class support for Labour was not high even in the late 1950s and will last only so long as the party 'delivers the goods'. Its failure to do so between 1966 and 1970 undoubtedly had a negative impact so far as support of this kind was concerned.

Among Conservatives too, however, partisanship has been diminishing. In 1963, according to Butler & Stokes, 75 per cent of those in occupational grades I–IV identified themselves as Conservative. By 1970 this proportion had fallen to 70 per cent.[42] The Essex study found the proportion in October 1974 to be as low as 65 per cent.[43] Part at least of the explanation for this *volte-face* by the middle classes is to be found in the fact that occupational grade II, which includes middle-ranking officials of the civil service, local authorities, nationalized industries and large private companies, is now largely a grade of employees. The growth of white-collar trade unionism among the professional classes, the bureaucrats, the supervisory and technical staffs, the managers of industry, has had a remarkable impact. Of those who had voted Conservative in 1970, but who had 'defected' in some way in February 1974, 41 per cent were or were married to trade union members. Even of those who remained loyal to the party in February 1974, a full 25 per cent came from a trade union household.[44] Since the level of working-class Conservative identifiers has remained steady at about a third, the trade union defection from the Conservative party could only have come, in the main, from the ranks of the middle classes. As they have evolved into unionized employees, the managerial groups no longer regard the Conservative party as their natural political home.

The weakening of the traditional class dichotomy in British politics may also be gauged from people's attitudes towards concepts and issues associated with the two-party system. Butler & Stokes found that only a quarter of their respondents thought of themselves as being to the 'left' or 'right' in politics. Over two-thirds did not think of themselves in terms of 'left' or 'right' at all. Even among those electors who believed in a relationship between class and party, only a minority saw the relationship in terms of class *conflict*.[45] When questioned in March 1969, less than one-third of an NOP random sample believed that trade unions exerted a good influence in this country, and almost two-thirds believed unions had too much power; even with classes C2 and DE the proportion was between 50 per cent and 59 per cent, and of Labour supporters it was 46 per cent.[46] The Essex study has, more recently, recorded a steady fall between 1964 and February 1974 in the proportion of Labour Identifiers who believe in more nationalization of Labour identifiers who believe in more nationalization, more spending on the social services, and the retention of close ties between the Labour party and the trade union movement. Nationalization, one of the most fundamental tenets of the Labour platform, has in fact come to be rejected by over half of Labour's own supporters.[47]

This is entirely consonant with the evidence presented in the second edition of Butler & Stokes, that the association between social class and partisan identification, which appears to have reached a peak with the generation first entering the electorate after 1945, has weakened considerably since the early 1960s, and especially since 1966. The partisanship of those first entitled to vote in the late 1960s is no stronger than the partisanship of those who came of age before 1918. Both generations were born into a political system in which the relationship between partisan affiliation and social class was far from clear-cut, and in which the major parties straddled social classes. The post-1945 Labour party has lost its cloth-cap image, the Conservative party its aristocratic undercarriage. The differences that exist between these two parties are not about the merits of the mixed economy and the welfare state, but simply about the way in which these institutions shall be managed.[48] The withering of the class alignment in British politics could not have a sounder base.

New voting alignments
If social class and occupational grade are no longer the major determinants of political choice, and if those votes that are given to the Conservative and Labour parties are given increasingly on a 'secular' basis, what other factors do determine the way in which people vote? On what precise

basis are votes still given to the two major parties? Why are votes being cast in larger numbers for the minor parties? What prompts electors not to give their votes to any part at all? There are two broad ways in which these problems can be tackled and they may be conveniently characterized as the 'predestination' approach and the 'free will' approach. The former stresses the range of other factors, such as sex, age, religion and region, which could provide clues to present voting behaviour, and which class has never completely overhauled. The latter emphasizes the empirical factors which have led voters to vote for minor parties, or not at all. The former is an essentially sociological approach, the latter is an essentially political one. These approaches are not mutually exclusive.

Sex, age, religion, region

By looking at voting patterns, not in terms of social class, but in terms of other basic background information, it is possible to suggest ways in which political preference is linked to, and is perhaps a reflection of, these other personal characteristics. Sex and age are the two most obvious variables. Opinion poll findings between 1964 and October 1974 show that women are more inclined to vote Conservative, or Liberal, than are men, a tendency which is very familiar in post-war politics.[49] The relationship between age and voting intention is, however, less easily reduceable to a simple generalization. The younger age-groups would appear to be more inclined to vote Labour, or Liberal, than the middle- or old-aged, and to have become more inclined to vote for a minor party over the past decade. But the pattern is by no means a consistent one. Between 1945 and 1966 those under 30 years of age consistently favoured Labour, but by margins varying from 1 per cent to 28 per cent.[50] In 1964 and 1974 the margin of support given to Labour by those under 35 also fluctuated.[51] Although the old-age pensioners favoured the Conservatives at both these elections, there have been times (e.g. 1951, 1959) when this group has favoured Labour. Those aged between 55 and 64 have displayed a similar volatility in their partisanship; the solid Conservative backing demonstrated by those in later middle age in the 1950s has evaporated. And although those aged between 35 and 54 have tended to be more Labour-inclined in recent elections, the margin of support has fluctuated a good deal.

Whether or not generalizations can be made about the correlation between age and voting, it would be dangerous to do so, because the comparison is not between like and like. Those who were in one age-group in 1964 were in the next age-group a decade later. In successive decades one would not, by this method, be measuring changes in the voting behaviour *of the same people*. Mortality rates differ from one age-group to the next. Rates of fertility, which largely determine the size and composition of the youngest voting group, are notoriously unpredictable. If class does not explain voting behaviour it is unlikely that age, or sex, or indeed any other single characteristic will do so.

The realization that this is so has led to the propagation of the idea of political generations, of studying groups of voters over a period of time and of looking at a variety of social, political, economic, religious and demographic variables associated with them. The easiest way of doing this is to use a 'panel', a sample of voters interviewed more than once over a desired time-span. Several studies of political behaviour in the 1950s used this method.[52] *Political Change in Britain*, by David Butler & Donald Stokes (1969) revolutionized the application of this technique so far as British political behaviour was concerned. In 1963 Butler & Stokes commenced an interview survey of 2009 voters chosen at random from 80 randomly-selected parliamentary constituencies in Great Britain. The panel, together with some other respondents added to ensure the continual accuracy of the sample, was re-interviewed after the general election of 1964 and again, with further additions, after that of 1966. The second edition of the work (1974) included the results of further panel interviews in 1969 and immediately after the 1970 general election. In all, 5,124 electors were interviewed between 1963 and 1970, and yielded over 7½ million separate items of information, which were analysed by computer. The British Election Study at the University of Essex is using the same approach and adding to the Butler & Stokes data.

The work of Butler & Stokes is not merely the most ambitious yet in terms of size and scope of the British electorate surveyed. It also made considerable use of 'open-ended' questions, in which respondents were at liberty to express their views in their own terms, and did not have to choose between two or three standard replies. Even to summarize all the findings would be beyond the scope of the present study. Some of them have been presented or referred to in previous chapters, and some of them have been questioned. Not all aspects of the electorate were surveyed by Butler & Stokes; the coloured population, for instance, received less than four pages, and little attention was paid to the Welsh and Scottish nationalist voters. Nonetheless, by monitoring the political and social characteristics of the same electors over a number of years Butler & Stokes were able to dispose of some popular fallacies about political choice, and also to point the way to a clearer understanding of the origins of partisanship and the mechanics of generational change.

Butler & Stokes found that the best guide to the way any voter is likely to cast his vote is not his social class, but the votes of his parents. Among people coming from homes where both parents were Labour or both Conservative, about 90 per cent formed their earliest party preferences along the same lines; where one parent was Labour and the other Conservative, the earliest party preferences of the children were likely to divide about 50–50 between the two parties. As the years pass, and the influence of the parental home diminishes, the political influence of parents grows less, but is still very strong; of homes where both parents were Labour, 81 per cent managed to instil Labour beliefs in their children; from wholly Conservative homes 75 per cent transmitted Conservative partisanship to their adult children.[53] It is only among individuals who begin life *without* a partisan lead from their parents that the class milieu becomes important. Even for these people, bereft of parental guidance, class is only one of a number of influences which step in to fill the gap. One of the most important is the impression which they gain of the parties as they reach the age of majority. It is clear from the reported first votes of new electors since 1935 that the favourable profile of the Labour party during the second world war helped Labour win the support of the young in 1945, that Labour's bad image in the 1950s lost it the support of first-time voters, and that the party's renaissance after 1959 attracted the new voters in 1964 and 1966.[54]

Once a partisan self-image is acquired, it hardens with age. As a voter becomes older, the inclination to change parties grows less, though it is by no means extinguished. In this sense, voters become more 'conservative' with age. But Butler & Stokes demonstrated convincingly that the so-called theory of 'senescent Conservatism', that people become more Conservative (with a big C) as they grow older, is quite wrong. The fact that, at the moment, the old tend to be more Conservative than the young, is not a reflection of their age *per se*, but of the time in which they were young. Voters who were 65 or over in 1974 came of age before 1931. Their chances of growing up in a Labour household were obviously much less than that of voters who came of age after 1945, and very substantially less than that of the new voters enfranchised in 1969.[55]

It is the dominance of the parental influence which led Butler & Stokes to conclude that, within the life of a single parliament, the deaths and coming-of-age of voters have almost as much effect upon the parties' fortunes as all the switches due to political moods or events.[56] The first point to grasp is that parents do not have identical numbers of children. The numbers of children born to wives of manual workers and non-manual workers during most of the period in which the present electorate was born were in the ratio 7:5, though this was partly offset by greater infant mortality in the working classes. To add to the problem this fertility imbalance poses for the Conservative party, working-class Conservatives have smaller families than working-class Labour supporters; on average the working-class Conservatives have 25 per cent fewer children. The second point is that women live longer than men, and middle-class people live longer than working-class people. The Conservative party has a greater share of the allegiance of women and of the middle classes. This gives the party some advantage to compensate for Labour's better fertility rate: fewer Conservative, or at least potentially Conservative children are born, but they are likely to live longer and to be able to vote in more general elections.

The electorate is not static. It is a constantly shifting mass. A party's support at one general election is composed of its electors at the previous general election, minus those who have left the country, plus those immigrants who are attracted to it, minus those supporters who have died, plus those who have come of age. By 1970 not less than 16 per cent of the 1959 electorate had been removed by emigration and death, and not less than 24 per cent of the 1970 electorate had been added since 1969 by immigration and coming-of-age. Of these processes, deaths and comings-of-age were by far the most important, accounting for over 90 per cent of the total 'turn-over' of the Conservative and Labour parties in the period.[57]

By analysing party support along these lines it is possible to calculate what proportion of a party's total advance can be attributed to political and what proportion to demographic causes. The results are startling. Butler & Stokes calculated that, between 1959 and 1964, Labour's net lead over the Conservatives increased to 4.3 per cent, as reflected in the replies of their panel; of this increase, the largest single component was provided by the turnover in the electorate (1.7 per cent), which was therefore three times as important for Labour as the net gain from making political converts (a mere 0.6 per cent).[58] Similarly, between 1966 and 1970 the Conservative lead over Labour increased to 6.5 per cent; the Conservatives performed well in winning converts (4.8 per cent), but almost half this effort was nullified by an adverse turnover in the electorate.[59]

Turnover in the electorate was, on this evidence, the biggest single factor in Labour's 1964 election victory, accounting for 40 per cent of their net lead in votes. Between 1966 and 1970 the Conservatives did well to win converts to their cause, and to get out the vote on polling day. But the turnover of the electorate, and in particular the entry of the newly-enfranchised young voters, favoured the Labour party and so prevented the Conservatives having an even greater victory. Clearly, the best thing a voter can do for his party is to live longer and have more children. The one election cry which the parties ought to make to their supporters, but never do, is: Be fruitful and multiply!

Knowledge of a voter's parental background is not by any means an infallible guide to his or her own partisanship. It is a very good guide, better than occupational grade. But it is only a measure of the *effect* of one aspect of political socialization; others include the media, friends, work mates, and honest political conversion and conviction. It is easy to argue that, as the older 'pre-Labour' generations die out, the Conservative party will be increasingly disadvantaged. This does not mean that electoral turnover will win election victories for the Labour party, and that party workers can therefore sit back and wait for the inevitable. As was argued earlier, class differences as they affect partisanship are themselves becoming less potent. The diminishing percentage of the electorate supporting either the Conservative or the Labour party may well mean that a generation of voters will grow up with no parental political influence, or with parental influence spanning a wide range of political choices. Class may come into its own once more. Or some new, unforeseen development might arise.

Two factors which at the moment are certainly less influential are the religious and the regional ones. In the nineteenth century religion was a most powerful root of political partisanship. Because the Conservative party championed the established Church of England, Catholics and Nonconformists turned to the Liberal party, which became the party of Dissent. Some of the most divisive issues in politics – Ireland in the early nineteenth century, Welsh Disestablishment, education—were above all religious ones. Religious groups who enjoyed second-class political status automatically became Liberal supporters. The Liberal party became a radical party in large measure because of these religious dimensions. Almost all Dissenters active in politics were Liberals, and most of the leading radicals were Dissenters.

The pull of religion was such that it could outweigh that of class. The Conservative revival in Lancashire in the late nineteenth century was made possible partly by vigorous exploitation of anti-Catholic feeling among working-class cotton operatives.[60] The Liberal traditions of the coal-mining communities, many of which (e.g. in Northumberland, Durham and South Wales) were strongly Dissenting, helped prevent the miners from affiliating to the Labour party till 1909; socialism was still tarred with the brush of atheism, and socialist support for Labour therefore had a negative effect on Nonconformists.[61] In Ireland, of course, religion was all.

Since the first world war religious influences upon British (but not Northern Irish) politics have declined markedly. The displacement of the Liberals, as the main opposition party to the Conservatives, by a class-based party, diluted the strength of the Nonconformist/Liberal and Anglican/Conservative alignments. Prominent Nonconformist families, such as the Chamberlains of Birmingham, joined the highest ranks of the Conservative party. The Irish issue was removed from the political forefront in 1921. Disestablishment and education ceased to be political issues. And there was a general decline in religious observance.

Butler & Stokes found that in the 1960s Anglicans and members of the Presbyterian Church of Scotland were almost equally divided in the support they gave to the Conservative and Labour parties. Methodists and Roman Catholics showed large Labour majorities, and the Liberals were more popular among Nonconformists than among members of established churches.[62] This apparent propensity for the Labour and Liberal parties among Catholics and Nonconformists is, however, more superficial than first appearances might suggest. Within all the church groupings class is strongly linked to party. Within the established churches of England and Scotland, the difference in partisanship between classes is nearly as great as in the country as a whole. Nonconformist support for the Liberal party is strongest among the older, middle-class electors; the difference between support for the Liberal party among Anglicans and Nonconformists of post-1945 generations is much less.[63] The strength of Labour support among Roman Catholics and Methodists is also explicable along class lines. Traditional Methodist strongholds, such as the north-east, the midlands and south Wales, are also working-class concentrations; it is class, not religion, which explains the voting patterns in these areas.[64]

Nowadays there are very few issues which divide people, politically, along religious lines. MPs who supported the 1967 Abortion Act have come under fire from Catholic voters and have no doubt lost Catholic votes as a result.[65] But many non-Catholics also oppose the 1967 Act, and it would be wrong to see this highly emotive issue purely in religious terms. The only instance of a definite link between religion and voting in modern Britain concerns the partisanship of the immigrant Irish Catholics, who carry with them a history of passionate opposition to the Conservative party and its links with the Protestant ascendancy in Ireland. In the major areas of Irish settlement (Liverpool, Glasgow, parts of north London), sectarian feeling has almost as strong a hold as in Ulster. Parliamentary candidates in these areas know that they will have to address themselves to Catholic audiences and to Irish issues. Where protestantism is particularly strong and militant, as on Clydeside, the Conservative party has become, albeit unwittingly, the 'Orange' party. The Labour party attracts the bulk of the Irish vote; Protestant sectarianism has, in the past, delivered a large number of working-class votes to the Conservatives.[66] Even here, however, religion is not a watertight explanation. The Irish immigrants of Clydeside, Merseyside, Camden and Islington would probaly vote heavily Labour in any case. The Ulster troubles have only reinforced a partisanship which is, for them, basically determined by occupational grade.

Regional variations in voting patterns are certainly very pronounced. Butler & Stokes found that the proportion of skilled manual workers (C2 class) supporting Labour varied from 79.9 per cent in Wales to 46.8 per cent in south-central England. The proportion of white-collar workers (C1 class) supporting Labour varied from 21.6 per cent in the south-west to 46.0 per cent in Wales. Conservatism in the professional and managerial classes (AB) was highest in the east-midlands (83.2 per cent) and lowest in Wales (58.0 per cent). Labour's proportion of the support given to the two main parties was on average 10 per cent higher in the combined regions of Scotland, Wales and the north of England than in the midlands and the south.[67]

This gives some credence to the continued existence of 'two nations', because only a third of the difference in Labour's strength between the north and west, on the one hand, and the midlands and south on the other, can be attributed to the fact that the working classes are thicker on the ground in the former areas than in the latter. There is a great deal of evidence to suggest that the neighbourhood in which people live is linked to the way they vote. The Conservative party does less well in coal-mining areas than its class support warrants, but does better than it deserves in seaside resorts. In mining towns, Labour obtained, in 1970, 79 per cent of the working-class vote and 50 per cent of the middle-class vote; in the resorts only 48 per cent of working-class support and 20 per cent of middle-class support.[68]

Does this mean that environment actually *influences* voting, that somehow the strong Labour support of miners will 'rub off' on to middle-class people in mining constituencies, and that the strength of Conservatism in the resorts will similarly 'rub off' on to working-class voters? To some extent it does. A working-class voter whose Labour attachment is weak, or weakening, will no doubt receive moral encouragement and support from living in a staunchly Labour constituency, working alongside rock-solid Labour workmates, meeting them in the pubs and clubs. The temptation to vote Conservative will diminish. But if such a voter lives in a Conservative environment the temptation may prove too great.

But another explanation is equally plausible. Seats which habitually return a heavy Labour poll are not likely to have flourishing, growing Conservative constituency parties. The Conservative campaign will be enacted merely for form's sake. By the same token, Labour constituency parties will be weak in very strong Conservative areas. In politics especially, nothing succeeds like success, and nothing fails like failure. Again, if the regional 'explanation' of voting held good, the rise of nationalist parties, and in particular the advances made by them in traditionally 'safe' Labour areas in Scotland and Wales, would not be explicable. In Scotland and Wales something has gone very wrong with the 'rubbing off' process. Regional differences in political support are not so much explanations of voting behaviour as simply reflections of it.

Third parties, local parties, no parties

It is no coincidence that the weakening of the class alignment has gone hand-in-hand with a surge in support for third parties. While this development has been most spectacular in Scotland and Wales, it has been no less marked in England. In parliamentary terms, the impact of the minor parties has been to sweep away the neat two-party system that characterized British politics in the quarter-century following the end of the second world war.

Although the parliamentary impact of the nationalist parties in Scotland and Wales was not felt until February 1974, the rise in support for the SNP and Plaid Cymru extended over a much longer period. Plaid Cymru, founded at the National Eisteddfod in Pwllheli in 1925, remained a small movement throughout the 1930s, '40s and '50s, though it fought some seats at every general election since 1929. Its breakthrough came in the 1960s, when rising support for the movement culminated in the victory of its president, Gwynfor Evans, in the Carmarthen by-election of July 1966. Labour won back Carmarthen in 1970. But in February 1974 Plaid Cymru captured Caernarvon and Merioneth. In

October, these seats were retained and Carmarthen was recaptured.

The SNP has a similar history. It was formed, in 1928, as the National Party of Scotland, by an amalgamation of a number of groups advocating Scottish Home Rule; a further amalgamation led to the adoption of the title Scottish National Party in 1934. At first the SNP enjoyed a large measure of support from Liberals and left-wing Labour supporters; the Clydeside group of Labour MPs actually supported Scottish Home Rule during the 1920s.[69] This support dwindled as the SNP adopted a more strident separatist tone. Its first parliamentary election victory, that of Dr. Robert McIntyre at the Motherwell by-election in April 1945, proved to be a false dawn; the seat was recaptured by Labour in the general election a few months later. The 1950s were lean years for the party, its membership reduced to a small hard core. In the early 1960s, however, it began to contest by-elections, with increasingly creditable results. In 1967 the party won the Lanarkshire seat of Hamilton from Labour. The seat was lost in 1970 but that of the Western Isles was gained. In November 1973 a second seat was won, that of Glasgow Govan. In the election of February 1974 the SNP lost Govan but retained the Western Isles, and won six other seats, two from Labour (Dundee East and East Stirlingshire) and four from the Conservatives (Aberdeenshire East, Argyll, Banff, and Moray & Nairn). All seven were retained in October; in addition four more Conservative seats fell to the party (Angus South, Dunbartonshire, Galloway, and Perth & East Perthshire).

In the 1960s it was fashionable to view the rising nationalist tide as a protest vote. In Wales, it was said, it was the backlash of rural, Welsh-speaking areas against (mis-)government from London, a cultural movement as much as a political one, based on a species of populist radicalism which had strong historic roots in Welsh politics. In Scotland, it could also be argued that the movement was essentially rural, and one of a transitory nature; general election results in the 1960s did not match up to expectations generated by by-election performance, and the gains (of 100 seats) at the Scottish local elections of May 1968 were almost wiped out three years later. A major work on Scottish voting behaviour, based on research carried out in the early 1960s, could afford to relegate the SNP to a few passing references.[70] In 1970 most of the new SNP votes in the area of greatest advance, in the north of Scotland, were won at the expense of the Liberals. The bastion of Plaid Cymru strength lay in the Welsh-speaking areas of west Wales, which had once been Liberal strongholds.[71] Neither nationalist party seemed to be capable of making sustained headway in urban areas, or of retaining support at general elections.

The nationalist performance since 1970 has proved these early judgments to have been most premature. In March 1972 Plaid Cymru came within 4,000 votes of capturing Merthyr from Labour, and almost quadrupled its vote in this English-speaking industrial constituency in the southeast of the Principality. As the 1974 election results showed, the party still does significantly better in rural than in industrial areas. Yet in the Welsh District Council elections of May 1976 the party made a net gain of 75 seats; it wrested control of Merthyr Tydfil from Labour and emerged the largest single party in the Rhymney Valley. The threat to Labour (Wales has never, apart from resorts and border counties, been an area of Conservative penetration) could not be clearer. In Scotland the main thrust of the nationalist advance since 1970 has been at the expense of the Conservatives. But in 1974 the SNP made headway at the expense of Labour as well; in October 1974 it took votes fairly evenly from both main parties.[72] Of the 41 seats held by Labour at that election, the SNP came second in 35, with 36 per cent of the vote. Though still the third Scottish party in terms of seats, it is now the second in terms of votes cast; the gap between its vote and the Labour vote in October 1974 was only 5.8 per cent.

The cumulative impact of Welsh and Scottish nationalism at general elections is shown in tables 5:5 and 5:6, which plot nationalist support in terms of the total Welsh and Scottish polls, in terms of the total electorates in each of the two countries, and in terms of the average percentage vote per candidate.

5.5 The performance of Plaid Cymru, 1959–74

Election	Candidates	MPs	Percentage of Welsh poll	Percentage of Welsh electorate	Average percentage vote per candidate
1959	20	0	5.2	4.3	9.0
1964	23	0	4.8	3.8	8.4
1966	20	0	4.3	3.4	8.7
1970	36	0	11.5	8.9	11.5
1974 (Feb.)	36	2	10.7	8.0	10.7
1974 (Oct.)	36	3	10.8	8.3	10.8

5.6 The performance of the Scottish National Party, 1959–74

Election	Candidates	MPs	Percentage of Scottish poll	Percentage of Scottish electorate	Average percentage vote per candidate
1959	5	0	0.8	0.6	11.4
1964	15	0	2.4	1.9	10.7
1966	23	0	5.0	3.8	14.1
1970	65	1	11.4	8.5	12.2
1974 (Feb.)	70	7	21.8	17.0	21.9
1974 (Oct.)	71	11	30.4	22.8	30.4

Clearly the progress of the SNP has been more spectacular than that of Plaid Cymru. The appeal of the Welsh party is to some extent a sectional one; its emphasis on the Welsh language won it support in the early days, but has been an obstacle in the way of progress in the industrial south, where the attitude of many Plaid Cymru supporters (that those who cannot speak Welsh are second-rate and could become second-class citizens) is much resented. The SNP is not burdened with a language problem. Its support is widespread and its no-nonsense appeal for separatism (as opposed to the mere devolution of power which the Welsh nationalist ask for) is easily comprehensible.⁷³ It has exploited the issue of North Sea Oil — 'Scottish oil' — with acumen. It has put Labour in Scotland on the defensive and caused a breakaway Scottish Labour Party (emphasizing Scottish socialist support for a large measure of home rule) to be formed in December 1975, with the adhesion of two of Labour's own MPs at Westminster.⁷⁴

There is still much research to be done in pinpointing the voters whom the SNP and Plaid Cymru have been able to attract. Such evidence as there is for Welsh nationalism suggests that Plaid Cymru voters are drawn equally from all classes in Wales.⁷⁵ The SNP, too, appears to have a 'cross-sectional' appeal, not based on socio-economic foundations and cutting across class divisions.⁷⁶ Neither in Wales nor in Scotland is nationalism wedded to the class structure.

A major element in the attraction of Scottish and Welsh voters to the nationalist parties has been growing and persistent dissatisfaction with government by remote control from London. This feeling is shared by people living in the north of England and the south-west.⁷⁷ In the past it was one of the planks upon which the Liberal vote rested. Between and including the general elections of 1945 and October 1974 a total of 93 Liberal MPs were returned to Westminster; 51 came from Welsh and Scottish constituencies, only 42 from English. Most of the English Liberal victories have been in seats remote from London; of the nine English seats won in February 1974, three were in Devon and Cornwall and one (Berwick) was in the far north. The Isle of Wight, which developed a peculiar inferiority complex often associated with separatist tendencies, can also be included in this category. The only seat which the Liberals captured in October 1974 was the Cornish administrative centre, Truro.

The strength of Liberalism would appear to have shifted from Scotland and Wales, which provided the majority of Liberal victories before 1974, to England. Between 1951 and October 1974 the average percentage vote per Liberal candidate fell in Scotland by about two-thirds and in Wales by about a half; in England it rose from 13 to 20 per cent. In

1974 only five Liberal MPs came from Wales and Scotland. But the English seats were still mainly on the celtic fringes of the country. The Liberal party has not been able to make much headway in capturing urban seats, particularly English urban seats held by Labour. Since 1945 the only Liberal seat to have been won from Labour unaided, and retained through more than one general election, is Rochdale, held since October 1972. Bolton West (1951–9) and Huddersfield West (1950–9) were held from Labour only because of a pact with the local Conservatives.[78] Birmingham Ladywood, won from Labour at a by-election in 1969, was lost the following year; Colne Valley, won from Labour in 1966, was also lost in 1970, though recaptured in February 1974. Where the Liberals have scored successes in English urban or suburban seats, they have been at the expense of the Conservatives, and have not been conspicuously long-lasting. Orpington, won in a spectacular by-election victory in March 1962, was lost in 1970. Cheadle, the Cheshire seat won in 1966, was also lost in 1970; substantially the same constituency, renamed Hazel Grove, was won in February 1974 but lost again in October. Sutton & Cheam, won in December 1972, was lost in February 1974 as was Ripon, won the previous July.

The performance of the Liberal party since 1945 is summarized in table 5:7.

5.7 **The Liberal vote, 1945–74**

Election	Percentage of UK poll	Percentage of UK electorate	Average percentage vote per candidate	Number of MPs Wales & Scotland	England	Total
1945	9.0	6.8	18.6	7*	5	12
1950	9.1	7.9	11.8	7	2	9
1951	2.6	2.1	14.7	4	2	6
1955	2.7	2.1	15.1	4	2	6
1959	5.9	4.6	16.9	3	3	6
1964	11.2	8.6	11.2	6	3	9
1966	8.5	6.5	8.5	6	6	12
1970	7.5	5.4	7.5	4	2	6
1974 (Feb.)	19.3	15.2	23.6	5	9	14
1974 (Oct.)	18.3	13.3	18.9	5	8	13

*Includes one Liberal MP returned for the University of Wales

The party has often done very well in by-elections and has a string of 'near-misses' to its credit. Its involvement in community politics has brought it much success in local government. But its general election performance has been disappointing. To a great extent this is the result of the first-past-the-post system, which means that the Liberal vote never realizes its potential in terms of seats. It is also a consequence of lack of concentration of its voting strength. The party prides itself on its 'classless' image, and makes a point of appealing to all sections of society. As table 5:8 shows, the tendency has been for the Liberal vote to become more evenly spread:

5.8 **Liberal party preference by class, 1964–74**
(NOP and Louis Harris)*

	AB	C1	C2	DE
		percentages		
1964	15	14	11	9
1966	11	11	8	7
1970	10	9	7	6
1974 (Feb.)	20	25	20	17
1974 (Oct.)	22	21	20	16

*NOP data from Nuffield election studies for 1964, 1966, 1970 and February 1974; Louis Harris data from Nuffield study for October 1974.

Liberal voters are also drawn fairly evenly from both sexes.[79] But, except in the remote celtic areas, where the social structure has changed less during the past 70 years and Nonconformity still has a political hold, the Liberals have no historic support upon which to build. Their support is indeed classless; over the past decade they have won votes relatively evenly from the two major parties.[80] On a rising tide the Liberal appeal is across the board. But to the extent that class acts like a reservoir, without which support for the Conservative and Labour parties would rapidly drain away, the Liberal vote does not incorporate any such holding mechanism. When it falls, both major parties gain, the party in the ascendant obtaining a proportionate advantage.[81] The image of the Liberal party is blurred so far as most electors are concerned. When polarization between the two major parties is strong, the classlessness of the Liberals is a liability; when it is weak, as in 1974, classlessness is Liberalism's greatest asset.

Support for the nationalist and Liberal parties is a further indication of the diminishing importance of class in British voting habits. The support given to other minor parties, mostly fringe groups, is in general far too small to permit the drawing of broad conclusions. Nonetheless, two of the fringe parties are worth mentioning in this context. One, the Communist party, is avowedly based on the working classes, conducts its campaigns in forthright class terms, and presumably expects class support. Yet, as table 5:9 shows, the average vote per Communist candidate in general elections has fallen almost continuously since 1945, when the party last returned MPs (two) to Westminster:

5.9 **Average Communist vote per candidate, 1945–74**

1945	4,894
1950	917
1951	2,164
1955	1,950
1959	1,717
1964	1,276
1966	1,090
1970	655
1974 (Feb.)	744
1974 (Oct.)	601

The best Communist result at any parliamentary election since 1950 was in Dunbartonshire Central in February 1974, where Jimmy Reid polled 14.6 per cent of the vote; but this was clearly a personal vote based on Reid's part in the 'work-in' following the collapse of Upper Clyde Shipyards in June 1971. The average percentage vote per Communist candidate was 1.7 per cent in February 1974 and 1.5 per cent in October; in 1945 it had been as high as 12.7 per cent, and stood at 4.4 per cent in 1951.

The fringe party which has made the biggest impact, relatively speaking, is the National Front, which emerged in 1974 as England's fourth party. The National Front was formed in 1966. The main brunt of its appeal is to the urban anti-immigrant vote and to the 'law and order' lobby, and these are by no means confined to working-class or immigrant areas. One study of its membership in a medium-sized industrial town in the north suggests that it is composed of a small middle-class and a larger working-class element; its appeal is to those alienated from both the Conservative and Labour parties.[82] This evidence of inter-class appeal is bolstered by the results of the 1974 elections. In February, National Front intervention caused a drop in the vote of Conservative, Labour and Liberal parties by about the same amount as the Front's support; in October the Front seems to have tapped a protest vote which would otherwise have gone Liberal.[83]

The average percentage vote of the National Front has dropped continuously from 3.6 per cent in 1970 to 3.1 per cent in October 1974. Yet it often does well in by-elections and has polled over 7 per cent of the vote in some constituencies at general elections.[84] It has established itself at local government level in towns such as Leicester and Blackburn where, in some wards, it is the second largest party.[85] Whether or not its fortunes are in the ascendant, such progress as it has made since 1970 is further evidence of the dwindling support for the two major parties, and of the crumbling of class alignments in British politics.

Voters who feel themselves alienated from the major parties may vote for minor ones. Even where they vote for the major parties, the criteria are likely to be secular; the support is *ad hoc*, not to be taken for granted. Voters may also vote for a candidate rather than for a party. A few years ago it was possible for one textbook to declare: 'Nearly all authorities agree that virtually no candidate, however outstanding, is worth more than 500 extra votes to his party.'[86] But even in the heyday of the two parties, 500 votes were not to be dismissed so lightly; in 1964 25 seats were won by majorities of less.[87] In February 1974 17 seats were held by less than 500 votes, and 23 in October. It is possible, moreover, that the personal following of a sitting MP may, in the long term, come to be worth as many as 2,000 votes.[88]

In an age of minority or near-minority governments, the personal vote which a candidate attracts is worth a great deal. It can be crucial in by-elections. The Liberal victories at Rochdale (October 1972) and the Isle of Ely (July 1973) were clearly due, in some measure, to the popularity and ebulliance of the Liberal candidates, respectively Cyril Smith and Clement Freud. Even in general elections, however, personal votes can make all the difference. An established MP, with a good constituency record, can expect to have built up a small personal following, worth on average about half-a-per-cent extra swing, perhaps as much as three per cent, and in some cases considerably more. A candidate who makes a dramatic personal impact, and who is prepared to work hard in the campaign, can sometimes pull off a major coup; the victories of George Reid (SNP, Stirlingshire East) and Stephen Ross (Liberal, Isle of Wight), who each increased their party's vote by a massive 23 per cent in February 1974, are clear examples.

Nor is it any longer true that 'voters vote for the ticket, not for the man or his ideas'.[89] The victories of S. O. Davies at Merthyr in 1970, Dick Traverne at Lincoln in March 1973 and February 1974, and Edward Milne at Blyth in February 1974, show that the personal followings of MPs can turn safe Labour seats into marginals, and have long term consequences. In the May 1976 District Council elections, Milne's Independent Labour Party in Blyth Valley won 11 seats, reducing the official Labour majority over all other parties to only three; at a by-election the following month, Milne's party deprived Labour of its overall majority on the district council. In Lincoln, Taverne's Democratic Labour Association retained control in the May 1976 elections; it and the Conservative party emerged as the only parties represented on the council.

A combination of strong personalities and local issues can, therefore, have a major impact. Like support for third parties, it reflects the weakening of class alignments and helps explain the fall in support for the two major parties. Between 1950 and 1966 there were rarely any 'maverick' general election results. Parliaments were composed of

Conservative and Labour MPs, with just a splash of Liberal colour. The fragmentation of Northern Irish politics in the late 1960s has resulted in the disappearance of the Conservative-allied Ulster MPs. But in 1974 more minor-party and independent MPs came from Great Britain than from Northern Ireland. Even supposing that the 12 Northern Irish MPs had all been allies of the Conservative party in February 1974, that general election result would still have been indecisive.

Two further developments in voting habits deserve consideration. The first is what might be called 'the ethnic dimension'. The second is the phenomenon of abstention.

The intense Labour proclivities of Irish immigrants have already been noted. According to the 1971 census, 1.3 per cent of the population of Great Britain was born in the Irish Republic. Most of these immigrants are to be found in the lowest occupational grades, as are most of those British citizens with Irish-born fathers. The Irish vote is therefore disproportionately anti-Conservative.[90] In October 1974 the 14 London constituencies with over 5 per cent Irish population polled an average Labour vote of 51.4 per cent, considerably higher than the Greater London average of 43.8 per cent. The five Birmingham seats with over 5 per cent Irish population returned an average Labour vote of 58.1 per cent, compared with the Labour vote, in Birmingham as a whole, of 49.8 per cent.

Another easily identifiable ethnic group are the Jews, of whom there were, in 1974, about 408,000, giving a Jewish electorate of about 300,000.[91] The Jewish vote would only be of interest to Jews, were it not for the fact that the British branch of the seed of Abraham is notoriously urban-dwelling, and its voting power highly concentrated. Over half Anglo-Jewry lives in London; nearly three-quarters of the remainder live in Manchester, Leeds, Glasgow, Brighton, Liverpool, Birmingham and Southend. Within London some boroughs (Barnet, Brent, Hackney, Redbridge, Tower Hamlets and Westminster) have Jewish concentrations over 20,000, and the political power of the Jews in the constituencies concerned is potentially considerable. Historically, as a 'dissenter' group, the Jews allied themselves with the Liberal party. Later, particularly as socialist-inspired immigrants arrived from Russia and Poland, and with the fascist threat as a constant companion, the Jews supported Labour. Since 1945, disillusionment with Labour policies towards Israel, and the inevitable move from the city-centres to the suburbs, have eroded Jewish support for the Labour party.

The residual effect of strong Labour roots can be seen in the breakdown of Jewish voting patterns in the Barnet constituency of Hendon North, where Jewish support for the Conservative candidate in the 1974 elections averaged 44 per cent, much less than the London & Southeast regional pattern of party preferences for comparable social classes (AB and C1) as given by Butler & Stokes, though, it must be said, much more than the percentage of Jewish support forthcoming for the Labour or Liberal candidates. There are Jewish areas of London which are solidly Labour (the historic 'East End'), but they are not, in the main, areas of expanding or young Jewish populations. It is safe to say that Jewish Labour voters, at least in London, are becoming fewer in relation to Jewish Liberals and Conservatives.

It is undeniable that Jewish electors are prepared to use their votes to support candidates with Jewish sympathies (primarily over Israel) and to punish those whose views are suspect. In Hendon North in 1974 the Conservative MP was able to save his increasingly-marginal seat by appealing specifically to Jewish voters on the Middle East issue. Elsewhere, both in London and the provinces, Jewish voters were assiduously wooed. In October 1974 Labour snatched Ilford North (Redbridge) from the Conservatives by a 778-vote majority in a campaign which revolved largely around persuading Jewish voters that the interests of Israel and of Soviet Jewry were better served by having a Jewish Labour MP at Westminster; Ilford North was the only London seat to change hands at that election. Now that such a fluid political situation exists in Great Britain, the Jewish vote is a minor but obviously not insignificant fact of political life.[92]

The ethnic group whose voting habits have aroused most interest are the coloured voters, the 'New Commonwealth' immigrants and their British-born children. Estimates of the number of New Commonwealth immigrants are difficult to arrive at and are the subject of some controversy. The 1971 census put the number of New Commonwealth-born at 1,140,000, or 2.1 per cent of the population. How many of these are registered electors is, however, open to doubt.[93] It seems reasonable to assume that the number of registered coloured voters (New Commonwealth-born plus their British-born children who have come of age) is in the region of 800,000. What is less doubtful is that they are overwhelmingly Labour supporters. Coloured immigrants are largely working-class. Most of them come from countries in which the British Conservative party is regarded as the embodiment of imperialism. When they arrive here they find that those most vociferous in their demands for a halt to coloured immigration, and for voluntary repatriation, are Conservatives, or ex-Conservatives like Enoch Powell.

The findings of the Harris Poll show that in the second half of 1970 69 per cent of coloured voters supported Labour. The Community Relations Commission found that as much as 81 per cent of the coloured vote went to Labour in the October 1974 election.[94] Like the Jews, the coloured voters are heavily concentrated in urban areas. In 1974 there were 59 seats which at both elections returned MPs with majorities smaller than the number of people in them born in the New Commonwealth; all 59 were urban constituencies and 29 were in London. Thirteen of the seats, held by the Conservative party in February, were won by Labour in October. This led the Community Relations Commission to conclude that 'without the minorities' support Labour would not have won more seats than the Conservatives in February 1974, and would not have won an overall majority in October 1974'. Such a conclusion is a little far-fetched. In one of the 13 seats, Ilford North, the Jewish vote was more significant than the coloured. Three of the remaining 12 had Labour majorities in October of less than 500 and four had majorities of between 500 and 1,000.

In seats as marginal as that, any number of factors, demographic as much as anything else, could account for the change in party support.

Moreover, although most coloured voters vote Labour, not all do so. In October 1974 9 per cent supported the Conservatives, and 10 per cent the Liberals. What can be said is that in certain urban constituencies the coloured vote, being so predominantly Labour, is a most important element in Labour's support, one it alienates at its peril.[95] This has not delivered the Labour party into the hands of coloured voters. But it has given coloured electors, as their spokesmen point out, a powerful political lever.[96]

So far this discussion has concentrated upon ways in which different groups of electors vote. Finally, it may be asked, what of those electors who do not vote? As has been argued in chapter four, the decision not to vote is as legitimate as the decision to cast a vote. Rational abstention can play an important part in determining individual constituency results. The British Election Study has isolated two groups of non-voters: those whose sense of partisanship is weak, who are more likely to be regular abstainers, and who are inclined to favour Labour; and those with a stronger sense of partisanship, who are likely to miss only an occasional election, who can more easily be persuaded to vote, and who are usually Conservative. Contrary to popular mythology, therefore, it is the Conservative party, rather than Labour, which has most to gain from a high turnout because, of those who are potential non-voters, and who can be persuaded to vote, a higher proportion are likely to be Conservative supporters.[97]

The emphasis which the Conservative party places upon the smoothness of its electoral machine is therefore not misplaced. Butler & Stokes calculate that between 1959 and 1964 differential turnout helped Labour to the extent of almost a fifth of its lead of 4.3 per cent; between 1964 and 1966 differential turnout contributed over a third of the net change in Labour's lead of 4.4 per cent; in 1970, by contrast, it helped the Conservatives by contributing over two-fifths of the Conservative lead of 6.5 per cent over Labour.[98]

Rational abstention is at its most potent for those voters who have previously been solid supporters of one party or another. The defeat of Dr. David Pitt at Clapham was undoubtedly due to the abstention of about 4,500 Labour supporters who would probably have voted for a white Labour candidate. It is possible that the unusually high 7.5 per cent swing to Labour in the west midland conurbations in February 1974 was party the result of a decision by Conservative anti-Common Marketeers to abstain rather than vote Conservative or follow Enoch Powell's advice and vote Labour.[99]

As a group the non-voters are growing in size. Between 1945 and 1964 they averaged 21.4 per cent of the electorate. Between 1964 and 1974 they averaged 25.2 per cent. That over a quarter of the electorate do not vote is important. That about half to two-thirds of these (over five million electors) deliberately choose not to do so is significant. At the very least it suggests that disenchantment with the entire electoral process, and with the political parties who run it, is growing. Paradoxically, these rational abstainers, by deliberately turning their backs on the election, help materially to decide its outcome.

Chapter Six

CONCLUSION

Unrepresentative democracy

Elections are complex social as well as political processes. Even the act of voting in the polling booth, the ultimate choice between competing teams of politicians, is replete with social implications. The ballot paper is a means by which politicians and their voting publics conduct a dialogue. Voting reinforces belief in the reality of political participation, and this helps underpin the citizen's belief in the legitimacy of the governmental system and allegiance to it. Conversely, non-voting is a repudiation, not merely of the party-political establishment, but of the constitutional framework within which the politicians operate.

It was the mistake of nineteenth-century reformers to have supposed that representative legislative institutions must necessarily result in democratic government. The electorate is not a body of shareholders meeting to pass judgment on the board of directors; it is a collective noun, nothing more. Electors do not reach joint decisions. Rather, it is the system of indirect representation of the electors which gives the illusion of electoral decision-making. And there is no doubt that the system of representation is itself at fault. It distorts the individual opinions of the electorate to such an extent that they are no longer recognizable. Universal suffrage is far from being achieved in practice. The issues in the election campaigns are often forced upon the electors by the politicians, and issues which electors regard as important are ignored. The campaign is, in any case, far less important in determining the outcome of the election than most politicians (and not a few voters) would like to admit. Its main function is to provide both with the illusion of participation – an important role but one which is totally unconnected with the theory or practice of British representative government. The number of voters who actually choose MPs is exceedingly small, and hardly a cross-section of electoral opinion.

A system of proportional representation would only cure some of these ailments. It would ensure that the composition of the House of Commons reflected much more accurately the preferences of the electorate as between the politicians who present themselves for election. It would not, in the last resort, prevent parliament from legislating contrary to the wishes of the people; it would make such an occurence more unlikely but it would not prevent it absolutely. The beauty of proportional representation is that, in a British context, it would deny in perpetuity the giving of legislative power to any one political group representing only a minority of electors. It would not prevent different political groups from compromising to agree on a set of measures for the government of the country. It would, indeed, encourage such a mechanism, for that would be the only way parliament's business could be carried on. In general this would be to the good. Nor would any reasonable observer deny that, in an emergency situation, measures might have to be taken which had not been submitted, for its prior approval, to the electorate. Winston Churchill's dictum that 'the responsibility of ministers for the public safety is absolute and requires no mandate', remains as true today as when it was first uttered in November 1935.[1] Yet, even under a system of proportional representation, there would be nothing in the system itself to prevent politicians from agreeing to measures which had nothing to do with the public safety, or a national emergency, but which had never been placed before the voters. Proportional representation, in short, would do much to make the House of Commons more representative. It would not prevent undemocratic or arbitrary rule.

Do such evils as undemocratic or arbitrary rule really

exist in Great Britain? The answer is twofold. Firstly, there are many measures passed by parliament, unconnected with emergency situations, which have never been approved by the voters: the abolition of capital punishment (1965); British entry into the Common Market (1972); the permission given to employers to disregard contractual salary arrangements which ran counter to the government's incomes policy (1975) – to name but a few. Secondly, the opportunities which the present electoral system give for arbitrary rule, even if seldom exploited, exist nonetheless and must remain a temptation for the ambitious and the unscrupulous elements too often to be found in public life.

That there is growing public disillusionment with representative democracy in this country is beyond doubt. A number of surveys have shown that, among ordinary voters, there is a widespread feeling of political impotence and a low opinion of politicians and of parliament.[2] A majority of voters do not feel that elections force governments to pay attention to what the people think. Hence, no doubt, the increasing resort to pressure groups, protest groups and 'direct action'. Hence, too, the use of by-elections and especially local elections to voice disapproval of government policies. It is a pity that local elections are too often fought on national issues. But politicians who explain away adverse local election results in terms of dissatisfaction with central government should reflect on why a supposedly democratic system has such consequences. At any given moment, the results of a by-election, or a trend in a set of local election results, may in fact be a better test of the state of public opinion than a general election. The loss of Orpington to the Liberals in 1962 reflected real and widespread dissatisfaction with the Conservative government. The defeat of Labour in the Greater London Council elections of 1967, giving control of London government to the Conservatives for the first time since 1931, was startling evidence of public rejection of Harold Wilson's government. Local government elections and by-elections are certainly no less significant than general elections as barometers of the national mood.

Some of the issues raised here are clearly beyond the scope of the present work. There is a body of opinion which, recognizing that parliament could be no less arbitrary for being elected, favours the adoption of a constitution, or 'Bill of Rights', which it might be beyond the authority of parliament, by itself, to alter.[3] This constitution might embody certain fundamental liberties, and would be capable of amendment only by a deliberately complicated and time-consuming process, perhaps involving ratification of amendments by majorities (possibly two-thirds majorities) of both houses of parliament and by a popular referendum. Guardianship of the constitution might be delegated to a new court of law (a 'supreme court') or to the House of Lords.

Some favour the reform of the upper house itself. The House of Lords retains, under the 1911 Parliament Act, its complete power of veto over any bill passed by the House of Commons to extend the life of parliament beyond the maximum five-year period between general elections. At present the presence of a hereditary element in the House of Lords is a deterrent against giving the upper house greater powers as a revising chamber. Clearly, an upper house from which the hereditary peers were removed, but the members of which were appointed solely by the political parties, would offer far too much in the way of patronage to the politicians; it was largely because of opposition on all sides to the proposed extension of patronage in this way that Harold Wilson was forced to abandon his proposed reform of the House of Lords in 1969.

Other ways might be found of appointing the members of the second chamber, perhaps by a wide variety of pressure groups and consumers' organizations; or the members could be elected on a territorial basis, as with the Senate of the United States of America. If devolution of power to Scotland and Wales proceeds to the extent of creating a federal system in the United Kingdom, an upper house elected in this way might become a distinct possibility. Even as at present constituted, the House of Lords has sometimes shown itself to be more responsive to national feeling than the House of Commons: it rejected the abolition of the death penalty in 1948 and 1956, and it rejected the Southern Rhodesia (United Nations Sanctions) Order in 1968.[4]

Many countries of the free world (such as Canada, Australia and the United States) use a second chamber as a way of stabilizing their democratic structures. But if such a chamber is not to be the poor relation within the legislative system its powers need to be considerable. And if they are considerable, the likelihood of a head-on collision between the two legislative houses increases. This happened in Australia in 1975, when the refusal of the Senate (controlled by the Liberal & Country coalition) to pass the financial legislation of the Labour federal government led the Governor-General, Sir John Kerr, to dismiss the Labour government and call a general election. That the Liberal & Country coalition won the election was regarded by its supporters as a vindication of the Governor-General's action. But the crisis was profound and has left a legacy of bitterness and recrimination.

Referendums
An alternative way of ensuring greater responsiveness to the wishes of the voters is to consult them directly on specific issues. Local referendums have been in use in Britain for over a century.[5] The Public Libraries Act of 1850 allowed ratepayers in England and Wales to decide whether free public libraries were to be established instead of or in addition to local museums; in 1853 the act was extended to Scotland and Ireland. Some aspects of the regulation of public houses in Wales and Scotland are decided by local polls. The 1932 Sunday Entertainments Act (until its replacement 40 years later) allowed local referendums on whether cinemas should be open on Sundays. From time to time local authorities have held referendums on a variety of subjects – comprehensive schools, for instance, and the sale of municipal undertakings.

The first use of a referendum for a national issue was on 8 March 1973 when, under the provisions of the Northern

Ireland (Border Poll) Act of the previous year, a referendum was held among Northern Irish electors to decide whether they wished Northern Ireland to remain part of the United Kingdom or be joined with the Republic of Ireland. In a 61 per cent poll, 591,820 votes were cast for the first alternative, and only 6,463 for the second. The Catholic minority largely abstained. Still, a vote of 55 per cent of the Northern Irish electorate in favour of continued union with Great Britain was convincing and decisive. The outcome was of course a foregone conclusion. The Conservative government at Westminster did not really need to consult the people of the province in this very formal manner to find out their views. The purpose of the referendum was to take the Border issue out of politics: in Northern Ireland, by demonstrating to the republicans that their views were not the views of the majority; and in relations with the Republic of Ireland, by being able to argue convincingly with southern Irish leaders that talk of the unification of Ireland was unrealistic, if not actually undemocratic. The referendum was held primarily to make life easier for the politicians.

This did not and does not detract from its worth. But it is a signpost to the limitations of a referendum as a means of consulting the people. The answer to any question depends to some extent upon the way it is asked. Who is to decide upon what issues referendums will be held? And in what manner will the result of a referendum be binding upon the government? All these problems were evident in the history of the first nationwide referendum in the United Kingdom, to decide on membership of the European Economic Community.

The Common Market referendum was a device adopted by Harold Wilson's Cabinet to prevent the break-up of the Labour party and the probable downfall of the government.[6] Both the Conservative (1961–3) and Labour (1967) governments had applied for membership of the European Economic Community, but had fallen foul of President de Gaulle's veto. The Labour party was deeply divided on the issue, the left wing and the trade union movement being in general very hostile to Common Market membership. The

Conservative party was less divided; a small section of the parliament party opposed membership, but most Conservative MPs supported it. In 1971 Edward Heath's government successfully negotiated entry, and in July 1972 the House of Commons passed the necessary legislation, the European Communities Act, by 301 votes to 284. Official Labour policy was that the terms of entry were not good enough and needed to be re-negotiated. But Wilson, no less than Heath, rejected the idea of a referendum on the issue.

During 1972 the hostile attitude of the bulk of the Labour party towards Common Market membership became more pronounced. Yet its attitude towards a referendum grew warmer. Some leading members of the party, including Harold Wilson, Roy Jenkins, Harold Lever and Shirley Williams, were avowed pro-Marketeers. Others, including Tony Wedgwood Benn, Michael Foot and Peter Shore, were vociferous anti-Marketeers. The idea of renegotiation followed by referendum became more attractive as a way of keeping the party together. For if the party was divided over the merits of the Common Market it could at least agree to abide by a referendum result. So it was that in February 1974 the Labour Manifesto promised 'a General Election or a Consultative Referendum' on the renegotiated terms.

Renegotiation was completed in March 1975. By then the Labour government had already committed itself to a referendum. The necessary legislation received the Royal Assent on 8 May. The referendum was held, at a cost of over £11 million, on 5 June. Electors were asked to vote 'Yes' or 'No' to the question 'Do you think that the United Kingdom should stay in the European Community (the Common Market)?' The results are set out in table 6:1.

6.1 **The Common Market referendum**

Total Electorate:	40,456,877
Total Voting	25,903,194
Spoilt Papers	54,540
'No' Vote	8,470,073
'Yes' Vote	17,378,581

Although a clear majority (67.1 per cent) of those voting was in favour of continuing membership of the Common Market, these voters represented a minority (42.9 per cent) of the entire electorate. Pro-Marketeers argued that this hardly mattered because those voting 'No' amounted to less than 21 per cent of the electorate. But it would be quite wrong to conclude, because of the low turnout (64.0 per cent) that over a third of the electorate could not have cared less about the issue. Many people felt – rightly – that by holding a referendum the politicians were dodging an issue which cut across party lines. During the passage of the referendum legislation there was some public discussion about the desirability of adding a third alternative on the ballot paper, to give voters an opportunity to say whether they wished the issue to be left to parliament to decide; a number of pro-Market Conservative MPs supported this idea, knowing that a majority in favour of Common Market membership would be forthcoming in the Commons but that the Labour party would be formally split in the process. The government naturally opposed the suggestion and it never materialized.

Clearly the wording no less than the timing of the referendum was crucial. Given the choice of *staying in* the Common Market, or pulling out, most of those voting chose to stay in. Suppose the referendum had been held before renegotiation, or even before entry, or that the wording had been different. Suppose the ballot paper had asked voters, not whether they wished to *stay in*, but whether they wished to *join* the Market. The result might have been very different. Before referendum day every household received, at the government's expense, three leaflets: one, *Why you should vote No*, produced by the National Referendum Campaign; one, *Why you should vote Yes*, produced by Britain in Europe; and a third, *Britain's New Deal in Europe*, produced by the Labour government and recommending the British people to vote for staying in the Common Market. The inclusion of a leaflet giving the government's recommendation was a subject of much controversy; it meant that voters received two 'Yes' leaflets and only one 'No' leaflet. A survey conducted by NOP in February 1975 found that if the ballot-paper wording had asked voters whether they accepted a government recommendation to *come out* of the Common Market, there would have been a 0.2 per cent majority, of those voting, in favour of this recommendation, as opposed to an 18.2 per cent majority for staying in, had the wording referred to a government recommendation to retain Market membership.[7]

Had Edward Heath held a referendum on membership in, say, 1971, before Britain joined the European Economic Community, he might have obtained a 'Yes' majority, but it would probably not have been as large as Harold Wilson obtained. On the other hand, had he called a general election on the issue he would probably have won handsomely, because general elections are rarely decided on one issue alone, and in any case the Labour party would have found itself in hopeless disarray. Harold Wilson chose to hold a 'consultative referendum'. In fact he made it clear that the government would abide by the verdict of a simple majority of those voting; in this sense the government regarded the referendum as 'binding'.[8] But had the verdict gone against Common Market membership, parliament would not have been bound in any way whatsoever. The government might have resigned, or fallen apart. British membership of the Community would have continued, at least until such time as a general election resulted in the return of a majority of anti-Market MPs. In fact great pains were taken to save MPs from the embarrassment of knowing that their constituents did not agree with their Common Market views. Although voting arrangements were similar to those for a general election, the counting of votes was by counties, not constituencies; this arrangement was passed in the Commons by a combination of 128 Labour MPs, 117 Conservatives, 12 Liberals and 15 nationalists, against 112 Labour MPs and 43 Conservatives.[9] The referendum result was a defeat for the Ulster Unionists, the SNP and Plaid Cymru, which all opposed Common Market membership. But the position of these parties in Northern Ireland, Scotland and Wales was hardly affected by the outcome.

As a public relations exercise the Common Market Referendum was a success. Its result did not bind parliament. But it was a participatory drama on a grand scale. The mechanics worked extraordinarily smoothly. It has whetted people's appetites for more referendums, on Scottish and Welsh devolution, for instance, and on capital punishment. Most western European states have provision for constitutional referendums. In Switzerland 50,000 electors may initiate legislation by calling it a constitutional amendment. In some individual states of the United States of America, voters may initiate legislation, or suspend legislation already passed by the legislature, by signing a petition. Such rights, especially when coupled with binding referendums, give real power to the voters. A consultative referendum, called at the behest of the politicians, and which cannot bind the legislators, is a poor alternative and one of limited value.

In any case, referendums are expensive. They are not a substitute for day-to-day parliamentary government. General elections are also expensive. Economic considerations would seem to rule out for the foreseeable future the realization of the only unfulfilled Chartist demand, for annual parliaments. At the same time, whatever mandate a government might claim when elected to office, it has no right to continue to claim three or four years later, when the opinions of the electorate, and indeed when the composition of the electorate, could be very different. The House of Commons ought to refer itself more frequently to the judgment of the electors and not, moreover, at times which suit the government of the day. Even if proportional representation is not adopted there seems to be a case either for shortening the maximum period between general elections, or for having fixed-period elections, say every four years, no sooner and no later.

A third possibility might be to elect a proportion of the House of Commons every year. The 635 MPs could be elected in batches of 127 every year, so that each one would face the electorate not less than once every five years. The constituencies to have an election in any one year would be in widely scattered parts of the country. The continual year-in year-out electioneering atmosphere would keep the MPs and political parties on their toes, ever watchful of the mood of the electorate and attentive to its wishes. An unpopular government would not be able to continue governing until the next general election, as at present; the re-election of one-fifth of the Commons every year would ensure that within two or three years the majority of such a government would disappear. Such a system would be more expensive than one election every four or five years, but less expensive than referendums or (as in 1974) two general elections in nine months followed by a referendum eight months later. Such a scheme would not, of course, be popular with the politicians. Like proportional representation, it gives more power to individual electors than most people in political life are willing to contemplate, let alone concede.

Do elections matter?
Herein lies a central difficulty surrounding the concept of British parliamentary democracy. It is the author's passionate belief that, given democratic rights, the overwhelming majority of people will exercise them responsibly. But the masses are as unloved and as distrusted today as they were a hundred years ago. The democratic principle must imply that governments exist to give voters what they, the voters, want, not what governments (however well intentioned) think they ought to have. This principle is not widely shared by those in positions of influence and authority.

In 1947 the Conservative politician and former minister Leo Amery categorically rejected the idea of 'political power as a delegation from the individual citizen through the legislature to an executive dependent on that legislature' as 'a weak and unstable' system of government.[10] What Amery wanted was strong, responsible government, not a constitution 'in which the active and originating element' was the voter. Two decades later Professor Bernard Crick, a member of the Fabian Society and a leading Labour theorist, wrote: 'the phrase "Parliamentary control" . . . should not mislead anyone into asking for a situation in which governments can have their legislation changed or defeated, or their life terminated (except in the most desperate emergency . . .). Control means *influence,* not direct power; *advice,* not command.'[11] The late Richard Crossman, when editor of the *New Statesman* in August 1970, argued 'Better the liberal elitism of the statue book than the reactionary populism of the market place'.[12] And, more recently, the former Conservative Cabinet Minister Lord Eccles has declared 'You cannot get policy made by people who are always looking over their shoulders to see what the people they represent would think'.[13]

Before 1974, in fact, the most the electorate could do was to pass post-mortem verdicts on what governments, backed by generally reliable parliamentary majorities, had already done. The experience of a minority government in 1974, and of near or actual minority government since then, has altered this picture. But it would be wrong to suppose that more frequent elections, or a system of proportional representation, or both, would by themselves give power to the voting public. As long as the myth of the mandate persists, and as long as manifestos contain detailed proposals rather than broad principles only, the manner in which politicians choose to interpret election results will continue to be essentially dishonest; claims of electoral support for measures proposed will continue to be made, even though this hardly conforms with the lack of attention paid by the electorate to the manifesto proposals themselves.

In this process the electorate is not entirely without blame. Over 200 years ago Rousseau pointed out:

> The people of England regards itself as free; but it is grossly mistaken; it is free only during the election of members of parliament. As soon as they are elected, slavery overtakes it, and it is nothing. The use it makes of the short moments of liberty it enjoys shows indeed that it deserves to lose them.[14]

The final sentence is not quoted as frequently as the first two, but its application to modern experience is just as relevant. Far too many voters pay too much attention to party images – images perhaps formed 30 or 40 years ago – and not enough to party policies. Present evidence suggests that more voters are thinking hard before they vote, switching parties, voting tactically, breaking out of old habits, being alert.[15] But Lord Bryce's vision of the 'average man' as 'the man of broad common sense . . . forming a fair unprejudiced judgment on every question' is as far from being realized today as it was half a century ago.[16] If voters find themselves burdened with unresponsive governments, in part at least they have only themselves to thank.

It is possible that a different electoral system would induce voters to think more about how to use their vote. But it would not by itself guarantee a lessening of political apathy. Nor would it lead to the election of a legislature whose composition more faithfully reflected the electorate as a whole. In terms of social class and occupational grade the House of Commons is an elite cutting across party lines. Table 6:2 shows the occupations of Labour and Conservative MPs returned in the general elections of 1951, 1964 and October 1974:

6.2 **Occupations of MPs, 1951, 1964 and October 1974**
(percentages)*

	Labour 1951	1964	October 1974
Professional	35	41	49
Business	9	11	8
Workers	37	32	28
Miscellaneous	19	16	15
	100	100	100
	Conservative		
Professional	41	48	46
Business	37	26	33
Workers	—	1	1
Miscellaneous	22	25	20
	100	100	100

*Based on figures in Butler & Sloman, *British Political Facts*, p.155.

The tendency has been for the professional classes to predominate, and for this predominance to grow at the expense both of manual workers and of the business classes. The public school element in the two major parties has decreased only marginally, and the proportion with a university education has increased (see table 6:3).

6.3 **Educational background of MPs, 1951, 1964 and October 1974**
(percentages)*

	Conservative Public School	University	Labour Public School	University
1951	75	65	23	41
1964	75	63	18	46
1974 (Oct.)	75	69	18	57

*Based on figures in Butler & Sloman, *British Political Facts*, p.155.

The House of Commons is, therefore, composed to a great extent of university-educated and, one ought to add, middle-aged males in the professional and business classes. The number of women MPs elected at a general election has never exceeded 28 (in 1964). The median age of Labour MPs has fallen from 52, in 1951, to 49 in October 1974; that of Conservative MPs has remained at about 47. The manual working classes, who form over 50 per cent of the population, are grossly under-represented in the Commons, as they are in the higher civil service.[17] It may of course be true that the 'political class' to be found in parliament is in fact best fitted to carry out the duties required of it; that solicitors, barristers, teachers, professional administrators, bankers and accountants between them provide a useful pool of parliamentary talent, and just the sort of expertise necessary to quiz ministers and grapple with a wide range of constituency problems. It may, indeed, be wrong even to suppose that the House of Commons *should* be a mirror of the nation in any respect – age, sex, social class, religion, or any other – except that of political views. But it is right to stress that the elite to be found in political leadership in the United Kingdom is one element of a wider elite, embracing the civil service, the professions, the leaders of commerce and industry, the media, and that such elitism is not likely to be put at risk by the adoption of a different method of electoral choice.

Finally it is worth remembering that British elections only elect legislatures. And while the House of Commons is the supreme law-making body in the United Kingdom, it is not the ultimate seat of *power*, and never has been. Bagehot tried to argue that effective power in mid-Victorian England had passed from the monarch to the Cabinet, 'a board of control chosen by the legislature, out of persons whom it trusts and knows, to rule the nation'.[18] There are no chapters in Bagehot on pressure groups, trade unions or employers' associations; there is no hint that the civil servants in Whitehall, by the advice they give to ministers, and by the information they withhold, may wield a great deal of power; there is no examination of the interaction between economic interest and legislative authority, though the history of railway regulation, factory legislation, or the abolition of slavery and the slave trade ought to have told Bagehot that wealth meant, if not power, at least a great deal of influence, and that the industrial producers, in and out of parliament, were a formidable bloc with whom only the most determined of Cabinets dared do battle.

To say that is not to embrace the Marxist interpretation, that ultimate power lies with those who *own* the means of production. But in a modern industrial society, as Great Britain is, heavily dependent on earning its keep through its manufacturing capacity and its technological expertise, the power of the producer groups is great indeed. A decision to build a factory, or not to build it, to invest capital or not to invest, to call a strike or not to call one, can affect the fortunes of the nation more directly and more rapidly than a piece of legislation which may take months to pass through parliament and even longer to put into effect. Even had Edward Heath been returned to power in February 1974 with a doubled majority, that would not have made one miner go below ground to dig one piece of coal. In that sense the election really was phoney, and by rejecting Heath the electorate at least demonstrated by its collective will that it realized a basic fact of modern political life. The budget which the Labour government presented in 1976, making proposed tax concessions dependent on trade-union agreement to an incomes policy limiting wage increases to 4½ per cent in the coming year, was not a lowering of parliament's stature, but a recognition that parliament is not all-powerful.

The corporative state has arrived. Power lies with the big economic battalions. What the Trades Union Congress wants, or what the Confederation of British Industry thinks, or what the Whitehall economists feel is right, is as relevant to the nation's welfare as the outcome of any general election. This does not mean that elections are not important. It means, rather, that elections are no longer about 'who governs', but about who chairs the meetings at which those with power and authority try to reach agreement. The fate of many meetings and many inquiries has been decided by the initial choice of chairman. In that sense elections are more important now than at the close of the second world war. To improve upon their ritualistic and representative functions is as necessary to the preservation of democracy, and hence of liberty, as is participation in them.

NOTES

Notes to Chapter One

1. P. G. J. Pulzer, *Political Representation and Elections in Britain*, 3rd edition, Allen & Unwin, 1975, p.17.
2. For the social acceptability of corruption, see J. Vincent, *Pollbooks: How Victorians Voted*, Cambridge University Press, 1967, p.10.
3. C. Hill, *The Century of Revolution 1603–1714*, Nelson, Edinburgh, 1961, p.276.
4. Sir L. Namier, *England in the Age of the American Revolution*, 2nd edition, Macmillan, 1961, p.25.
5. E. Burke, *Works*, vol. III, Thomas M'Lean, London, 1823, p.20.
6. Quoted in J. B. Owen, *The Eighteenth Century 1714–1815*, Nelson, London, 1974, p.291.
7. *The Times*, 28 July 1976, p.2; 11 August, p.13. My italics.
8. G. Alderman, *The Railway Interest*, Leicester University Press, 1973, p.12.
9. E. N. Williams, *The Eighteenth-Century Constitution 1688–1815*, Cambridge University Press, 1960, p.128.
10. Quoted in N. Gash, *Politics in the Age of Peel*, Longmans, 1953, p.17.
11. ibid., pp.24, 75.
12. H. J. Hanham, *The Reformed Electoral System in Great Britain, 1832–1914*, Historical Association, London, 1968, p.35.
13. A. H. Birch, *Representative and Responsible Government*, Allen & Unwin, 1964, p.51.
14. A. Beattie, ed. *English Party Politics*, vol. I, Weidenfeld, 1970. pp.94–5.
15. D. Beales, *From Castlereagh to Gladstone 1815–1885*, Nelson, London, 1969, p.119.
16. J. S. Mill, *The Admission of Women to the Electoral Franchise*, London, 1867.
17. J. S. Mill, *Considerations on Representative Government*, London, 1861, Chapter viii.

18 ibid., chapter vii.
19 Beales, op. cit., pp.202–4.
20 ibid., p.244.
21 H. J. Hanham, *Elections and Party Management: Politics in the time of Disraeli and Gladstone*, Longmans, 1959, pp.12–14.
22 L. M. Helmore, *Corrupt and Illegal Practices*, Routledge, 1967, passim.
23 D. Butler & A. Sloman, *British Political Facts 1900–1975*, 4th edition, Macmillan, 1975, p.200.
24 M. Ostrogorski, *Democracy and the Organization of Political Parties*, trs. F. Clarke, vol. I, Macmillan, 1902, p.584.
25 ibid., p.586.
26 ibid., p.588.
27 W. C. Costin & J. S. Watson, *The Law and Working of the Constitution*, vol. II, A. & C. Black, London, 1964, p.326.
28 S. H. Beer, *Modern British Politics*, 2nd edition, Faber, 1969, p.120.
29 Quoted in ibid., p.118.
30 D. E. Butler, *The Electoral System in Britain 1918–1951*, Oxford University Press, 1953, pp.6–7. [Cited hereafter as Butler, *The Electoral System*.]
31 ibid., pp.7–10; R. L. Leonard, *Elections in Britain*, Van Nostrand, London, 1968, p.18.
32 D. Butler & M. Pinto-Duschinsky, *The British General Election of 1970*, Macmillan, 1971, p.263.
33 F. W. S. Craig, *British Electoral Facts 1885–1975*, Macmillan, 1976, p.104.
34 The phrase is Pulzer's, op. cit., p.180.
35 D. E. Butler & R. Rose, *The British General Election of 1959*, Macmillan, 1960, p.40.
36 F. Stacey, *The Government of Modern Britain*, Oxford University Press, 1968, p.248.
37 Professor Richard Rose. *The Problem of Party Government*, Macmillan, 1974, p.411, has identified four issues upon which Mr. Heath's government acted contrary to its 1970 election pledges (nationalization, government spending, admission of immigrants and abolition of the Stormont government in Northern Ireland), and three issues upon which the previous Labour government acted in a like manner (the maintenance of a free health service, housing, and the Common Market).
38 M. Benney, A. P. Gray & R. H. Pear, *How People Vote*, Routledge, 1956, pp.140–141.
39 J. Blondel, *Voters, Parties and Leaders*, Penguin, Harmondsworth, 1976, pp.73–8.

40 R. Rose, *Influencing Voters A Study of Campaign Rationality*, Faber, 1967, also does not deal with manifestos or mention the word in his index.
41 D. Butler & D. Stokes, *Political Change in Britain*, 2nd edition, Macmillan, 1974, pp.370–4.
42 On this point see R. H. S. Crossman, *The Politics of Pensions*, Liverpool University Press, 1972, p.24.
43 D. Butler & D. Kavanagh, *The British General Election of February 1974*, Macmillan, 1974, p.48. [Cited hereafter as Butler & Kavanagh, *February 1974*.]
44 D. Butler & D. Kavanagh, *The British General Election of October 1974*, Macmillan, 1975, pp.55–60. [Cited hereafter as Butler & Kavanagh, *October 1974*.]
45 The figure is taken from Butler & Stokes, op. cit., p.22; the percentage of those subscribing to a local party dropped from 14 per cent in 1964 to 10 per cent in 1970.
46 It is true that in 1945 the Labour manifesto warned: 'We give clear notice that we will not tolerate obstruction of the people's will by the House of Lords'. This was not a pledge to pass a Parliament Act, and no details of such a measure were included in the manifesto. On the subject of the European Economic Community, the 1970 Conservative manifesto said: 'Our sole commitment is to negotiate; no more, no less'.
47 Quoted in H. J. Hanham, ed., *The Nineteenth-Century Constitution 1815–1914*, Cambridge University Press, 1969, p.147.
48 The resolution which the Lords passed on 30 November 1909 read: 'That this House is not justified in giving its consent to this Bill [the budget] until it has been submitted to the judgment of the country': *House of Lords Journals*, 1909, p.453.
49 *SNP & You Aims & Policy of the Scottish National Party*, 4th edition, Edinburgh, 1974, p.4.
50 The relationship between votes and seats is sometimes expressed in terms of the 'cubic law', which states that if votes are cast in the proportion A:B, seats will be won in the proportion $A^3:B^3$. The veracity of this 'law' depends, *inter alia*, on the accuracy of constituency boundaries and the absence of big majorities and minor parties. The 'law' worked reasonably well in the early 1950s, but is now only of historic interest, and is best ignored.
51 Conservative Action for Electoral Reform pamphlet, *Support Electoral Reform*.
52 Quoted in ibid.
53 For a comprehensive guide to PR, see E. Lakeman, *How Democracies Vote*, Faber, 1970, and S. E. Finer, ed., *Adversary Politics and Electoral Reform*, Anthony Wigram, London, 1975.

54 Butler, *The Electoral System*, p.191.
55 M. Steed in Butler & Kavanagh, *February 1974*, p.328.
56 M. Steed, loc. cit., p.329.
57 Butler, *The Electoral System*, p.187.
58 M. Steed in D. E. Butler & A. S. King, *The British General Election of 1966*, Macmillan, 1966, p.293. [Cited hereafter as Butler & King, 1966.]
59 M. Steed in Butler & Kavanagh, *February 1974*, p.329.
60 *The Report of the Hansard Society Commission on Electoral Reform*, Hansard Society, London, 1976, pp.37–40.
61 It is described in full in ibid., p.52.
62 These prognostications of AMS are taken from P. Kellner, 'Fall of the Big Parties', *Sunday Times*, 13 June 1976, p.5; AMS would have produced small but workable Conservative majorities in 1955 and 1959, and STV would have given Labour a working majority in 1966 of between 10 and 20 seats.
63 Letter from Peter Morrison, Conservative MP for the City of Chester, *The Times*, 16 June 1976, p.15.
64 The example of the Fourth French Republic is often cited as an argument against PR. Between December 1946, when the constitution of the Fourth Republic came into operation, and May 1958, when the Fifth Republic commenced, France had 22 governments. But strict proportionality by party lists was only in operation until June 1951. During the period 1946–51 there were eight ministries. This works out at an average duration of just under 7 months per government, which is about the same as the average for the entire period 1946–58. Frequent changes of government were not, therefore, due to PR, but to the instability of post-1945 French politics and society.
65 M. Steed in Butler & Kavanagh, *October 1974*, pp.339–40.
66 *Royal Commission on the Constitution 1969–1973*, vol. I: Report, Cmnd. 5460, Her Majesty's Stationery Office, 1973, paragraphs 788 and 1140; vol. II: Memorandum of Dissent, Cmnd. 5460-I, paragraph 249.
67 *Our Changing Democracy – Devolution to Scotland and Wales*, Cmnd. 6348, H.M.S.O., 1975.
68 *The Times*, 20 August 1976, p.1.
69 Ronald Butt, in the *Sunday Times*, 18 July 1976, p.13, calculated that if the 81 seats were elected by the plurality system, the results, assuming the voting pattern to be the same as for the October 1974 general election, would give Labour 44 seats, the Conservatives 31, and the Scottish National Party and the Ulster Unionists 3 each; there would be no Liberal or Plaid Cymru representatives.

Notes to Chapter Two

1. *The Times*, 16 June 1976, p.2.
2. In Scotland, the assessor of the county or large borough.
3. Butler, *The Electoral System*, pp.50–51, 138.
4. *The Times*, 29 July 1976, p.3; 6 August, p.2; a further revelation in this case was that an alien had mistakenly been allowed to vote in the name of a qualified voter.
5. P. G. Gray, T. Corlett & P. Frankland, *The Register of Electors as a Sampling Frame*, Central Office of Information, London, 1950.
6. P. G. Gray & F. A. Gee, *Electoral Registration for Parliamentary Elections*, Government Social Survey, London, 1967. Some of this inaccuracy was due to voters becoming 21 years of age during the currency of the register. Such voters – 'Y' voters – could only vote after 20 October. By the Representation of the People Act of 1969 this system was replaced by one involving the placing of the 18th birthday date by the names of young voters on the register; they become eligible to vote as soon as this date is reached.
7. As widely quoted at the time: eg in *The Times*, 14 October 1974, p.2, and Butler & Sloman, op. cit., p.186.
8. M. Steed in Butler & Kavanagh, *October 1974*, p.333.
9. N. Deakin, ed., *Colour and the British Electorate 1964*, Pall Mall Press, London, 1965, p.7.
10. D. Lawrence, 'Race, Elections and Politics', in I. Crewe, ed., *British Political Sociology Yearbook*, vol. 2 ('The Politics of Race'), Croom Helm, London, 1975, p.69.
11. *Participation of Ethnic Minorities in the General Election October 1974*, Community Relations Commission, London, 1975, pp.13–14.
12. Because the constituency was a very safe Conservative seat; their impact on local elections is, however, more problematical.
13. Butler, *The Electoral System*, p.137.
14. D. E. Butler & A. King, *The British General Election of 1964*, Macmillan, 1964, pp.226–7. [Cited hereafter as Butler & King, *1964*.]
15. Butler & Pinto-Duschinsky, op. cit., p.333.
16. Butler & Kavanagh. *February 1974*, pp.242–3.
17. Butler & Kavanagh, *October 1974*, pp.244–5.
18. *Report of the Speaker's Conference on Electoral Law*, Cmnd. 3202, 1967.
19. In February 1974 the percentage fell to 2.0 per cent, because the general election was held on a much fresher register.
20. Craig, op. cit., p.74.
21. In February 1966 the Speakers' Conference (Cmnd. 2917, 1966) voted 11 to 11 on the question of publishing two registers a year; the Speaker then used his casting vote to defeat the proposal.

22 Butler, *The Electoral System*, p.57. If an election is declared void, a new election is held. An election may, however, be deemed by the courts to have been an 'undue' election; in such a case, the successful candidate is unseated and another candidate is declared elected in his place. There have been three such instances since 1918. In Fermanagh & South Tyrone (1955) the successful candidate was disqualified as a felon. In Mid-Ulster (also 1955) the successful candidate was similarly disqualified. At Bristol, South-East (1961) Viscount Stansgate (Anthony Wedgwood Benn) was disqualified as a peer.
23 D. G. Neill, 'The Election in Northern Ireland', in D. E. Butler, *The British General Election of 1951*, Macmillan, 1952, pp.220–35.
24 Butler & Kavanagh, *February 1974*, p.244.
25 A. P. Hill, 'The Effect of Party Organisation: Election Expenses and the 1970 Election', *Political Studies*, xxii (1974), pp.215–217.
26 Butler & Pinto-Duschinsky, op. cit., p.334.
27 Butler & Kavanagh, *October 1974*, p.244.
28 ibid., p.242.
29 Butler & Kavanagh, *February 1974*, p.228.
30 *The Times*, 4 November 1975, p.7.
31 *Report of the Committee on Financial Aid to Political Parties*, Cmnd. 6601, 1976, p.26.
32 Butler & Kavanagh, *February 1974*, p.128.
33 Butler & Pinto-Duschinsky, op. cit., p.102; Rose, *The Problem of Party Government*, p.221; *The Times*, 5 August 1976, p.4.
34 Sir Philip Magnus, Unionist MP for the University of London, 1906–1921, had formerly been a minister at the West London Synagogue.
35 The full story is told in Leonard, op. cit., pp.64–5.
36 *The Times*, 2 July 1976, p.4; the fact that the allocation of television time does not depend in general upon the number of candidates does not affect the argument.
37 Craig, op. cit., p.79; lost deposits in the university seats (totalling £2,850) were forfeited to the universities, not the Treasury.
38 Butler & Kavanagh. *October 1974*, p.272.
39 J. F. S. Ross, *Parliamentary Representation*, 2nd edn, Eyre & Spottiswoode, London, 1948, pp.204–7.
40 *The Report of the Hansard Society Commission on Electoral Reform*, p.20.
41 A reform proposed by Professor F. Stacey, op. cit., pp.12–13.
42 Cmnd. 3275, 1967.
43 *Report of the Committee on Financial Aid to Political Parties*, Cmnd. 6601, 1976, p.xv.
44 Beales, op. cit., pp.85–6.

45 ibid., p.244.
46 Butler, *The Electoral System*, p.208.
47 H. G. Nicholas, *The British General Election of 1950*, Macmillan, 1951, p.4.
48 Butler, *The Electoral System*, p.193.
49 D. Butler, 'The Redistribution of Seats', *Public Administration*, xxxiii (1955), pp.125-47.
50 M. Kinnear, *The British Voter*, Cornell University Press, Ithaca, 1968, p.62.
51 M. Steed in Butler & King, *1964*, pp.357-8; Butler & King, *1966*, pp.293-5.
52 M. Steed in Butler & Pinto-Duschinsky, op. cit., p.415.
53 P. Bromhead, *Britain's Developing Constitution*, Allen & Unwin, 1974, p.181; M. Steed in Butler & Kavanagh, *February 1974*, pp.324-5. The calculation must be very approximate because of the impact of the lower voting age.
54 *The Times*, 5 July 1976, p.2.
55 ibid., 16 June 1976, p.15.
56 M. A. Busteed, *Geography and Voting Behaviour*, Oxford University Press, 1975, pp.9-21.
57 Excluding the seat allotted to Queen's University, Belfast.
58 In October 1974 the 13 Glasgow seats represented an average of 44,768 electors each; the six most northerly and westerly Scottish constituencies (Caithness & Sutherland, Western Isles, Orkney & Shetland, Ross & Cromarty, Inverness and Argyll) had an average of 29,392 electors each.
59 This calculation assumes that the parties would have obtained the same percentage of seats.
60 *Disturbances in Northern Ireland Report of the Commission appointed by the Governor of Northern Ireland* [Cameron Commission], Government of Northern Ireland, Belfast, Cmd. 532, 1969, p.57.
61 ibid., p.59.

Notes to Chapter Three

1 Since 1950 only one 'independent' MP has fitted this definition: Frank Maguire, elected for Fermanagh in October 1974; but he has strong connections with the Republican movement in Northern Ireland.
2 Quoted in Butler & Kavanagh. *February 1974*, p.104.
3 Butler & Stokes, op. cit., p.31.
4 G. Wallas, *Human Nature in Politics*, Constable, London, 1908, pp.82-3.

5   E. Burke, 'Thoughts on the Cause of the Present Discontents' (1770) in *Works*, John C. Nimmer, London, 1899, vol. I, p.530.
6   On party discipline, see G. Alderman, op. cit.; H. B. Berrington, 'Partisanship and Dissidence in the Nineteenth-Century House of Commons', *Parliamentary Affairs*, xxi, 1967–8, pp.338–74; and R, J. Jackson, *Rebels and Whips*, Macmillan, 1968.
7   Butler & Sloman, op. cit., p.136.
8   ibid., p.126.
9   A. H. Birch, *Small-Town Politics A Study of Political Life in Glossop*, Oxford University Press, 1959, pp.81–2; M. Benney, A. P. Gray & R. H. Pear, *How People Vote A Study of Electoral Behaviour in Greenwich*, Routledge, 1956, p.132.
10 Butler & Stokes, op. cit., p.21.
11 Quoted in Rose, *The Problem of Party Government*, pp.157–8.
12 For a good discussion of local party hierarchies see Blondel, op. cit., pp.88–112; see also Benney et. al. op. cit., p.47.
13 A. H. Birch, *Small-Town Politics*, p.84; F. Bealey, J. Blondel & W. P. McCann, *Constituency Politics*, Faber, 1965, pp.274–81.
14 W. L. Guttsman, 'The British Political Elite and the Class Structure', in P. Stansworth & A. Giddens, eds, *Elites and Power in British Society*, Cambridge University Press, 1974, p.38.
15 A. H. Birch, *Small-Town Politics*, p.81; Bealey et al, op. cit., p.404.
16 Beer, op. cit., p.258.
17 A. Ranney, *Pathways to parliament*, Macmillan, 1965, pp.48-50.
18 Stacey, op. cit., p.56.
19 Ranney, op. cit., p.74.
20 L. D. Epstein, *British Politics in the Suez Crisis*, Pall Mall Press, 1964, pp.98–119.
21 Pulzer, op. cit., p.79.
22 Butler & Kavanagh, *February 1974*, p.208.
23 Ranney, op. cit., pp.42–48; the candidate was Andrew Fountaine, the constituency Chorley (1950), the grounds Fountaine's attitude to Jews.
24 Stacey, op. cit., pp.53–4.
25 See Craig, op. cit., pp.85–6; Butler & Kavanagh, *February 1974*, p.213, *October 1974*, p.217.
26 P. Paterson, *The Selectorate*, Macgibbon & Kee, London, 1967, pp.98–9.
27 M. Harrison, *Trade Unions and the Labour Party since 1945*, Allen & Unwin, 1960, p.81.
28 In 1973 the proportion was 11 per cent, and in 1974 19 per cent; see Rose, *The Problem of Party Government*, p.236, and *Report of the Committee on Financial Aid to Political Parties*, Cmnd. 6601, 1976, p.35.

29 Ranney, op. cit., p.164.
30 ibid., pp.188–191.
31 ibid., p.181.
32 The cases of S. O. Davies and Dick Taverne have already been discussed (see p.69). E. J. Milne was rejected by his constituency Labour party because of his campaign against corruption amongst Labour councillors in the north-east; he was returned as the Independent Labour MP in February 1974. Margaret McKay was rejected by her constituency party largely, it would appear, because of her pro-Arab views; she did not contest the seat in 1970. Her successor as Labour candidate at Clapham, Dr. David Pitt, lost the seat; as a coloured candidate, his disadvantage was obvious.
33 *The Times*, 6 July 1976, p.2.
34 Pulzer, op. cit., p.67.
35 Frank Tomney, 'How the odds are stacked against a Labour MP facing the sack', in *The Times*, 5 July 1976, p.12.
36 M. Rush, *The Selection of Parliamentary Candidates*, Nelson, London, 1969, p.276.
37 Ranney, op. cit., pp.62–5.
38 L. W. Martin, 'The Bournemouth Affair: Britain's First Primary Election', *Journal of Politics*, xxii, 1960, pp.654–81.
39 *The Times*, 1 April 1976, p.4; 5 April, p.4. See also A. H. Hanson & M. Walles, *Governing Britain*, revised edn., Fontana,1975, p.59.
40 *Report of the Hansard Society Commission of Electoral Reform*, p.19.
41 Leonard, op. cit., p.76.
42 Steed in Butler & Pinto-Duschinsky, op. cit., p.405; Butler & Kavanagh, *October 1974*, p.345.
43 Ranney, op. cit., p.34.
44 Leonard, op. cit., p.75.
45 Butler & King, *1966*, p.209.
46 Paterson, op. cit., pp.51–4.
47 *The Times*, 13 July 1976, p.10.
48 Guttsman, loc. cit., p.39; Paterson, op. cit., pp.97–8.
49 Butler & Kavanagh, *October 1974*, p.214.
50 The Labour party contested three Irish seats; otherwise the Northern Irish parties were left to do battle amongst themselves.
51 Another method of calculating swing is to base the calculation on the votes cast for the two major parties only – the 'two-party' swing; yet another variant – 'electorate swing' – is calculated from the proportions of the total electorate voting for the major parties. These methods are in some respects less abstract than 'conventional' swing, but are not widely used outside the works psephologists write for each other.

52 Leonard, op. cit., p.27; the three were Darlington (1951), Glasgow, Pollock (1964) and Cheadle (1966).
53 The twelve were: Bolton East, Bolton West, Bosworth, Cannock, Clapham, Dudley, Gloucester, Leek, Oldham West, Pembrokeshire, Rossendale, and Walthamstow West; Dudley, Oldham West and Walthamstow West were Labour gains.
54 *The Times*, 10 October 1974, p.16; *The Economist*, 23 February 1974, p.26.
55 Aristotle, *Politics*, trans. H. Rackham, Loeb Classical Library, Heinemann, London, 1967, book IV, chapter 4, p.301.
56 Television broadcast, 7 February 1974.
57 Television broadcast, 8 February 1974.
58 Buter & Kavanagh, *February 1974*, pp.92–3. The usefulness of private polls and canvassing feedback is doubtful. The polls, which are expensive, do not tell the party faithful anything they would not be able to learn from other sources, such as polls published in newspapers and opinion poll data published elsewhere. There is no evidence that the private polls put one party in exclusive possession of vital information. When the news from the private polls is bad (as it was for the Conservatives in October 1974) they serve only to depress party morale. Canvassing is a notoriously unreliable method of reading the voters' minds; canvassing feedback, and reports from regional and area organisers, are generally far too optimistic and wildly inaccurate.
59 Butler & Kavanagh, *February 1974*, pp.229–31.
60 Quoted in Butler & Stokes, op. cit., p.23; Butler & Stokes themselves (ibid., pp.352–5) obtained similar though not quite so depressing results.
61 ibid., pp.361–8.
62 Butler & Pinto-Duschinsky, p.146.
63 Butler & Kavanagh, *February 1974*, p.79.
64 ibid.
65 ibid., pp.232–3.
66 Butler & Kavanagh, *October 1974*, p.230.
67 In 1970 the Conservative manifesto was entitled *A Better Tomorrow*. The summary produced for distribution in Wales was called *A Better Tomorrow for Wales*, and mentioned such things as the Milford Haven Oil Terminal, the University Hospital of Wales in Cardiff, and the Mid-Wales Rural Development Board.
68 Quoted in Butler & Kavanagh, *October 1974*, p.232.
69 Butler & Pinto-Duschinsky, op. cit., pp.438–9; Butler & Kavanagh, *February 1974*, pp.62–3; *October 1974*, pp.235–6.
70 J. Trenaman & D. McQuail, *Television and the Political Image*, Methuen, 1961, pp.58–60.

71 Blondel, op. cit., 83.
72 Deakin, op.cit., *passim*.
73 R. W. Johnson & D. Schoen, 'The "Powell effect": or how one man can win', *New Society*, 21 July 1976, p.169.
74 Butler & Pinto-Duschinsky, op. cit., pp.328, 340, 412.
75 Butler & Kavanagh. *October 1974*, p.351.
76 Butler & Stokes, op. cit., p.297; in 1963 the first four were (in order): social welfare, housing, economic problems and education; in 1970 they were: economic problems, social welfare, taxation and housing.
77 Butler & Kavanagh, *October 1974*, p.236.
78 Butler & Kavanagh, *February 1974*, p.62.
79 See M. J. Le Lohé, 'Participation in Elections by Asians in Bradford' and G. Alderman, 'Not Quite British: The Political Attitudes of Anglo-Jewry', in I. Crewe, ed., *British Political Sociology Yearbook*, vol. 2, Croom Helm, 1975, pp.84–122 and 188–211.
80 Butler & Kavanagh. *February 1974*, p.225.
81 Butler & King, *1966*, p.285; in some cases, such as Eton & Slough and Leyton, it rose by over 5 per cent, and in Brighton, Kemptown, by 7.9 per cent.
82 Butler & Kavanagh, *October 1974*, p.338.
83 See chapter two.
84 Butler & Pinto-Duschinsky, op. cit., p.410.
85 ibid., pp.288–9; 342. The authors of the February 1974 Nuffield study make a similar point in relation to the Labour party; Labour regional agents told them of two marginal seats where organization was 'appalling' and which would probably be lost. Both seats showed 'a handsome swing' to Labour: Butler & Kavanagh, *February 1974*, p.248.
86 The seats are listed in Butler & Kavanagh, *October 1974*, p.227.
87 There were 20 seats with pro-Conservative swings in October 1974; in 10 of them, Conservative and Labour candidates occupied the top two places. Of the 20, only three were on the critical list.
88 None of the 15 listed seats which the Conservatives were defending in October had been won by them in February.
89 Bolton East was recaptured in February 1974, Bolton West and Rossendale in October. The Clapham Seat was swallowed up in the redrawing of boundaries.

Notes to Chapter Four

1 See Rose, *Problem of Party Government*, pp.71–3; Butler & Pinto-Duschinsky, op. cit., p.336; Butler & Stokes, op. cit., p.423.
2 The most remarkable example of pressure by the electorate during this parliament was over a proposal to break faith with consumers of

off-peak (night-rate) electricity by increasing the charges for this type of electric current so that it would have cost more than half the price of day-time electricity, contrary to pledges given over a number of years by the electricity boards. There was an outcry from consumers, and the proposal was dropped.

3   Plato, *Republic*, tr. A. D. Lindsay, Everyman's Library edn, Dent, 1935, book III, pp.99–100.
4   W. Bagehot, *The English Constitution*, Fontana edn, 1963, ch. II.
5   R. Rose, *Politics in England*, Faber, 1965, pp.224–7.
6   Butler & Stokes, op. cit., p.466.
7   R. H. S. Crossman, *The Diaries of a Cabinet Minister*, Hamish Hamilton, 1975, 1976, 1977.
8   *New Society*, 17 June 1976, pp.630–2.
9   It is worth noting that in recent years two Privy Councillors and former ministers have been found guilty of lying: John Profumo, Secretary of State for War under Harold Macmillan, who resigned in June 1963 after admitting he had lied to the House of Commons about his relationship with Miss Christine Keeler; and John Stonehouse, Postmaster-General under Harold Wilson, who in August 1976 was jailed for seven years on a variety of charges, including fraud.
10 M. Abrams & R. Rose, *Must Labour Lose?*, Penguin, 1960, p.23.
11 Rose, *Politics in England*, p.221.
12 *A Better Tomorrow*, p.12.
13 David Blundy in the *Sunday Times*, 1 August 1976, p.3.
14 Quoted in *The Times*, 12 June 1976, p.20; the italics are mine. Note the assumption that the electors are not competent to decide for themselves what is in the best interests of their own children.
15 I. Crewe, T. Fox & J. Alt, 'Non-Voting in British General Elections 1966–October 1974', in C. Crouch, ed., *British Political Sociology Yearbook*, vol. 3, Croom Helm, 1977, p.67.
16 Butler & Stokes, op. cit., p.21.
17 ibid., p.22.
18 I am grateful to Ladbrokes for this information; in the two general elections of 1974 the amounts taken by this firm were £970,000 and £750,000.
19 I am grateful to William Hill for this information; the firm also informs me that, if either party is at long odds on, large industrial organizations will invest several thousand pounds as an insurance against 'various contingencies'.
20 Butler & Stokes, op. cit., pp.355, 475.
21 Professor Rose found, in a pre-election survey in Stockport in March 1964, that only 9 per cent of his sample were annoyed by the campaign: Rose, *Politics in England*, p.90.

22 See R. Rose, *The Problem of Party Government*, Macmillan, 1974, pp.63, 214.
23 D. A. Kavanagh, *Constituency Electioneering in Britain*, Longmans, 1970, p.84.
24 Butler & Pinto-Duschinsky, op. cit., pp.321–2; Butler & Kavanagh, *February 1974*, pp.249–51; Butler & Kavanagh, *October 1974*, p.246.
25 This discussion of the press is confined to the most widely read national daily newspapers. Specialist national dailies, such as the *Financial Times* and the *Daily Worker* (later *Morning Star*) are not included; neither are Sunday papers, evening papers or provincial dailies. The circulation of the specialist papers is small. That of the provincials and the evening papers is local, and their content is locally orientated. The circulation of the seven leading Sunday papers is much larger; in 1974 the *News of the World, Observer, Sunday People, Sunday Mirror, Sunday Express, Sunday Telegraph* and *Sunday Times* had a combined Sunday circulation of 22,100,000. The Sundays are, however, much more in the nature of entertainment magazines. Butler & Stokes, op. cit., p.115, found that few of their respondents derived campaign information from a Sunday newspaper, and fewer still from an evening paper.
26 Ostrogorski, op. cit., vol. I, p.409.
27 ibid., p.410.
28 The information in this paragraph is based on C. Seymour-Ure, *The Political Impact of Mass Media*, Faber, 1974, pp.166-7, and the same author's contributions to Butler & Kavanagh, *February 1974*, pp.182–3, and Butler & Kavanagh, *October 1974*, pp.166–7.
29 Butler & Stokes, op. cit., p.116.
30 ibid., pp.117–9.
31 H. G. Nicholas, *The British General Election of 1950*, Macmillan, 1951, p.176.
32 Seymour-Ure, *The Political Impact of Mass Media*, p.229.
33 ibid., p.230.
34 ibid., p.168.
35 Butler & Stokes, *Political Change in Britain*, 1st edn, Penguin Books, 1971, p.292.
36 ibid., p.293.
37 ibid., p.285.
38 Unpublished Butler & Stokes data from their 1963 survey, reported in Seymour-Ure, *The Political Impact of Mass Media*, p.169, shows that only four per cent of respondents specifically mentioned politics when asked what they liked about their paper.
39 On the newsreels, see N. Pronay, 'British Newsreels of the 1930s', *History*, lvi, 1971, pp.411-8; lvii, 1972, pp.73–72.

40 R. B. McCallum & A. Readman, *The British General Election of 1945*, Macmillan, 1947, pp.142–3.
41 D. E. Butler, *The British General Election of 1951*, Macmillan, 1952, pp.75–7.
42 Seymour-Ure, *The Political Impact of Mass Media*, p.209.
43 D. E. Butler & R. Rose, *The British General Election of 1959*, Macmillan, 1960, pp.92–3.
44 Seymour-Ure, *The Political Impact of Mass Media*, pp.209–10; see also H. Grisewood, 'The BBC and Political Broadcasting in Britain', *Parliamentary Affairs*, xvi, 1962–3, pp.42–5.
45 Butler & Rose, op. cit., p.76.
46 Seymour-Ure, *The Political Impact of Mass Media*, p.210.
47 Butler & Stokes, op. cit., 1st edn, p.271.
48 Butler & King, *1964*, p.162.
49 Butler & King, *1966*, p.127.
50 Butler & Pinto-Duschinsky, op. cit., p.203.
51 Ostrogorski, vol. I, p.408.
52 Butler & Pinto-Duschinsky, op. cit., p.312.
53 Seymour-Ure, *The Political Impact of Mass Media*, p.213; see also Butler & King, *1966*, p.188.
54 ibid., pp.146–7.
55 Butler & Pinto-Duschinsky, op. cit., p.207; Butler & Kavanagh, *October 1974*, p.142.
56 Butler & King, *1964*, p.162.
57 Butler & King, *1966*, p.139.
58 Butler & Kavanagh, *February 1974*, p.158; *October 1974*, pp.153–4.
59 Since 1970 no party broadcast on television has attracted an audience of more than 26 per cent (Conservative broadcast, 22 February 1974); the average is 21.6 per cent: Butler & Pinto-Duschinsky, op. cit., p.227; Butler & Kavanagh, *February 1974*, p.341; *October 1974*, p.161.
60 Butler & Kavanagh. *February 1974*, p.165.
61 On this episode see J. G. Blumler, 'Producers' attitudes towards Television Coverage of an Election Campaign', in R. Rose, ed, *Studies in British Politics*, 2nd edn, Macmillan, 1969, pp.220–45.
62 Butler & Kavanagh, *October 1974*, p.163.
63 *The Times*, 12 November 1975, p.4.
64 Lord Windlesham, *Communication and Political Power*, Cape, 1966, chapter three.
65 Butler & Rose, op. cit., pp.21, 28.
66 ibid., pp.25, 27.
67 Quoted in Butler & King, *1966*, p.33.
68 ibid., p.93.

69 Butler & Pinto-Duschinsky, op. cit., pp.224–5; Butler & Kavanagh, *February 1974*, p.161.
70 In Butler & Pinto-Duschinsky, op. cit., p.225.
71 R. Rose, *Influencing Voters. A Study of Campaign Rationality*, Faber, 1967, pp.58, 181.
72 Butler & Pinto-Duschinsky, op. cit., p.64.
73 Butler & Stokes, op. cit., 1st edn, pp,513-16. J. Trenaman & D. Mcquail, in their examination of the effects of television on attitudes and voting during the 1959 campaign (*Television and the Political Image*, Methuen, 1961) found no evidence that the viewing of party broadcasts had affected voting or the attitudes of electors to the Labour and Conservative parties.
74 J. G. Blumler & D. McQuail, *Television in Politics: Its Uses and Influence*, Faber, 1968, pp.43, 159, 169–70.
75 Butler, *The British General Election of 1951*, p.97.
76 Butler & King, *1966*, p.188.
77 Seymour-Ure, *The Political Impact of Mass Media*, pp.225-6.
78 Butler & Kavanagh, *October 1974*, p.162.
79 Butler & Stokes, op. cit., 1st edn, p.513.
80 Stacey, op. cit., p.306.
81 Blumer & McQuail, op. cit., pp.197-207, 263-79, in their examination of the impact of television on the 1964 election, found that exposure to television was associated with a marked rise in Liberal support. There is little doubt that the increased attention paid by all the media to the Liberal party since the Orpington 'breakthrough' of 1962 has given it much valuable publicity, and brought its policies firmly to the attention of the voting public.
82 For a full discussion of the pros and cons of each system, and variations upon them, see C. A. Moser & G. Kalton, *Survey Methods in Social Investigation*, 2nd edn, Heinemann, 1971.
83 R. Hall, 'The Chances of Getting a Wild One', *Sunday Times*, 7 June 1970, p.9. For a discussion of sampling error see F. Teer & J. D. Spence, *Political Opinion Polls*, Hutchinson, 1973, pp.24–7.
Using the formula $S = \pm 1.97 \sqrt{p(100-p)/n}$, where S is the Sampling Error, p is the percentage shown by the sample, and n is the size of the sample, 95 per cent of all values of p will lie within the range shown by the value of S.
84 See M. Steed in Butler & Pinto-Duschinsky, op. cit., p.392.
85 F. A. Stacey, *British Government 1966–1975*, Oxford University Press, 1975, p.19.
86 For further evidence in refutation of the classic bandwagon and boomerang theories, see Teer & Spence, op. cit., pp.131–3.
87 *The Times*, 14 October 1974, p.2.

88   ibid., 12 October 1974, p.4; this assertion was supported by Mr. Humphrey Taylor, managing director of Louis Harris, who said 'he had data showing that quite a large number of Labour supporters stayed at home because they did not want to give Labour a big majority'.
89   Leonard, op. cit., p.137.
90   Cmnd. 3550, 1968, p.6.
91   Stacey, *The Government of Modern Britain*, p.310.
92   Butler & Kavanagh, *October 1974*, p.187.
93   Butler & Pinto-Duschinsky, op. cit., p.187.
94   Quoted in Butler, *The British General Election of 1951*, p.88.
95   Additionally, the evidence of the polls between elections can influence the Prime Minister in his choice of a dissolution date: see Stacey, *The Government of Modern Britain*, pp.306–10, and chapter one, above.
96   For the history of the private polls see Butler & Pinto-Duschinsky, op. cit., pp.189–98; Butler & Kavanagh, *February 1974*, p.135; *October 1974*, pp.197–207; Seymour-Ure, *The Political Impact of Mass Media*, p.226; and Teer & Spence, op. cit., pp.154–75.
97   Butler & Kavanagh, *October 1974*, p.204.
98   T. Forester, 'The Opinion Poll Industry', *New Statesman*, 4 October 1974, p.454.

Notes to Chapter Five

1   Quoted in N. O'Sullivan, *Conservatism*, Dent, 1976, p.118.
2   Vincent, op. cit., p.125.
3   ibid., pp.92–3.
4   J. A. Thomas, *The House of Commons 1832–1901*, University of Wales Press, Cardiff, 1939, pp.4–5, 14–15.
5   Vincent, op. cit., pp.67–70.
6   ibid., pp.58–60.
7   ibid., p.23; and see T. Nossiter, 'Voting Behaviour 1832–1872', *Political Studies*, xviii, 1970, 380–9.
8   *Annual Register*, 1877, part 1, pp.3–4.
9   Thomas, op. cit., pp.14–15.
10 H. Pelling, *The Social Geography of British Elections 1885–1910*, Macmillan, 1967, pp.418–20.
11 ibid., pp.30, 43; the Scottish voting figures also reveal a strong correlation between party and social status: ibid., pp.392, 403, 411.
12 The discussion in this and the following paragraph is based on R. Williams, *Keywords*, Fontana, 1976, pp.51–9.

13 T. H. Marshall, *Citizenship and Social Class*, Cambridge University Press, 1950, p.92.
14 M. Kahan, D. E. Butler & D. E. Stokes, 'On the Analytical Division of Social Class', *British Journal of Sociology*, xvii (1966), 123–130.
15 Butler & Stokes, op. cit., p.75. [Except where otherwise indicated, all references to Butler & Stokes in this chapter are to the second edition.] A further difficulty, with which political sociologists have hardly begun to grapple, is that the systems of class divisions they use invariably refer to men. The majority of the electorate are women, yet they are categorised mainly in terms of the positions on the scale occupied by their fathers or husbands!
16 H. Durant, 'Voting Behaviour in Britain, 1945–66', in R. Rose, ed, *Studies in British Politics*, 2nd edn, Macmillan, 1969, p.166.
17 Pulzer, op. cit., p.102.
18 R. M. Punnett, *British Government and Politics*, 3rd edn, Heinemann, 1976, p.70.
19 Butler & Stokes, op. cit., 1st edn, p.137; 2nd edn, p.183. In 1964 NOP found that 47 per cent of Conservative support came from classes C2 and DE, and that 18 per cent of Labour support came from classes AB and C1: Pulzer, op. cit., p.110.
20 Bagehot, op. cit., p.248.
21 See, for example, Bob Jessop, *Traditionalism, Conservatism and British Political Culture*, Allen & Unwin, 1974, passim; R. Samuel, 'The Deference Voter', *New Left Review*, i, 1960, 9–13; R. T. McKenzie & A. Silver, *Angels in Marble: Working Class Conservatism in Urban England*, Heinemann, 1968, chapter four.
22 ibid., p.109.
23 ibid., pp.92–7.
24 ibid., pp.183–5.
25 Butler & Stokes, op. cit., p.186.
26 ibid., p.168.
27 McKenzie & Silver, op. cit., p.188.
28 F. Parkin, *Middle Class Radicalism*, Manchester University Press, 1968, passim.
29 G. C. Moodie & G. Studdert-Kennedy, *Opinions, Publics and Pressure Groups*, Allen & Unwin, 1970, p.57.
30 B. Hindess, *The Decline of Working Class Politics*, MacGibbon & Kee, London, 1971, passim; and see chapter three above.
31 Butler & Stokes, op. cit., 1st edn, pp.128–31.
32 On this see ibid., pp.132–5 and Pulzer, op. cit., p.112. But home-ownership can have an effect, as Butler & Stokes themselves admit: Butler & Stokes, op. cit., 1st edn, p.134, 2nd edn, p.107; and see above, p.157.

33 I. Crewe, B. Sarlvik & J. Alt, 'The Why and How of the February Voting', *New Society*, 12 September 1974, p.672.
34 Butler & Pinto-Duschinsky, op. cit., p.388; Butler & Kavanagh, *October 1974*, p.334.
35 Crewe et al, *New Society*, 12 September 1974, p.669.
36 I. Crewe, B. Sarlvik & J. Alt, *Partisan Dealignment in Britain 1964-1974*, University of Essex mimeograph, 1976, pp.5, 14, and figure 4. I am grateful for permission to cite material from this paper.
37 As partisanship hardens with age, the new generation of voters may well develop and transmit a very weak sense of party identification. This possibility bristles with implications which are, however, beyond the scope of the present work.
38 Crewe et al, *Partisan Dealignment*, pp.27-8 and table 15.
39 See above, p.161.
40 McKenzie & Silver, op. cit., p.112.
41 ibid., p.115.
42 Butler & Stokes, op. cit., p.203.
43 Crewe et al, *Partisan Dealignment*, table 19; these figures are somewhat higher than those given in table 5:1 above. The decline, measured by averaging the AB and C1 percentages, is even steeper.
44 Crewe et al, *New Society*, 12 September 1974, p.672.
45 Butler & Stokes, op. cit., pp.85, 468.
46 Jessop, op. cit., pp.96–7.
47 Crewe et al, *Partisan Dealignment*, table 6.
48 Butler & Stokes, op. cit., pp.193–205.
49 Butler & King, *1964*, p.296; Butler & Kavanagh, *October 1974*, p.278; Durant, loc. cit., p.168.
50 ibid., p.169.
51 Butler & King, *1964*, p.296; Butler & Kavanagh, *October 1974*, p.278.
52 E.g, M. Benney, A. P. Gray & R. H. Pear, *How People Vote*, 1956; R. S. Milne & H. C. Mackenzie, *Straight Fight*, 1954 and *Marginal Seat*, 1958.
53 Butler & Stokes, op. cit., pp.51–2.
54 ibid., p.51.
55 ibid., pp.62–5.
56 This paragraph is based on ibid., pp.221–33.
57 ibid., p.242.
58 ibid., p.256.
59 ibid., p.263.
60 Pelling, op. cit., p.259; R. Blake, *The Conservative Party from Peel to Churchill*, Fontana, 1972, pp.87-8, 94, 111.

61 R. Gregory, *The Miners and British Politicas 1906–1914*, Oxford University Press, 1968.
62 Butler & Stokes, op. cit., p.156.
63 ibid., pp.160–66.
64 S. Koss, *Nonconformity in Modern British Politics*, Batsford, 1975, p.225.
65 E. J. Milne, *No Shining Armour*, John Calder, London, 1976, p.203.
66 Pulzer, op. cit., p.116. The strength of Labour victories on Clydeside and Merseyside since 1964 suggests that the fervour of Protestant sectarianism among the working classes there is declining.
67 Butler & Stokes, op. cit., pp.126–8.
68 ibid., pp.131–7.
69 G. Donaldson et al, 'Scottish Devolution: The Historical Background', in J. N. Wolfe, ed., *Government and Nationalism in Scotland*, Edinburgh University Press, 1969, p.11.
70 I. Budge & D. W. Urwin, *Scottish Political Behaviour*, Longmans, 1966.
71 Butler & & Pinto-Duschinsky, op. cit., pp.402–3.
72 Butler & Kavanagh, *October 1974*, p.348.
73 J. P. Cornford & J. A. Brand, 'Scottish Voting Behaviour', in Wolfe, op. cit., p.27.
74 *The Times*, 27 July 1976, p.1.
75 A. B. Philip, *The Welsh Question: Nationalism in Welsh Politics 1945–1970*, University of Wales Press, Cardiff, 1975, pp.150–1.
76 W. Miller, 'The Scottish Voter', *The Scotsman*, 15 October 1975, p.10; D. H. Jaensch, 'The Scottish Vote 1974: A Realigning Party System?', *Political Studies*, xxiv, 1976, 306-19.
77 Butler & Stokes, op. cit., p.139.
78 C. Cook, *A Short History of the Liberal Party 1900–1976*, Macmillan, 1976, p.135.
79 See note 49 above.
80 Butler & Stokes, op. cit., pp.79 and 138; Steed in Butler & Kavanagh, *February 1974*, pp.316–7.
81 Butler & Stokes, op. cit., pp.256, 263.
82 D. Scott, 'The National Front in Local Politics: Some Interpretations', in Crewe, ed, *British Political Sociology Yearbook*, vol. 2, pp.214–38.
83 Butler & Kavanagh, *February 1974*, p.351; *October 1974*, p.336.
84 Community Relations Commission, op. cit., pp.39–42; the Front's best performance was in the West Bromwich by-election of May 1973, when it polled 16.0 per cent of the total vote.
85 *The Times*, 1 June 1976, p.2; *Jewish Chronicle*, 21 May 1976, p.6.
86 Leonard, op. cit., p.147.
87 Pulzer, op. cit., p.132.

88 P. M. Williams, 'Two Notes on the British Electoral System', *Parliamentary Affairs*, xx, 1966, 25.
89 Pulzer, op. cit., p.132.
90 Butler & Stokes, op. cit., pp.218–9.
91 These statistics are based upon the estimates of the Research Unit of the Board of Deputies of British Jews.
92 G. Alderman, 'Not Quite British: The Political Attitudes of Anglo-Jewry', in Crewe, ed, *British Political Sociology Yearbook*, pp.188–211; 'How Jews Vote', *Jewish Chronicle*, 19 July 1974, p.10; 'Where Being Jewish Counts', ibid., 25 October 1974, p.14.
93 See chapter two above.
94 Community Relations Commission, op. cit., pp.17–19.
95 The Bradford example is a case in point; see chapter three above.
96 *The Times*, 2 July 1976, p.4; 16 November 1976, p.5.
97 I. Crewe et al, *British Political Sociology Yearbook*, vol. 3, pp.99–101.
98 Butler & Stokes, op. cit., pp.256, 261, 263.
99 R. W. Johnson & D. Schoen, 'The "Powell effect": or how one man can win', *New Society*, 22 July 1976, p.170; Steed in Butler & Kavanagh, *February 1974*, p.332.

Notes to Chapter Six

1 House of Commons Debates, 5th series, vol. 317, col. 1105, 12 November 1935.
2 See, for example, G. A. Almond & S. Verba, *The Civic Culture*, Princeton University Press, 1963, p.102; *Royal Commission on the Constitution 1969–1973*, vol. 1: Report, Cmnd. 5460, 1973, pp.85–100; Jessop, op. cit., p.103; Butler & Stokes, op. cit., pp.29-30.
3 On this, see F. Stacey, *A New Bill of Rights for Britain*, David & Charles, Newton Abbot, 1973, especially pp.149–57; and Lord Hailsham's 1976 Dimbleby Lecture, reported in *The Times*, 15 October 1976, p.4.
4 Almost half the Butler & Stokes panel of respondents favoured a negotiated settlement; the proportion agreeing with sanctions fell from 29 per cent in 1966 to 19 per cent in 1970: Butler & Stokes, op. cit., p.465.
5 This paragraph is based on S.Alderson, *Yea or Nay? Referenda in the United Kingdom*, Cassell & Collier Macmillan, 1975, chapter 3.
6 On the history of the decision to hold the referendum see D. Butler & U. Kitzinger, *The 1975 Referendum*, Macmillan, 1976, pp.1–67, and P. Goodhart, *Full-Hearted Consent*, Davis-Poynter, London, 1976, passim.
7 Butler & Kitzinger, op. cit., p.60.
8 Goodhart, op. cit., p.89.

9   Butler & Kitzinger, op. cit., p.63.
10 L. S. Amery, *Thoughts on the Constitution*, 2nd edn, Oxford University Press, 1964, pp.17–18.
11 B. R. Crick, *The Reform of Parliament*, revised 2nd edn, Weidenfeld, 1970, p.80.
12 Leading article in the *New Statesman*, 7 August 1970, quoted in Goodhart, op. cit., p.21.
13 *The Times*, 18 February 1977, p.12.
14 J. J. Rousseau, *The Social Contract*, trs, G. D. H. Cole, Everyman's Library edn, Dent, 1913, p.83.
15 Opinion polls in February 1974 suggested that more votes switched during the three-week election campaign than in any previous British election: Butler & Kavanagh, *February 1974*, p.112.
16 James Viscount Bryce, *Modern Democracies*, Macmillan, 1921, vol. 1, p.168.
17 Blondel, op. cit., p.194.
18 Bagehot, op. cit., p.67.

APPENDIX

General Election Results, 1945–1974
(Votes Cast; MPs in brackets)

Election & Electorate	Con.	Lab.	Lib.	Com.	Nat. Front	Welsh & Scot. Nat.	Others
1945 33,240,240,391	9,972,010 (210)	11,967,746 (393)	2,252,430 (12)	102,780 (2)	—	46,612 (0)	753,617 (23)
1950 34,412,255	12,492,404 (298)	13,266,176 (315)	2,621,487 (9)	91,765 (0)	—	27,288 (0)	272,004 (3)
1951 34,919,331	13,718,199 (321)	13,948,883 (295)	730,546 (6)	21,640 (0)	—	18,219 (0)	159,107 (3)
1955 34,852,179	13,310,891 (345)	12,405,254 (277)	722,402 (6)	33,144 (0)	—	57,231 (0)	230,807 (2)
1959 35,397,304	13,750,875 (365)	12,216,172 (258)	1,640,760 (6)	30,896 (0)	—	99,309 (0)	110,890 (1)
1964 35,894,054	12,002,642 (304)	12,205,808 (317)	3,099,283 (9)	46,442 (0)	—	133,551 (0)	169,422 (0)
1966 35,957,245	11,418,455 (253)	13,096,629 (364)	2,327,457 (12)	62,092 (0)	—	189,545 (0)	170,569 (1)
1970 39,342,013	13,145,123 (330)	12,208,758 (288)	2,117,035 (6)	37,970 (0)	—	481,818 (1)	354,094 (5)
1974 (Feb.) 39,753,865	11,872,180 (297)	11,645,616 (301)	6,059,519 (14)	32,743 (0)	76,865 (0)	804,554 (9)	848,685 (14)
1974 (Oct.) 40,072,971	10,462,565 (277)	11,457,079 (319)	5,346,704 (13)	17,426 (0)	113,843 (0)	1,005,938 (14)	785,549 (12)

GUIDE TO FURTHER READING

A number of works dealing with British politics contain substantial bibliographies which include material on elections. Amongst these are R. M. Punnett, *British Government and Politics*, 3rd edn, Heinemann, 1976; P. G. J. Pulzer, *Political Representation and Elections in Britain*, 3rd edn, Allen & Unwin, 1975; J. Blondel, *Voters, Parties and Leaders*, revised edn, Penguin, 1976; and R. Rose, ed, *Studies in British Politics*, 3rd edn, Macmillan, 1976. Also useful is K. I. Macdonald, ed, *The Essex Reference Index: British Journals on Politics and Sociology, 1950–1973*, Macmillan, 1975. Two indispensible works of reference are F. W. S. Craig, *British Electoral Facts 1885–1975*, 3rd edn, Macmillan, 1976, and D. Butler & A. Sloman. *British Political Facts 1900–1975*, 4th edn, Macmillan, 1975. Individual constituency results are tabulated in *The Times House of Commons* and F. W. S. Craig, *British General Election Results*, Macmillan, four volumes covering the period 1832–1970.

The evolution of the British electoral system during the twentieth century is best treated in D. E. Butler, *The Electoral System in Britain since 1918*, 2nd edn, Oxford University Press, 1963, which should be supplemented by the works of Punnett and Pulzer cited above, and by F. Stacey, *The Government of Modern Britain*, Oxford University Press, 1968, and *British Government 1968–1975*, Oxford University Press, 1975. Each general election since the second world war has been the subject of a Nuffield election study. The series began with a survey of the 1945 election by R. B. McCallum & A. Readman; the 1950 election was covered by H. G. Nicholas; David Butler wrote those for 1951 and 1955, and has co-authored each one since: 1959 with R. Rose, 1964 and 1966 with A. King, 1970 with M. Pinto-Duschinsky, and the two for 1974 with D. Kavanagh; the Nuffield studies are published by Macmillan. By-elections have been surveyed by C. Cook & J. Ramsden, eds, *By-Elections in British Politics*, Macmillan, 1973.

A Nuffield study of *The 1975 Referendum*, by D. Butler & U. Kitzinger, appeared in 1976. It was outclassed by P. Goodhart, *Full-Hearted Consent*, Davis-Poynter, 1976.

Proportional representation is best treated in E. Lakeman, *How Democ-*

racies Vote, Faber 1970, which should be supplemented by *The Report of the Hansard Society Commission on Electoral Reform*, published in 1976.

There have been a number of studies of individual constituencies and local political organization. Among these may be mentioned F. Bealey, J. Blondel and W. P. McCann, *Constituency Politics* [Newcastle-under-Lyme], Faber, 1965; A. H. Birch, *Small-Town Politics A Study of Political Life in Glossop*, Oxford University Press, 1959; and M. Benney, A. P. Gray & R. H. Pear, *How People Vote A Study of Electoral Behaviour in Greenwich*, Routledge, 1956. A. Ranney. *Pathways to Parliament*, Macmillan, 1965, and M. Rush, *The Selection of Parliamentary Candidates*, Nelson, 1969, deal more generally with the problems of candidate selection, The relationship between central and local party organizations is dealt with very fully in P. Paterson, *The Selectorate*, Macgibbon & Kee, 1967, R. Rose, *The Problem of Party Government*, Macmillan, 1974, and the *Report of the Committee on Financial Aid to Political Parties*, Cmnd 6601, 1976.

R. Rose's *Influencing Voters*, Faber, 1967, probes the assumptions behind electoral campaigns and campaign management. The views of candidates are examined in D. Kavanagh, *Constituency Electioneering in Britain*, Longmans, 1970. The effects of the mass media have been the subject of several recent studies; C. Seymour-Ure's *The Press, Politics and the Public*, Methuen, 1968; the same author's *The Political Impact of Mass Media*, Constable, 1974; J. Trenaman & D. McQuail, *Television and the Political Image*, Methuen, 1961; J. G. Blumer & D. McQuail, *Television in Politics*, Faber, 1968; and Grace Wyndham Goldie, *Facing the Nations Television and Politics 1936-1976*, Bodley Head, 1977.

The pitfalls of political opinion polls are examined in F. Teer & J. D. Spence, *Political Opinion Polls*, Hutchinson, 1973, and by R. Rose in an essay, 'Opinion Polls and Election Results', in his *Studies in British Politics*, which also contains a number of important articles concerned with media research.

Political sociology is an expanding field. For a general introduction to political behaviour see R. Rose, *Politics in England Today*, Faber, 1974. The seminal work is by D. Butler & D. Stokes, *Political Change in Britain*, 2nd edn, Macmillan, 1974; there is a critique by I. Crewe, 'Do Butler and Stokes Really Explain Political Change in Britain?', *European Journal of Political Research*, ii, 1974. Working-class conservatism is examined in R. T. McKenzie & A. Silver, *Angels in Marble*, Heinemann, 1968, and R. Jessop, *Traditionalism Conservatism and British Political Culture*, Allen & Unwin, 1974. *The British Political Sociology Yearbook*, published by Croom Helm, contains articles reflecting current research and conceptual and methodological debate; the first two volumes, 1974 and 1975, were edited by I. Crewe, the third, 1977, by C. Crouch.

I. Crewe and B. Sarlvik are co-directors of the British Election Study at the University of Essex; J. Alt is the study's senior research officer. No comprehensive account of its findings has as yet appeared, but of particular interest to students of elections are 'The Why and How of the February Voting', which appeared in *New Society* in September 1974 and is reprinted in *Studies in British Politics*, 'Partisan Dealignment in Britain 1964–1974', in the *British Journal of Political Science*, vii, 1977, and W. Miller, 'The Scottish Voter', in *The Scotsman*, 14, 15 and 16 October 1975. There is no recent study of Welsh voting behaviour. The party preferences of ethnic minorities are examined in the second volume of *The British Political Sociology Yearbook* and in the Community Relations Commission's study of the *Participation of Ethnic Minorities in the General Election October 1974*, published in 1975.

There is no contemporary study of the part played by elections in the workings of what is termed parliamentary democracy, although many of the works already mentioned naturally deal, inter alia, with this problem. The works of J. F. S. Ross, *Parliamentary Representation*, 2nd edn, Eyre & Spottiswoode, 1948, and A. H. Birch, *Representative and Responsible Government*, Allen & Unwin, 1964, are now dated, but still thought-provoking. *Adversary Politics and Electoral Reform*, Anthony Wigram, 1975, edited by S. E. Finer, does contain much material bearing upon the ways in which the present electoral system shapes politics and political communication in this country.

INDEX

Abortion, 97
Absentee voters, 46-7
Acts of Parliament
  Reform (1832), 9, 13-4, 16, 22-3, 58
  Reform (1867), 9, 15-6, 18, 58
  Municipal Franchise (1868), 17
  Ballot (1872), 9, 16
  Corrupt Practices (1883), 9, 16
  Reform (1884), 9, 16-7
  Redistribution (1885), 16, 18, 58
  Parliament (1911), 21
  Representation of the People (1918), 9, 21-2, 23, 43, 54, 58-9
  Representation of the People (1928), 21
  Redistribution (1944), 59
  Representation of the People (1948), 22, 46
  Representation of the People (1949), 124
  Television (1954), 124
  Redistribution of Seats (1958), 61
  Abortion (1967), 175
  Commonwealth Immigration (1968), 105
  Representation of the People (1969), 23, 50, 127, 212
  Industrial Relations (1971), 108, 110
  Northern Ireland (Border Poll) (1972), 196-7
Additional Member System, 37-8
Age, voting behaviour and, 168-9
Aliens, 43, 46, 212
Alternative Vote, 21, 33-4, 36
Amery, L. 202
Aristotle, 93
Arbtrary rule, 193-4

Bagehot, W., 106, 156, 206
Betting, 112-3
Boundary Commissions, 59-65
Broadcasting, 122-33

Burke, E., 11, 14, 19, 70-1
Business vote, 21
By-elections, 125, 161-2

Cabinet, 106-7
Campaigns, 93-103, 125-6, 133-8
Candidates
  choice of, 73-87, 93
  educational background of, 86-7
  personal vote of, 184-6
  women as, 83-5
Capital punishment, abolition of, 98, 105, 194
Catholics
  parliamentary candidates, 85
  voters, 173-5
Chartism, 14-5, 58, 201
Class, 148-67
Coloured voters, 45-6, 57, 99-100, 189-90
Committee on Political Broadcasting, 117, 124-5, 127, 131-2
Common Market, 97, 136, 210
  Referendum (1975), 28, 197-201
Communist party, 131, 184
Comprehensive education, 110-1
Conservative party
  Central Office, 129
  funds of, 52-3
  marginal seats, 101-2
  National Union, 18
  origins of, 148-9
  press and, 117, 119
  working-class support for, 154, 156-8, 165, 171-2
Constituencies, unequal representation of, 29-30
Constitution written, 195
Corporative state, 207
Corrupt practices, 10, 17, 43
Crick, B., 202
Crossman, R. H. S., 107, 134, 203
Cubic Law, 210

Index

Demographic factors in party support, 171-3
Deposit, 54-6
Differential abstention, 142
Dissolution of Parliament, 23-4
Distribution of seats, 58-68

Eccles, Lord, 203
Eire, citizens of, 43
Elections
  cost of, 56
  eligibility to stand at, 53-4
  expenses at, 49, 54-8
  frequency of, 201
Elites, 205-6
Embourgeoisement, 159, 164
Ethnicity, 187-90

Female suffrage, 15, 17, 20-1
First-past-the-post system, *see under* Plurality system
Fox, C. J., 11

Generational change in the electorate, 169-73

Hansard Society Commission on Electoral Reform, 37, 56, 83
House of Lords, 34, 194, 210
  1909 budget and, 210
  constituency bounbaries and, 62
  plural voting and, 21
  veto of, 20, 27, 28

Immigration, 98-9
Institute of Practitioners in Advertising, 153
Interests, representation of, 12
Irish voters, 175, 187

Jews
  parliamentary candidates, 85
  voters, 99-100, 175-7

Labour party
  Celtic fringe and, 66-7
  constituency parties, 159
  constitution, 20, 26
  election strategy (1959-64), 109
  funds of, 51-2
  marginal seats, 100
  middle-class support for, 158-9
  origins of, 19, 151
  postal vote and, 47
  press and, 116-9
Labour Representation Committee, 19
Liberal party
  campaigns, 97
  candidates, 80
  media and, 138
  National Liberal Federation, 18
  origins of, 16, 149-50
  press and, 117, 119
  support for, 181-4
Lunatics, voting provisions affecting, 43

Mandate, 12, 14, 28-9
Manifestos, 24-8, 96, 129, 136
Marginal seats, 88-9, 91-3, 100-2
Marx, K., 152
Marxism, 149, 206
Media, the 114-38 *passim*
Members of Parliament
  independence of, 69
  local reputations of, 102,
  occupations and educational background of, 204-5
  women as, 205
Mill, J., 15
Mill, J. S., 15, 152
Minority government, 38-9, 105, 203, 218-9
Monarchy, 106

National Front, 52, 55, 99, 131, 184-5
Nationalism, 65-6, 177-81
Nationalization, 108
Newspapers, 115-22
  press conferences, 129
Newsreels, 122-3
Nonconformists, 149
  parliamentary candidates, 85-6
  voters, 173-5, 183

Index

Non-voting, 112, 161, 190-1
Northern Ireland, 97-9
  election abuses in, 48-9, 67-8
  under-representation of, 60, 65

Opinion polls, 138-46
  162
  code of practice, 145
  private polls, 94, 133-4, 139, 146, 217
Osborne judgment, 19, 21
Ostrogorski, M., 19, 115

Parental influence in voting, 170-1
Parliamentary reform, 9-22 *passim*
Personation of voters, 48-9
Plaid Cymru, 56, 88, 200
  broadcasting and, 126, 131-2
  campaigns, 97
  growth of, 177-81
Plato, 106
Plurality system, 30, 38, 40
Plural voting, 21-2
Political parties, 69-73
  activitists in, 71-3
  ballot papers, names on, 50
  broadcasting, control of, 124-8, 131-2
  broadcasts by, 98, 131-2, 134-5, 145
  growth of, 14, 18-19
  leaders, salience of, 95-6, 129-30
  printed propaganda of, 128-9
Poll books, 149
Postal vote, 46-8, 142
Pressure groups, 51
Primary elections, 81-3
Proportional representation, 15, 32-9, 193
  opposition to, 35, 38, 41
Public relations firms, 133-4

Quota sampling, 139-40

Random sampling, 139-40
Referendums, 196-202
Regional factors in voting behaviour, 176-7
Religion

of parliamentary candidate, 85-6
of voters, 173-5
Rousseau, J. -J., 203
Royal Commission on Electoral Systems (1909-10), 21

Safe seats, 102-3
Sampling error, 140, 143, 222
Scotland, over-representation of, 60, 65-6
Scottish Labour Party, 181
Scottish National Party, 29,88, 90-1, 200
  campaigns, 97
  growth of, 177-81
  the media and, 131-2, 138
Second chamber, 195-6
Senescent Conservatism, 171
Sex, voting behaviour and, 168
Single Transferable Vote, 34-6, 40
  in Northern Ireland, 68
Socialism, decline of, 164, 166-7
Speaker's Conference on Electoral Law
  (1916-7), 34
  (1965-8), 47, 56, 144, 212
Swing, 88-93, 147, 216
  'late swing', 142

Tactical voting, 39, 112
Trade Unions,
  financial support for Labour party, 51, 77-8
  sponsorship of parliamentary candidates, 76-8, 86
Trades Union Congress, 110, 116-7, 119
Turnout, 22, 112-3, 160-1, 190

Undue elections, 213
Undue influence at elections, 49
Universal manhood suffrage, 15, 21
University seats, 17, 21, 34, 69
  abolition of, 22

Void elections, 48, 213
Volatility of the electorate, 160-3
Voting age, lowering of, 22

Voting qualifications, 42-3

Wales, over-representation of, 60, 65-6
Wallas, G., 70
West German electoral system, 37
Whigs, 149-50

Zinoviev letter, 120-1, 133